Sunset

COOKING BOLD AND FEARLESS

Sunset

COOKING

BOLD AND FEARLESS

RECIPES BY CHEFS OF THE WEST

ILLUSTRATIONS BY HARRY O. DIAMOND

PUBLISHED BY SUNSET PUBLISHING CORP., MENLO PARK, CA

First Edition and Printing November 1957

Reprinted April 2000

Copyright 1957

SUNSET PUBLISHING CORP., MENLO PARK, CALIFORNIA

Publishers of *Sunset*, The Magazine of Western Living

Printed in U.S.A.

Library of Congress Catalog Number 57-14558

ISBN #0-376-02338-4

NOTICE

contents

Chefs of the West
The Art of Cooking...by men...for men

"Have played leading roles as ambassadors of taste for more than 17 years"

# of cooks bold and fearless

We address this book to all who stand ready to cast away caution in the pursuit of cooking adventure. Does the boot fit?

Your guides have been hand picked for this assignment. They come from that elite corps of men cooks known as *Chefs of the West*. They lead by example—test them by tasting.

Chefs of the West have played leading roles as ambassadors of taste for more than 17 years.

On the pages of *Sunset Magazine,* the first *Chefs* won tall white caps for published contributions to cookery in March, 1940. Ever since, a monthly column in *Sunset* has brought in new members until the total is now about 800.

This book represents the *crème de la crème*—471 outstanding recipes carefully chosen from the grand total of almost 1,000.

To bold, fearless cookery, *Chefs* bring courage and imagination.

The courage of the male cook as he confidently takes over the kitchen is—shall we say—boundless.

The spur to creative cookery might be just something that "rings a clear bell-like reflex in the small peaked campanile of my memories," testifies one *Chef*. (But after the flash of inspiration, a *Chef* might

"Rings a clear bell-like reflex in the small peaked campanile of my memories"

spend hours, days—or even years—perfecting the final recipe.)

Others draw inspiration from some food they have tasted on their travels. Recipes have always been important items of international exchange. In the past they moved slowly from border to border. But in this air age, you never know when you might be eating a dish that some *Chef of the West* picked up only last week in Saudi Arabia.

Many *Chefs* acknowledge a debt to some particular foreign cookery that has enriched our repertoire. Although we Westerners pay our sincere respects to French cuisine, we are not overawed by it. Up and down the Pacific Coast, we find too many good foreign influences to give exclusive homage to any one.

Sometimes such an influence can be traced directly to the use of one particular ingredient. We are reminded of how soy has gone island-hopping across the Pacific, with a last jump from Hawaii to us.

"Might spend hours, days, or even years"

We might also note, in passing, that *Chefs* make bold and free with herbs in their cooking. Herbs are not staple foodstuffs, nor are they strictly flavorings; they are more aptly called seasonings. Wherever food is well esteemed, served with ceremony, and tasted with apprecia-

"We are reminded of how soy has gone island-hopping across the Pacific"

tion, you are likely to find herbs used well in cookery. *Chefs of the West* are always experimenting with herbs as they strive to season with just the right touch.

One's approach to cooking may be peculiarly personal. Every man who grows his own fruit or vegetables, hunts his own game, or catches his own fish, develops an attachment to these foods and it carries over to his preparation of them. Some men who do little in the kitchen are master cooks over a barbecue or a campfire. The inner prompting may be just an unusually hearty appetite. Or it may be a deeper urge—understood by most male campers and by all the early Western pioneers—to prove that man can produce some of the good things of life with nothing but his bare hands and the minimum elements of subsistence.

We all know the old fireside pastime, probably invented by the cave man, in which someone begins the telling of a story and each person in turn adds his bit to what went before. Every *Chef of the West* who experiments with an old recipe participates in a similar process. Sometimes new developments follow one another in chain reaction. Sometimes they pop up without apparent relation to each other—as they sometimes do in

science when scientists all over the world are working on the same problem.

There's a little of the scientist in most *Chefs.* Bold flights of free fancy are fine, but the responsible scientist puts theories to test and states his results with precision. Before the *Chef* will sign his name to a recipe, he runs through one last trial with measuring spoons, cups, tapes, calipers, and timers ready.

There's a little of the artist in him, too. In the creation of a recipe, he knows that one very important final process is negative. It consists of throwing out every detail that doesn't contribute to the desired effect—a certain balance, a contrast, perhaps a dominant flavor.

"If the majority vote is favorable"

"One last trial with measuring spoons, cups, tapes, calipers, and timers ready"

Final test is the tasting by an impartial jury. (*Sunset* tests every *Chef* dish by preparing it and serving it to a panel of taste-testers.) If the majority vote is favorable, the recipe is ready to publish to the waiting world.

Chefs of the West have set a lively pace for other practitioners of the culinary arts. We see every likelihood that this happy state of affairs will continue.

appetizers

HUNTER'S HORS D'OEUVRES

Hunters, and also their fortunate guests, may relish these delectable by-products of a successful expedition. They concern duck giblets (or those of geese or pheasants, for that matter). "These little tidbits, usually thrown away, can be converted into delicious morsels to serve as appetizers," says *Chef* Kendrick Morrish, of Orinda, California. His very simple formula involves a bottle of beer.

"Happen to have wild duck on hand"

If you don't just happen to have wild duck giblets on hand, chicken giblets will do very nicely.

>   2 pounds (1 quart) gizzards and hearts
>   2 bay leaves
>   1 clove garlic
>   1 teaspoon salt
>   1 bottle or can (12 oz.) of beer
>   Butter or margarine

At the duck club or in the kitchen, use a sharp knife to cut giblets in pieces, each about the size of one good bite. Place giblets in saucepan with bay leaves, peeled garlic, salt, and beer. Cover and simmer for 2 hours, regulating heat so that all liquid is boiled out at the end of that time. Sauté giblets in butter for a few minutes, stick a toothpick in each, and serve hot. The result will be tender and juicy and will create a demand for more. Serves 8 to 10.

A slight variation of this formula makes a good creamed dish: Instead of boiling off all liquid, allow a little of the final thickened liquor to remain in the pan.

Make a cream sauce separately and blend with the liquor. (For extra fanciness add mushrooms, either fresh cooked or canned.) Heat and serve on toast.

Ken Morrish

Banker and writer.
Orinda, Calif.

PIROSHKI STROINSKA

"Turkey is sufficient in itself," advises J. D. Dunshee of Phoenix, Arizona. "So, retain the liver to be used later with this recipe. To call it by its Polish name, it is *Piroshki Stroinska.* This is a snack dish, liver supreme. We found that monosodium glutamate in the filling, plus a crisp pastry crust, gave a mouth-watering effect that had us reaching for another as long as they were within reach."

We made minor changes in Mr. Dunshee's proportions to fit our convenience. And, to us, it seemed easier to make turnovers larger than the 1½-inch circles prescribed. But we did so with a clear conscience because we know Mr. Dunshee's philosophical approach: "A recipe is an outline, so to speak, for good cookery, rather than an iron-clad rule too sacred to modify." We agree wholeheartedly.

>   2 tablespoons butter
>   1 tablespoon flour
>   1 can (4 oz.) mushrooms
>   1 teaspoon monosodium glutamate
>   1 turkey liver (2 chicken or rabbit livers)
>   chopped
>   1 teaspoon onion juice or grated onion
>   1 tablespoon minced parsley
>   2 large stuffed olives, chopped
>   Salt and pepper to taste
>   Rich pastry

Melt butter and brown slightly. Blend in flour. Drain mushrooms, retaining liquid. Add enough water to mushroom liquid to make ½ cup. Stock may be substituted for mushroom liquid. Add liquid to blended butter and flour. Chop mushrooms and add to sauce with other ingredients. Cook slowly for about 10 minutes, or until mixture is reasonably thick.

Make a rich pastry and roll it very thin. Cut into small circles, fill each with ½ to 1 teaspoon of the liver mixture, and make into turnovers, moistening the edges of the pastry so that the filling will not leak out during the baking. Press edges with tines of fork. Bake in a very hot oven (450°) for 7 to 10 minutes, or until lightly browned. Serve hot. Makes approximately 100 turnovers from 2½-inch pastry rounds. Leftovers can be stored in freezer or refrigerator freezing compartment. Be sure to reheat before serving.

J. H. Dunshee

Doctor
Phoenix, Arizona

CEVICHE

Chef George C. Booth, one of our specialists in Latin American cooking, says "I have heeded your call for simple recipes." He submits *"Ceviche*—served all along the Pacific Coast from Acapulco to Lima as a snack, appetizer, hors d'œuvre, or

"I asked the waitress for the recipe. She said the cook had gone home."

full meal." He learned to like it in Panama during the war. But he couldn't find the recipe until last summer when he revisited El Rancho, one of his favorite Panama eating places.

"I asked the waitress for the recipe, but she said the cook had gone home. I went to the kitchen and, by fast talk and *plata*, got the heavenly secret."

It is only fair to mention that this dish won't be favored by those who avoid anything that might be called "raw fish." However, *Chef* Booth makes a point worth making when he says, "Ceviche is not raw; it cooks at room temperature in the lime juice. In fact, the chef at El

Rancho said, 'Cook it outside the ice box.' Any good dry fish will do, but corbina is the classic."

> 2 fillets (approximately 2 pounds) fresh corbina, diced
> 2 cups chopped onions
> ¼ cup minced green chili peppers (more or less according to your preference)
> 2 teaspoons salt
> 2 cups lime juice

Combine corbina with other ingredients and allow to marinate for 4 hours at room temperature. Chill in the refrigerator before serving. Serves about 20 as an appetizer.

Geo C Booth

Teacher
Long Beach, Calif.

CHICKEN LIVER APPETIZERS

Bacon, chicken liver, and anchovy are well suited to one another. Bacon and anchovy are salty, but the combination doesn't seem salty at all. Some of our taste testers who wouldn't walk across the room for either chicken livers or anchovy were eating this snack with relish.

Wrap one anchovy fillet around each well chilled or partially frozen chicken liver; then wrap a 3-inch bacon strip around the anchovy. Secure with toothpicks. Cook in hot deep fat (375°) for 3 minutes or until bacon is crisp. (The bacon strip keeps the anchovy from disappearing.) Drain on paper toweling. Serve hot.

Joseph Coco

Restaurant owner
San Francisco, Calif.

TONY'S COCKTAIL CHEESE

> 1 pound *each* of Roquefort and Monterey Jack cheese
> 1 teaspoon finely chopped green onion tops
> 1 teaspoon finely chopped parsley
> 1 medium sized onion, minced
> 1 large clove garlic, minced
> ¼ teaspoon rosemary
> 2 teaspoons A-1 sauce
> Dash of Tabasco sauce
> Sherry

Take equal parts of Roquefort and Monterey Jack cheese (or cream cheese) and crumble into a mixing bowl. To each 2 pounds of the cheese add all the accompanying ingredients except sherry.

Mix thoroughly, adding enough sherry to give mixture a creamy consistency. Serve on butter crackers.

TONY HILL
Utility serviceman
Fresno, Calif.

HOLIDAY HORS D'OEUVRE

Chill red eating apples. Slice in thin wedges with skins left on. Mix paste of ⅓ Blue or Roquefort cheese and ⅔ cream cheese. Place cheese in center dish. Stick tips of apple wedges into cheese or encircle dish. Provide cheese or butter knife.

Geo. R. Miller

Los Angeles.

SAUERKRAUT BALLS

        1 medium sized onion, chopped
        1 tablespoon salad oil or melted margarine
        1⅓ cups chopped cooked ham
        ½ clove garlic, mashed or minced
        6 tablespoons flour
        ½ cup beef broth
        3 cups sauerkraut, thoroughly drained,
            then chopped
        1 tablespoon chopped parsley

Batter:

        1 egg
        2 cups milk
        2½ cups flour
        ½ cup dry bread crumbs

Brown chopped onion lightly in oil or margarine. Add chopped ham and garlic. Brown slightly. Stir in flour and cook thoroughly. Add broth, sauerkraut, and parsley and mix thoroughly. Cook a few minutes more until mixture is thick enough to shape into croquettes. Cool; form into balls about 1 inch in diameter.

Beat egg, milk, and flour together to form a fairly heavy batter. Dip sauerkraut croquettes in batter and roll in bread crumbs. Fry in hot deep fat (375°) for 2 minutes, or until croquettes are firm and light brown.

Serve on toothpicks for hors d'oeuvres. Makes about 6 dozen small croquettes. If desired, make into larger balls and serve as main course of dinner with mashed potatoes and other side dishes.

Edward Leicht

Expeditor
Mountain View, Calif.

FISH PERUVIAN

        2 pounds red Spanish onions
        2 cups red wine vinegar
        2 cups water
        1 clove garlic
        1 bay leaf
        2 or 3 red chili peppers
        1 teaspoon mustard seed
        12 whole cloves
        1 large stick cinnamon (if available)
        Sea bass, swordfish, or rock cod, cut into
            serving-sized pieces, the amount depend-
            ing upon the number to be served

Peel the onions and cook them in boiling salted water until they are tender but still firm enough to hold together. Pack them loosely into wide-mouthed jars. Combine the vinegar, water, garlic, bay leaf, peppers, mustard seed, cloves, and cinnamon in a saucepan; bring to a boil, and pour over the onions. (See that each jar, if more than one is used, contains a portion of each seasoning.) Seal the jars and keep at room temperature for at least 24 hours.

Broil or fry the fish cuts and set aside. About an hour before serving, prepare:

Fish Sauce

        2 onions, minced
        1 clove garlic, minced
        ¼ cup olive oil
        1 cup tomato sauce
        1 cup water
        1 bay leaf
        1 teaspoon oregano
        1 teaspoon rosemary
        1 teaspoon sweet basil
        6 cloves
        Salt and pepper to taste

Sauté the onions and garlic in olive oil until golden, then add the tomato sauce, water, and remaining ingredients. Simmer for 10 to 20 minutes, adding water as necessary to keep the sauce relatively thin.

On a flat serving plate, arrange a bed of crisp lettuce leaves. Place the fish cuts in the center. Remove the onions from the jars, cut them in halves, and lay them face up in a ring around the fish. Pour the sauce over onions and fish. Garnish with ripe olives and slices of hard-cooked egg. Chill thoroughly before serving.

CHARLES M. BELSHAW
Food processor
Oakland, Calif.

BOSTON CAFÉ DIABLE

    2 jiggers brandy
    1 jigger Jamaica rum
      Thin peel of 1 orange
    4 whole cloves
    1 bay leaf
    ½ stick cinnamon
    4 lumps sugar
    3 tablespoons whole roasted coffee beans
    4 demi-tasses strong black (use drip or
      Silex) coffee

Pour brandy and rum in chafing dish. Add orange peel, cloves, bay leaf, cinnamon, 3 sugar lumps, and coffee beans; heat and set aflame in the following way: Dip up small amount of liquor; place sugar cube in ladle and set aflame. Lower ladle with blazing contents into chafing dish and let it flame; add coffee slowly, gently lifting and pouring with ladle to keep contents burning. When flames die down, remove coffee beans and ladle coffee into demi-tasse cups.

Executive
Los Angeles, Calif.

SHRIMP-VITOUS SPREAD

    ½ pound shelled cooked shrimp
    2 stalks celery, including the tops
    2 sprigs parsley
    ¼ green pepper
    ⅛ teaspoon Tabasco, or to taste
    ¼ teaspoon garlic salt
      Pepper to taste
    ½ teaspoon paprika
    5 tablespoons mayonnaise

Use a blender, or a food chopper with a medium blade to cut shrimp, celery, parsley, and green pepper. Add all remaining ingredients, with the mayonnaise last, so you can add more of it if needed to give mixture a nicely spreading consistency. (Note that the recipe contains no salt.) Serve on thinly sliced rye bread, pumpernickel, or crisp rye crackers.

Dentist
Seattle, Washington

IA O TAHITI

An exotic treatment of sole comes to us from Ross A. Urquhart. We have known the dish as I'a Ota, appreciated in the South Seas as an hors d'oeuvre. For a first-course serving, it will bring you culinary kudos. If the idea of eating uncooked fish startles you at first (it did us, too), be assured that the delicate slices are cooked literally by the lime juice. After one taste of this Tahitian delight, you'll have no more qualms!

    4 fillets of sole (or very thin slices of halibut)
    ½ cup fresh lime juice
    2 onions, sliced
      Salt and pepper
      Coconut milk
    1 cup sour cream
      Whites of 2 hard-cooked eggs
      Chopped parsley and chives

Cover the fish with lime juice and sliced raw onions, sprinkle with salt and pepper, and let marinate for 8 to 10 hours. Strain off marinade and cover fish with coconut milk thickened with sour cream, chopped egg whites, parsley, and chives. Serve very cold on a bed of romaine. Serves 4.

Real estate broker
Los Angeles, Calif.

SHRIMP DELIGHT

By popular demand, the shrimp (or the prawn, depending on the size you prefer) has played a great many successful performances in the chafing dish. Here is another, presented by *Chef* Tom Vinnedge of Portland, with a somewhat exotic assortment of supporting ingredients.

He recommends spearing the shrimps from the chafing dish with toothpicks and placing them on small crackers to eat as appetizers. If you should happen to have any of this dish left over, you can always enlarge on it by adding some other favorite seafood and serving the whole over rice or noodles.

> 1 medium sized onion, chopped fine
> ½ green pepper, sliced
> 3 pepperoncini (small, green pickled peppers) chopped
> 1 teaspoon pepperoncini liquid
> 1 clove garlic, minced (optional)
> 3 tablespoons cooking oil
> ½ teaspoon salt
> ⅛ teaspoon pepper

Sauté the above ingredients quickly, adding salt and pepper to taste. Then add the following:

> 1 small can (8 oz.) tomato sauce
> ½ cup chili sauce
> 1 tablespoon vinegar

(After you measure out the chili sauce, rinse out the cup with the vinegar.) Let the whole mixture come to a simmer, then add the final touches:

> ¼ teaspoon curry (or to taste)
> 1 pound (15 to 20 count) prawns, cooked, shucked, and cleaned

Since prawns of this size are too large to go on crackers, we cut them in half. Let the mixture continue to simmer until the prawns just heat through. This recipe makes enough appetizers to serve 6 persons easily.

Tom Vinnedge

Import-export
Portland, Oregon

ZAKUSKA

We recommend this dish wholeheartedly to the Western stream fisherman.
You can make it up in quantity, preserve it, and use it weeks afterward. Sunday is a good day to dedicate to such a production. The Russian name, *Zakuska*, means "little bits" or, roughly, "appetizer"— serve it thus on Sunday or on any other day of the week.

> 2 large trout or a 4 to 6-pound salmon, filleted
> Salad oil
> 2 onions, chopped fine
> 1 large can (No. 2½) tomatoes
> 2 bottles (2¼ oz. each) of capers and liquid
> 2 small cans (4 oz. each) button mushrooms
> 1 can (4 oz.) chopped ripe olives
> 3 or 4 carrots, sliced and cooked
> 6 thin lemon slices
> 1 teaspoon whole black peppers
> 1 bay leaf
> ½ teaspoon salt

Brown fish fillets (no flouring) in salad oil and place to one side. Brown onions in same oil, then add all remaining ingredients and simmer a few minutes.

Alternate fish and sauce in a large casserole. Cover and bake in a slow oven (300°) for 1 hour. Pack in sterilized jars, seal, and keep in refrigerator. Makes about 4 pints, depending on size of fish.

Serve as an appetizer (antipasto). Fish will absorb sauce but still remain in identifiable pieces if not cooked too long.

Adolf Knoflock

Los Altos, Calif.

PICKLED SALMON

We recommend this as an appetizer. *Chef* Fred Fahlen makes a suggestion that may not fit everyone's taste: that fishermen take a jar of it along for munching on during an all-day excursion. There's a theory that to catch a fish you have to think like a fish. (Eating fish, thinking like fish, and catching fish.) *Chef* Fahlen of Scandinavian ancestry, is obviously a far-gone fisherman.

> 1 pound piece of salmon
> Water
> 1 small onion
> 6 whole allspice
> 1 teaspoon salt
> 1 cup white vinegar
> 1 cup water
> ¾ cup sugar
> 1 medium sized onion
> 10 whole allspice

"To catch a fish, you have to think like a fish"

Cover salmon with cold water. Add onion, allspice, and salt. Simmer until barely tender (don't overcook). Let cool in the stock. Drain. Break into pieces and pour over it pickling liquid made by combining the vinegar, water, and sugar. (Pickle mixture should be quite sweet.) Slice onion over top, sprinkle in allspice, cover. Let fish stand in pickle mixture for at least 4 hours. Remove and serve with the onion rings. Serves 8. (If any salmon is left over, keep it refrigerated.)

FredDahlen

Hope Island, Washington

CHICKEN BITS IN TERIYAKI SAUCE

Chicken (or rabbit, veal, or almost any
    quick cooking meat)
1 cup sherry
4 cloves garlic
Ginger root (crushed)
¼ cup soy sauce

Cut raw meat in small pieces and soak at least one hour in the sherry-garlic-ginger root mixture (this brings out the essence of garlic). Shortly before cooking time, add the soy sauce. Flour pieces, then fry in deep fat. Serve very hot.

Another good hors d'oeuvre idea for small meat balls, pieces of raw fish, or small bits of broiled steak: Mix 2 tablespoons dry mustard with enough hot water to make a paste. Then add soy sauce, about ½ cup or to taste. Impale bits of meat on a toothpick, dip into this sauce, and consume immediately.

CJ Fern

Lihue, Kauai, T. H.

SHRIMPS JACQUES

2 cups water
2 cups white wine
1 carrot, cut up
3 stalks celery
3 branches parsley
½ lemon, cut in two
1 teaspoon paprika
2 tablespoons salt
32 medium sized, uncooked (green) shrimps

Combine all ingredients, except shrimps, and bring this court bouillon mixture to a boil. Add the fresh shrimps. Cook 10 minutes *only*. Drain and shell shrimps. Prepare sauce.

Sauce for Shrimps Jacques:

2 tablespoons anchovy paste
2 tablespoons mayonnaise
4 tablespoons sour cream
2 tablespoons garlic vinegar
2 tablespoons catsup
Dash of thyme
Dash of Worcestershire sauce
½ teaspoon salt
¼ teaspoon monosodium glutamate
4 hard cooked eggs, chopped
1 teaspoon capers

Mix all ingredients, except eggs and capers; put through a coarse sieve. Add the finely chopped eggs, pour over the shrimps, and mix well. Sprinkle capers over all. Let stand three hours in the refrigerator. Serve on crisp lettuce leaves. Serves 4.

Doctor
La Jolla, Calif.

PICKLED PRAWNS

    2 pounds raw jumbo prawns (about 12 to 15
        count)
    6 cups boiling water
    1/3 cup rock salt
    1/4 cup vinegar

Drop prawns into boiling water to which salt and vinegar have been added. Bring water rapidly to a boil again and cook from 6 to 8 minutes, depending on size of the prawns. Remove from heat and let stand while preparing pickling liquor.

Pickling liquor:

    1 cup water
    2 tablespoons mixed pickling spices
    3 tablespoons brown sugar
    1/2 cup vinegar
    1 tablespoon rock salt
    1 tablespoon red table wine
    1 clove garlic, crushed

Simmer the pickling liquor ingredients together. When they are thoroughly heated, remove prawns from cooking water and drop into the pickling liquor. Let stand at least overnight. Serves about 8 as appetizer.

Research engineer
Seattle, Washington

After the first trial, you may want to cut down a little on the rock salt. It depends on your taste, and what you serve with the prawns.

CLAM RADONSKY

Instead of hauling out canvas and easel for his expression of a picturesque landscape, Bill Herb turns to pots and pans, griddles and grills. One masterpiece worthy of an exhibition is a dish he calls Clams Radonsky. He uses Washington clams, found along the coast as far south as central California but known locally as butter clams. However, he says, "Use any clams you can split."

If you find it more convenient, you may prepare clams the night before and keep them under refrigeration ready for the dénouement.

    Small to medium sized clams
    Salt
    Pepper
    Flour
    Bacon drippings

Leave clams in salt water overnight or for a few hours, so they will rid themselves of most of their sand. Open clams by cutting through muscles, taking care not to jar the pail and cause remaining clams to "button up tight." Leave meat in shells. Remove stomachs, rinsing under faucet to remove bits of sand that may cling to the "ruffle."

Mix together salt, pepper, and flour and sift over clams. Heat griddle, greasing with bacon drippings. Place clams, meat side down, on griddle and fry. Clams will steam tender and juicy under shells, becoming brown and crisp where they touch griddle. They are done when the shells turn white.

Serve at once, preferably with large cubes of delicious, hot, cheese-coated bread.

Cheese Bread Cubes

    1 loaf white sandwich bread, unsliced
    1/2-pound package sharp Cheddar cheese spread
    2 cubes (1/2 lb.) butter
    2 cloves garlic

Use day-old bread. Remove crusts. Cut once through the center the long way. Cut halves into 2-inch cubes. Mix together equal parts sharp cheese spread and butter, both previously softened at room temperature. Thoroughly blend in the minced garlic—do not be modest with garlic; a good emphatic flavor is desirable. Cover bread cubes generously with cheese-butter-garlic mixture and place in hot oven until heated through. Serve hot.

Executive, paper manufacturing
Bellingham, Washington

Soups

"Have ladles, spoons, and fingers ready for the attack"

PUGET SOUND BOUILLABAISSE

You can always be sure that bouillabaisse will contain a mixture of fishes, but you never know just what the individual formula may be. For instance, in France (where bouillabaisse apparently originated), you might find carp, eel, whiting, sole, and lobster in one soup pot; and red snapper, perch, cod, sea bass, and Spanish mackerel in another.

Tuck bibs or aprons under your chins. *Chef* Clinton R. Vitous is about to lift the lid off another mysterious pot labeled "Puget Sound Bouillabaisse." Have ladles, spoons, and—yes—fingers ready for the attack. This is no time to be over-fastidious.

Dr. Vitous has filled it with toothsome morsels. "To me," he says, "this has clam chowder beat hollow. I use no bacon, fat, oil, or butter to detract from the wonderful fish flavor."

We have here a real Northwest adaptation of the famous cosmopolitan dish, with salmon, halibut, fresh crab, shrimp, and mushrooms, all natives and plentiful along the Pacific Coast. *Chef* Vitous coaxes the cooking process along through an afternoon, but you won't hurt the product by cutting down to the shorter time we have indicated in the recipe.

2 stalks celery with tops
1 large onion
2 cloves garlic
1 slice fresh halibut, 1½ inches thick
1 slice fresh salmon, 1½ inches thick
1 large fresh crab
1 pound kippered salmon
¼ pound shelled fresh shrimp
15 small clams in the shell
1 can (8 oz.) tomato sauce
½ pound fresh mushrooms, halved
2½ quarts water
    Salt and pepper to taste
    Grated Parmesan cheese

Cut celery, onion, and garlic in several pieces—no need to be fussy, as it all cooks up anyway. Then add the fish.

Put in the halibut and salmon slices whole. Scrub the crab, clean, then disjoint the legs and crack them up a bit, and cut the body meat in a few pieces. Break up the kippered salmon with fingers and remove its skin and as many bones as possible. Add shrimp. Scrub clam shells well with a vegetable brush. (I like the small butter clams; they give the served bowl an interesting look.)

Add tomato sauce, mushrooms, water, and salt and pepper to taste. Bring to a rolling boil. Then cover tightly, turn heat down to simmer, and cook for about 45 minutes.

Serve in bowls (dig down deep in the kettle) and sprinkle with grated Parmesan cheese (gives a good flavor, also, if you add some during the cooking). In the Latin-American countries, a slice of lemon always accompanies any soup; try it with this one. Crunchy garlic French bread and a tossed salad complete the meal. You'll be surprised how filling this dish is. Serves 8 generously.

Clinton R. Vitous

Dentist
Seattle, Washington

BOUILLABAISSE TACOMA

If Paul Bunyan ever ate seafood, his favorite dish must have been "bouillabaisse" (the well-established English pronunciation is bool-ya-BASE). It takes a good man to make it and a big man to do it full justice in the eating. The French soldiers who marched into Paris as revolutionists in 1792 are supposed to have gained their great strength from a heavy diet of "Bouillabaisse Marseille."

From Paul Bunyan's Northwest lumber country—good sea food territory, too—*Chef* A. B. Woodworth of Tacoma submits his version of a bouillabaisse.

This is "real, not amateur, bouillabaisse," says he. "I will caution anyone trying this recipe not to be dismayed by the specified quantities and not to cut them down because I assure you this as it is presented is the pure quill."

The pure quill, the real McTavish, the genuine bouillabaisse does not follow a very tight formula. One authority notes that there are as many types as there are French villages on the Mediterranean, but "whatever its origin, the basic ingredients of bouillabaisse never change. Olive oil, garlic, and saffron must always be included in this aromatic epicurean fish and shellfish combination.

"Any variety of American fish may be used," he continues. "The French often select four or five different kinds of fish as well as three or more types of shellfish.

The proportion is usually two to one; that is, there are twice as many pounds of fish as shellfish."

"Crowd in a wild assortment of fish"

Chef Woodworth does remain faithful to the three basic ingredients. He does crowd in a wild assortment of fish in near-gargantuan quantity. (The ratio of shellfish to other fish is more nearly one to one.) However, we are going to indulge his extravagant whim, adding only one word of advice: Use the kinds of fish you like best in quantities that please you most.

No thickening is indicated, but when you do your last-minute testing and tasting with a long handled spoon, you may find that some is advisable.

        2 leeks
        2 medium-sized carrots
        1 medium-sized onion
        4 tomatoes, peeled
        ¼ cup olive oil (or your favorite salad oil)
        1 pound mackerel
        1½ pounds sea bass, red snapper, or kindred fish
        1 dozen clams
        5 cups water
        5 cups tomato juice
        2 cloves garlic, chopped fine or mashed
        1 pinch saffron
        1 tablespoon chopped parsley
        3 teaspoons salt
        ½ teaspoon nutmeg
        ½ teaspoon pepper
        6 drops Tabasco (or use your own judgment)
        1 dozen oysters
        1 pound green shrimp, shelled and cleaned
        2 lobsters about 1½ pounds each, or
            equivalent amount of crab meat

Chop vegetables. Sauté slowly in the oil. Cut all larger pieces of fish into approximately 1-inch cubes. In a large kettle, combine the sautéed vegetables, all the liquids, all the seasonings, and all sea food except the shrimp and the lobster or crab. Bring to a boil quickly, then turn heat to simmer. Cook for 5 minutes, then add the shrimp and lobster or crab and cook for 15 minutes longer.

Be careful never to let the mixture boil

"Last-minute testing and tasting with a long-handled spoon"

rapidly at any time, as this tends to break up the fish. Serve in a soup plate over your favorite. garlic bread, or serve the bread as a side issue. Will serve 10 average people (easily), but only eight enthusiasts.

A.B. Woodworth

Tacoma

FRIJOLES RIO BLANCO

For bean lovers who enjoy the real McSanchez—*frijoles* in Latin American hot style—here is a soup that should make a one-dish supper for a wintry Sunday evening.

Chef George C. Booth considers himself an expert on beans.

"Understand that I was born in the wilds of southern Oregon and spent my early years with a prospector and his wife. Beans were my staple for years. Then add more time in logging and construction camps, a hitch in the Marines, three years in the Navy in the last war, and time in Mexico. For years I have been cognizant of the Mexican habit of cooking rice and beans and hominy and beans, but I couldn't get over my *gringoismo* enough to go for that. It took Peru last summer to open a new vista.

"During a Naval Reserve cruise, I took a train trip up the Andes with 60 sailors. We were dropped off at Rio Blanco, about 12,000 feet up and waited around 3 hours for the down train. There were only 2 stores and a cantina, a llama, a cold white stream, and a dozen people. The sailors photographed the llama from every angle and ate sandwiches brought from the ship. I tried a plate of beans in the cantina and bowed to a genius greater than my own. Here is the recipe as reconstructed in my own kitchen":

    2 cups dried navy beans
    ½ pound ham hock or chopped salt pork
    6 cups water
    1 teaspoon oregano
    2 cloves garlic, chopped
    1 large onion, chopped
    1½ teaspoons soda
    1 tablespoon salt
    1 teaspoon pepper
    1½ cups dry split peas
    1 large onion, sliced
    4 stalks celery with tops, finely sliced
    4 medium sized carrots, sliced thin
    2 medium sized green peppers, sliced
    2 fresh or dry hot chili peppers (optional), chopped
    1 teaspoon dry marjoram
    2 cups Burgundy

Cook beans, ham or salt pork, water, oregano, garlic, chopped onion, soda, salt, and pepper together for 2 hours. Then add all other ingredients except wine and cook for 1½ hours more. Add wine 45 minutes after vegetables have been put in.

The soup puréeist may want to colander his soup, but I like it straight. Serve hot from the pot. Serves 10 to 12.

Geo. C. Booth

Teacher
Long Beach, Calif.

KAILUA FISH CHOWDER

    2 (2 pounds each) mullet (or any white fish) filleted and diced
    3 to 5 chili peppers
    1½ cups chopped onions
    ½ cup chopped salt pork (or bacon)
    1½ cups diced raw potatoes
    7 cups fresh or canned milk
    1 cup cream
    1 pinch baking soda
      Salt, pepper, and paprika
    1 tablespoon butter

Save skin, heads, and bones of fish. Place in a saucepan, add chili peppers and 2 cups of water. Simmer for about 20 minutes to make stock. In a heavy pan, fry onions and salt pork until quite brown, then add strained stock. (Strain carefully, as one bone will spoil the whole chowder.) Add potatoes, and simmer until they are cooked, about 15 minutes. Add milk, cream, and a pinch of baking soda to prevent milk from curdling. When the chowder comes to a boil, add diced fish, a dash of paprika, butter, and seasonings. Let simmer gently. If chowder is too thin, add a few soda crackers. Don't omit the chili peppers! This recipe will make 10 to 14 servings.

Rear Admiral USN
San Francisco, Calif.

TROUT CHOWDER

    4 strips bacon, diced
    1 large onion, finely diced
    3 or 4 good sized potatoes, thinly sliced
    2 or 3 carrots, diced or grated
      Salt, pepper, and thyme to taste
    8 seven-inch trout (or equivalent)
      Lump of butter

Cook diced bacon and pour off fat. Stir in diced onion and sauté lightly. Add potatoes, carrots, and seasonings, with enough water to cover all ingredients. Simmer in a deep, covered skillet or kettle until vegetables are done and a thickened sauce has formed from potatoes. This will take from 30 to 40 minutes at high altitudes. In the meantime, prepare the trout by making a V-cut along all fins; remove with the bones; cut off heads and tails. Place trout gently on top of simmering chowder and replace cover until trout are done. Using two forks, split trout down the back through fin cut and carefully remove backbones and ribs. They will come out in one piece. Stir up the mixture and serve, after adding the lump of butter for more flavor. Serves 4 hungry campers.

Life insurance
Portland, Oregon

CLAM CHOWDER LOCKWOODII

We seldom meet a clam chowder that speaks so well for itself as the one submitted by R. H. Lockwood of Portland. Although we don't altogether agree with one of our taste testers that you have to be cold to really appreciate it (hot), we must say it would be mighty welcome out on a sail or on a cold day in camp.

"Have to be cold to really appreciate it"

    3 cans (7½ oz. each) minced clams or
        I cup chopped steamed clams and
        I cup clam nectar
    1½ cups chicken stock
    2 medium size potatoes, finely diced
    I cup celery, very finely sliced
    I small white onion, chopped
    I tablespoon parsley, chopped
    I small carrot, chopped
    ½ teaspoon monosodium glutamate
    I teaspoon salt
    ¼ teaspoon black pepper, freshly ground
    ¼ teaspoon thyme (optional)
    I cup undiluted evaporated milk
    ½ cube butter

Drain liquid from minced clams; add it (or clam nectar) to all remaining ingredients except clams, evaporated milk, and butter. Simmer for 30 minutes. Drain stock in another saucepan; set aside ⅔ cup of the vegetables. Purée remaining vegetables in blender; return to stock. Add reserved vegetables, minced clams, evaporated milk and butter.

Heat for 10 minutes, keeping it just below the boiling point. Serves 6.

Bookkeeper (retired)
Portland, Oregon

"The underwater cowboy at the abalone roundup"

ABALONE CHOWDER

You might gather from the dictionary that abalone is used for food only in the Oriental nations, but many Westerners know better—including Claude E. Wendt of Soledad, California. In fact, at Carmel, deep in abalone country, a gay group of artists and writers first sang the famous "Abalone Song" to celebrate their personal discovery of this delicacy.

In this superior version of "Boston" or "White" clam chowder, *Chef* Wendt substitutes abalone for clams and mushroom soup for milk. The underwater cowboy at the abalone roundup may prefer to eat his catch in steaks, but we suggest he save the trimmings for this chowder.

    1 pound fresh or frozen abalone
    2 slices bacon, minced
    1 small onion, chopped
    ½ cube (¼ cup) butter or margarine
    1 cup diced potatoes
    ½ cup diced carrots
    3 tablespoons minced green pepper
    ¼ cup sliced celery
    1 tablespoon minced parsley
    1 can (10¾ oz.) cream of mushroom soup
    4 soup cans water
    4 beef bouillon cubes
    ½ teaspoon salt
    ¼ teaspoon pepper
    6 drops Tabasco sauce
    1 tablespoon Worcestershire sauce
    ½ teaspoon powdered garlic or bottled
        garlic purée
    1 tablespoon monosodium glutamate

Put abalone through the fine blade of the food chopper. Fry bacon until light brown in a 5-quart cast iron or cast aluminum Dutch oven. Add abalone, onions, and about 1 tablespoon of the butter and fry about 10 minutes over medium heat, stirring continually so they will not burn.

Melt the remaining butter in a skillet; then add potatoes, carrots, pepper, celery, and parsley, and fry until light brown.

Add the soup, water, and bouillon cubes to the abalone mixture in the Dutch oven and simmer until the cubes are dissolved. Then add all the seasonings and cook for about 40 minutes, boiling slowly. Finally, add the potatoes and other vegetables from the skillet and cook for 20 minutes, boiling very slowly.

This will serve about 6 hungry people.

Claude E. Wendt
Department manager
Soledad, Calif.

ABALONE SOUP

    2 medium-sized onions, chopped
    1 cup sliced celery and chopped leaves
    1 to 2 tablespoons bacon drippings
    4 medium-sized potatoes, diced
    1 can (No. ½) canned abalone pieces
        (approximately 1 cup)
    1 cup water
    3 cups milk
        Chopped parsley to taste
    1 bouillon cube
    ½ teaspoon monosodium glutamate
        Salt, pepper, and other seasonings to taste

Lightly sauté chopped onion and celery in bacon drippings in the bottom of a pressure cooker. Add the diced potatoes, abalone, and water. Cover and cook at 15 pounds pressure for 10 minutes. Cool cooker slowly. Remove lid and stir in milk, parsley, bouillon, monosodium glutamate, and seasonings. Cover and simmer for 15 minutes. Add frozen succotash, or anything else that intrigues you, for the last cooking. Serves 4.

Paul B. Johnson

Sierra Madre, Calif.

PARSLEY ROYALE

Parsley can be more than a green garnish. You might even be tempted to plant an extra row of it in your garden once you've discovered what an aristocratic soup it makes.

        1 slice bacon, diced
        4 tablespoons finely chopped onion
        2 tablespoons finely chopped celery
        2 cups water
        2 cups finely chopped parsley
        1 tablespoon butter or margarine
        1 pint milk
        3 teaspoons salt
            Freshly ground pepper to taste
        2 egg yolks, slightly beaten

Fry bacon in a deep skillet until crisp. Add onion and celery; sauté until onion is golden brown. Add water and parsley; cover and simmer for 20 minutes. Add butter, milk, and seasonings; allow to come almost to a boil; strain through a fine sieve. Stir a small amount of the soup into the egg yolks; return mixture to the skillet. Stir continuously over low heat until soup thickens slightly. Serve with croutons. Serves 4 to 6.

Frank P. Newby

Ventura, Calif.

POTATO CREAM SOUP

Chef Banner R. Brooke of Portland speaks up for a school of cookery—most strongly represented in the Northwest— that leans more heavily on the goodness of basic ingredients than on variety of seasonings.

"This is potato soup," says *Chef* Brooke. "It is not a chowder and is best if not burdened with the host of additions commonly suggested. Call it 'Poor Man's Soup' or 'Vichysoisse'; it's still really a simple cream soup—the most appealing."

        2 medium sized potatoes
        1 medium sized onion
        1 tablespoon salt
            Water
        1 cup evaporated milk
        1 tablespoon butter or margarine
        ½ teaspoon pepper
            Grated Parmesan cheese, or chopped chives

Quarter both the peeled potatoes and the onion. Salt and cover with water in a saucepan with a lid. Cover and boil until onions are well cooked. Mash onion and potatoes with a fork. Add evaporated milk, butter, and pepper. Sprinkle each bowl with grated Parmesan cheese—or chopped chives—or both, and serve hot. Serves 4 or 5.

Dr. Banner R. Brooke

Physican (retired)
Portland, Oregon

GREEN SOUP

        6 cups of beef and ham stock
        1 cup minced raw spinach
        ½ cup minced green onion
        ½ cup mixed greens (kale, sorrel, beet tops—
            your choice) minced
            Bouquet of parsley, celery, rosemary, and
            other herbs to taste
        1 tablespoon flour
        5 tablespoons sour cream
        3 hard cooked eggs

Bring the stock to boil slowly. Add the spinach, onions, mixed vegetable greens, and bouquet of herbs tied together so you can easily remove them later, and let simmer slowly for 1 hour. Remove pan from fire and discard bouquet of herbs. Mix flour with sour cream, gradually adding a little of the hot soup as you do so, until the mixture is fairly thin and smooth. Add mixture to soup pan, return it to the fire, and stir the soup until it thickens slightly and just comes to a boil. Serve with some slices of hard boiled egg in each soup bowl, and add additional sour cream, if desired. Serves 6 to 8.

Abe Zwellinger

North Hollywood, Calif.

BEAN SOUP COLBY

Chef Edward P. Colby captivated our taste testers with a soup developed much as a chemist might develop a new compound in his test tube. He started—sensibly enough these days—with a canned soup. Some might find minor fault with the appearance·of this soup—it does look a little like chocolate pudding. The remedy is easy: Make the blob of whipped cream on each serving generous enough to cover the whole surface. (If you'd rather, use sour cream.)

    1 can (10½ oz.) black bean soup
    1 cup milk
    1 large clove garlic, mashed
    ½ teaspoon hot salsa sauce (or a few drops
        Tabasco)
    ½ teaspoon fresh ground ginger, or ¼
        teaspoon dry powdered ginger
    1 small can (4 oz.) Vienna sausage, chopped
    1 teaspoon olive oil
    ¼ cup mayonnaise
        Whipped cream (optional)
    4 to 6 teaspoons chopped chives

Put bean soup and milk in saucepan and mix thoroughly; then add garlic, salsa, ginger, and chopped sausage. Stir olive oil into mayonnaise, shake or stir together vigorously, then add to the soup. Simmer for 20 minutes, stirring occasionally. If you don't mind the calories, put a generous blob of whipped cream on each serving before topping it with chives. Serve piping hot. Serves 4.

Edward P. Colby

Lanakai, Oahu, T. H.

POTLATCH CHOWDER

Potlatch is the Chinook Indian name for a festival of trading, gambling, love-making —a colorful spectacle which, unfortunately, is gradually disappearing from the Northwest.

By the size and splendor of his potlatch, you could judge an Indian's importance in his community. An abundance of foods, a heavy attendance, numerous and costly gifts to the most distinguished guests— all marked a true man of distinction. Sometimes an Indian would save for a lifetime in order to give one large unforgettable potlatch.

Customs have changed in the Northwest in the last hundred years. But people have not lost their love of feasting on copious goodness such as *Chef* A. B. Woodworth of Tacoma has crowded into one memorable "Potlatch Chowder." It should give you a high chief's rating with your guests.

"In this I use a much-overlooked mollusk, the horse clam — easily dug, and found in large numbers on Pacific Coast beaches. (Also known as the *Gaper clam*, up to eight inches long, up to four pounds in weight, lives in mud bottoms of bays and inlets from San Diego to Alaska.)

"Hope you have a large container, because this recipe makes two gallons. It is expected that on most occasions this will be the main dish and it will be strictly a chowder party. Green salad may be added if necessary.

"If you wish to prepare this for future reference, it can be frozen, kept handy for drop-in guests, and it will be good as new."

This dish is big and full-bodied. The blend of 18 ingredients can scarcely be harmed by an individual substitution. Don't like parsnips? Subtract them; add more clams. Use canned minced clams if you don't have the fresh handy.

    3 pints ground horse clams
    ½ pound bacon, sliced and cut in ¼-inch pieces
    4 medium to large potatoes, diced
    4 medium onions, diced
    3 cloves garlic, minced
    2 parsnips, diced
    4 medium carrots, sliced
    6 large, outside pieces celery, sliced
    1 green pepper, chopped
    1 can (No. 2) whole kernel corn
    1 can (No. 2) tomatoes
    1 large can (No. 5) tomato juice
        Rind of 1 lemon, grated or
        very finely chopped
    1 tablespoon salt
    1 teaspoon pepper
    1 teaspoon nutmeg
    ½ teaspoon Tabasco sauce
    3 tablespoons Worcestershire sauce

It will take about six horse clams to make three pints. (Actually, any kind of clam will suffice.) Take the clam out of the shell. Cut off neck. Scald and peel off outer skin. Slit and wash out sand. Clean out stomach by squeezing out all dark substances. Grind up all that is left—digger, neck, outside of stomach, and so on. It's all good except the stomach contents.

"An overlooked mollusk, the horse clam"

Fry bacon and put in pot, drippings and all. Put in all other ingredients. Bring to a boil, then turn heat down to simmer until vegetables are done. If the chowder appears to be too thick, add water. But don't carry this to the dilution stage. Slow cooking is important!

Serve in bowls of any size appropriate to the occasion. Should serve anywhere from 10 to 30 people, depending on whether it is preliminary or main event.

A. B. Woodworth
Tacoma

LAMB'S CLAM CHOWDER

Now here's a recipe for clam chowder that certainly rates in the granddaddy-of-them-all class. Preparations should be deliberate and unhurried, in the manner of New England. Roland T. Lamb, of Inverness, California, says, "The recipe has been in our family for over 50 years and originally came from Worcester, Mass., via Boston."

A chowder "baked" in the oven may be new to your food experience. It's recommended as the main dish for a fall or winter lunch or dinner. "If possible," says Roland Lamb, "the chowder should be prepared the previous day so it can stand overnight. If that is inconvenient, try to make it sufficiently in advance so it can cool in the milk and then be reheated—it may be necessary to add more scalded milk."

The architect's specifications call for "Tomales Bay cockleshells," but if you don't live on Tomales Bay, as he does, you may have to accept some alternates. Fortunately, almost every section of beach along the Pacific Coast yields some sort of small succulent clam (2 to 3 inches) be it bent-nose, cockle, littleneck, chione, or razor.

    4 quarts live clams (Tomales Bay cockleshells,
        or other small clams)
    1 pound box pilot crackers, or similar water
        and flour crackers
    3 to 4 quarts milk
    1 pound fat salt pork, sliced and cut into
        very thin strips
    6 medium sized potatoes, sliced
    6 onions, sliced
      Pepper to taste
    ½ cube butter

Scrub clams, place in a pot, partially cover with water, and steam until the shells open. Remove meat from shells and place on dish for use later. Strain the clam juice, or broth, and save. Break the crackers into pieces about the size of a potato slice and soak in about 2 cups milk until soft.

In a large round casserole, place:

    1 layer of salt pork, covering bottom
        of pan,
    1 layer of sliced raw potatoes,
    1 layer sliced raw onions,
    1 layer steamed clams,
    1 layer soaked pilot crackers.

Pepper each individual layer, but add no salt. Repeat each layer in above order until all pork, potatoes, onions, and clams have been used. Put 1 layer of butter on the last layer of crackers. Pour strained clam broth over top of chowder. Cover casserole and bake very slowly at 300° for 3 hours, adding a little water if the dish starts to dry out (take a peek into the oven every now and then).

After chowder bakes 3 hours, scald milk, add to hot chowder, and stir gently. (The chowder should not be thin.) Place on asbestos plate, or other protective device, on top of range and keep *below* boiling point until ready to serve. Or—better—allow to cool in the milk; reheat slowly to serve. Serves 15.

Roland T. Lamb
Retired
Inverness, Calif.

LENTIL-PEA PURÉE

G. W. Phillips, Lt., USN, admits he is a "frustrated chemist at heart." Before your mind leaps to some wild picture of a mad scientist turned loose in the kitchen laboratory, let us hasten to say that the spirit of scientific inquiry is an excellent attribute for a *Chef of the West*. This candidate has long "cast a covetous eye" on our culinary order.

It is unfair to judge a lentil-pea dish on appearance alone. Its color is God-given. You can always float a slice of lemon, a sprig of parsley, or a blob of sour cream, on top for some contrast in color as well as flavor. The tomato is a refreshing surprise in this combination.

```
½-pound piece salt pork
 2 quarts water
½ pound lentils
½ pound split peas
 1 large onion, diced
 1 can (8 oz.) tomato sauce
   Salt and pepper to taste
```

Brown salt pork on all sides in a large, heavy kettle. Add water, lentils, peas, and onion; cover and simmer for 2 hours, or until lentils are very tender. Add tomato sauce and heat. Remove pork. Purée through strainer or food mill; salt and pepper to taste. Serve with a scattering of croutons, a sprinkle of Parmesan cheese, or just plain. Serves 6 to 8.

Lieutenant, USN
Chula Vista, Calif.

PURÉE OF LENTIL SOUP DE LOS REYES

A good reliable soup is the mainstay of many a *Chef*. This soup, contributed by Charles L. Palmer, is practically a whole meal. Above all, it should be served hot, lest it resemble adobe. We suggest more consommé and water.

"It really is a lot of work to make," says *Chef* Palmer, "but worth it, especially if a liquidizer can relieve the strain of mashing ingredients through a sieve." (A food mill will do the job, too.)

"Let me say here that a poor sauterne will make all the difference in the flavor, adversely. I use a fine, light chablis. Any equivalent wine will do."

```
 1 pound dried lentils
 2 carrots
½ bell pepper
 1 stalk celery
 1 clove garlic
 2 sprigs yerba buena, or 3 leaves mint
 2 link sausages
 2 bay leaves
½ teaspoon thyme
 1 teaspoon salt
¼ teaspoon, each, oregano, sage, black pepper
⅛ teaspoon, each, ginger, nutmeg
 1 pinch dried rosemary leaves
 5 cups water
```

Wash and soak lentils for 1 to 2 hours. Cut carrots, bell pepper, and celery into small pieces. Strip leaves off yerba buena or mint. Place ingredients in a covered pan and simmer overnight, or 6 to 8 hours, adding more water if necessary.

When thoroughly cooked and soft, remove from fire and cool. Lift out and discard the sausages and bay leaves. Mash the remaining mixture through colander, or put through liquidizer. This should produce purée about the consistency of a thick pudding. Store in refrigerator.

To serve 4 persons, add 1 can condensed consomme (or more) to each 4 cups of purée and cook to desired consistency.

Ladle into individual soup bowls and put into each 2 tablespoons of fine light chablis or sauterne wine and 1 pat of butter. Serve at once.

Publicity
Fresno, Calif.

UN-ELABORATE ONION SOUP

Chef K. L. Boosey of San Jose, California, names this "Un-elaborate Onion Soup." Instead of using a bouillon or consommé for the base, he makes a beef stock and then conveniently forgets to take out the beef. In place of the usual Parmesan cheese, he uses Romano cheese —wrapped in aluminum foil and kept in the refrigerator between bouts with the un-elaborate onion—and grates it fresh each time.

1 large beef knuckle bone, sawed into 4 pieces
1 pound lean beef stew meat
  Water
1 tablespoon salt
4 small bay leaves
16 large onions
½ cup olive oil
1 teaspoon salt
  Pepper to taste
2 heaping tablespoons grated Romano cheese
¼ cup sherry
  Rye toast, croutons, or sour French bread

Cover bones and beef with water, add salt, bay leaves, and water; bring to a vigorous boil, and then simmer about 4 hours, or until meat falls to pieces and marrow is cooked out of the bone. Let this stock get cold; then lift all the hard fat off the top and discard. Remove bones and bay leaves. Finely shred the stew meat and put back in the stock. Slice onions on the bias. Fry in olive oil over medium to fast heat, and turn constantly until onions are a deep golden brown all the way through. Sprinkle with the teaspoon of salt as you fry

At this stage, both stock and fried onions can be put in the refrigerator and kept for several days if desired.

When ready for onion soup, combine onions and stock, add pepper to taste (salt as necessary) and the Romano cheese, and bring to a boil (no more). Add wine and serve in hot bowls with a sprinkling of Romano cheese and (a) slice of rye toast in bottom of the bowl, (b) croutons, or (c) fresh sour French bread (best of all). With the shredded meat and the bread, this can be a whole meal that will serve 12 people.

K L Boosey

Credit manager
San Jose, Calif.

TURKEY SOUP TEPIC

Sufferers from holiday malaise sometimes welcome the man who serves a savory soup as heartily as lost travelers in the Alps are supposed to welcome that big shaggy dog carrying a small cask of "XXX" under his muzzle. *Chef* George C.

Booth plays the role of shaggy dog in this story; and just to confuse the geography, we'll shift the locale to Mexico.

"We'll shift the locale to Mexico"

"Last Christmas we drove down the West Coast Highway to Guadalajara. At Tepic we enjoyed a soup furnished by the lordly Mexican *guajolote* (turkey), a concoction at once restful and soothing, but exciting to the taste buds. I obtained the recipe and shall be proud to share it."

  Remnants of turkey
3 quarts water
1 bell pepper, seeded and chopped
1 medium onion, chopped
1 clove garlic, chopped
1 cup celery tops, chopped
3 sprigs parsley, chopped
1 bay leaf
2 teaspoons salt
  Pepper to taste
8 oz. package medium sized noodles
1 cup cream or evaporated milk

Put turkey bones, skin, any bits of leftover meat, and dressing remnants in the 3 quarts water. Add the chopped vegetables, bay leaf, and seasonings, and simmer for 3 hours. Strain through a colander fine enough so that only the clear soup is saved. Cook the noodles until they are just tender. Add to barely boiling soup and cook another 20 minutes. Turn off heat, add the cream, stir, and serve. Serves 8.

Geo. C. Booth

Teacher
Long Beach, Calif.

"The fish, which we did eat in Egypt freely, the cucumbers, the melons, and the leeks, and the onions, and the garlick"

CHICKEN AND CUCUMBER SOUP

If you want to build a really cool soup, what material is more logical than the proverbial cool cucumber, whose merit as a garden vegetable has been recognized at least since the time of Moses?

"We remember the fish, which we did eat in Egypt freely; the cucumbers, and the melons, and the leeks, and the onions, and the garlick."—*Numbers* xi, 5

This recipe uses cucumbers, some onions, too, and some chicken stock to give it a good rich base. It gives you cucumber without the seeds—the essence of cucumber minus what some people consider its less desirable substance. Actually, as *Chef* Ed Fitzharris points out, you can serve the soup either cold or hot; and you can make it with either sweet cream or sour cream. If the latter, add after the soup has cooled.

    3 large cucumbers
    2 tablespoons butter.
    3 cups chicken stock or canned chicken broth
    3 tablespoons flour
    1 medium sized onion, sliced
    1 cup milk
    1 cup cream
      Salt and pepper
      Minced parsley
      Chopped green onion

Peel and slice cucumbers, removing seeds. Cook in butter over low heat for 10 minutes. Gradually add flour, then chicken stock, stirring continually. Put onion, sliced very thin, into milk and bring just to a boil. Put through strainer to remove onion, and add milk to soup. Push soup through a sieve or food mill; stir in cream, season with salt and pepper to taste, and chill. Serve cold with sprinkling of green onion and parsley on top. Serves 8.

Public relations consultant
San Francisco, Calif.

CRAB LEGS BETHESDA

Heat together 1 can cream of spinach soup, 1 can tomato soup, and ¼ teaspoon of either basil or rosemary. Add 4 tablespoons sherry and pour into hot soup dishes. Put 4 crab legs into each serving.

Real estate
Bellevue, Washington

COD CHOWDER NEU STYLE

Chef Frank M. Neu of Redlands, California, used Pacific Coast cod for this chowder, and we believe it is a happy choice. All of the several fish sold locally as cod have rather solid flesh which does not cook to pieces in chowder. We believe that the thick fillets probably taste better in chowder than they do when they are either baked or fried.

chowder

"Anything from clams to whale meat . . . properly subdued by seasoning, of course"

On the point of classical controversy, *Chef* New sides with the New York school by using tomatoes instead of milk. His really unique seasoning touch is the tablespoon of lemon juice.

    2 slices bacon
    1 medium-sized onion, minced
    1 teaspoon salt
    ⅓ teaspoon pepper
    1 teaspoon minced parsley
    1 teaspoon dried basil, crushed
    1 teaspoon dried thyme, crushed
    1 bay leaf
    1 pint (2 cups) boiling water
    1 pound cod fillets, fresh or frozen, cut in
        small chunks
    ½ cup cooked tomatoes
    1 medium-sized potato, cubed
    1 tablespoon lemon juice

Cut bacon in small pieces and fry until crisp. Add minced onion and sauté. Add all seasoning and herbs and stir well; then add the boiling water, fish, tomatoes, potato, and lemon juice. Let simmer 20 to 30 minutes, or until potatoes are done, stirring occasionally. Serve hot with crackers. Serves 4.

Frank M. New

Veterans affairs
Redlands, Calif.

GAZPACHO

This iced soup, a favorite in Mexico and Central and South America, is a fine beginning for a dinner with a Latin flavor. After it, serve enchiladas, a hot vegetable, a tossed green salad, and hot French bread. If you wish to venture beyond this classical combination, serve guava jelly and cream cheese with crackers for dessert.

    4 large, very ripe tomatoes, peeled and
        chopped
    1 large cucumber, peeled and diced
    1 onion, finely minced
    1 green pepper, finely minced
    ½ cup French dressing (1 part wine vinegar
        and 3 parts olive oil, with salt, freshly
        ground black pepper, and garlic to taste)
    1 cup tomato juice
      Seasonings to taste

Mix the vegetables, French dressing, and tomato juice. Rectify the seasoning and put the soup into the refrigerator to chill.

Serve in soup dishes with an ice cube in each. The Latins serve their *gazpacho* over sippets of toast, but I prefer to pass croutons with this American version.

Bill Comstock

Pasadena, Calif.

CREAM OF ONION SOUP

    2 pounds red onions
    ¼ pound (1 cube) butter or margarine
    1 can beef bouillon
    3 cups water
    1 package Italian bread sticks, about
        2 cups crushed
    ½ pint heavy cream
      Salt and pepper

Peel onions and slice so they are paper thin. Dump them in a big kettle in which the large hunk of butter is melting over a slow fire. Throw in the bouillon and water. Now break up the bread sticks (this makes the soup thick or *à la purée*). Stir in crumbs and let her simmer all day, not boil. Just before serving add cream and season to taste with salt and pepper.

Electrical manufacturer
Los Angeles, Calif.

AVOCADO SOUP À LA MEXICANA

3 green chili peppers
2 medium-sized avocados
Salt
1 tablespoon minced coriander or parsley
6 cups rich stock, chicken preferred

Mince the chilis very fine and mash with avocados that have been peeled. Press through potato ricer, season with salt to taste; divide in 6 equal parts, one for each plate. Sprinkle with some coriander or parsley. Add to each plate one cup of hot stock. Serve very hot with *tortillas*.

MAX WILMARTH
Manhattan Beach, Calif.

CREAM OF AVOCADO SOUP

Like works of art in other fields, this avocado soup by *Chef* Wilbur G. Graf of

"Like works of art in other fields"

Tucson, Arizona, seems so logical, so inevitable, that you ask, "How could it have been made in any other way?" Actually, it has been made in a good many other ways, with flour or jellied consommé for thickening, and with a variety of other additives. However, this way is the simplest and also one of the best—

1 large ripe avocado
2 cans (14½ oz.) evaporated milk
1 pint (2 cups) fresh milk
½ teaspoon celery salt
½ teaspoon garlic salt
¼ teaspoon monosodium glutamate
Salt and pepper to taste

Peel avocado, remove seed, and run it through a blender or press through a sieve. Beat the evaporated milk into the avocado pulp; then stir in the fresh milk. Add seasonings and heat enough to blend all ingredients. Serve hot with garlic croutons, or allow it to cool and serve cold. Serves 6 to 8.

Wilbur G. Graf

Tucson, Arizona

BORSCH

Both the spelling and the pronunciation of borsch are confusing to us who speak English. In various cook books you may find it spelled bortsch, borsh, borsch, or borsht. The stickler is one letter in the Russian alphabet which has no counterpart in English. We can only come close with the sound "tsch," as in Tschaikowsky. If you have trouble saying borsch, try putting the soup and the music together—BORSH-TSCH(aikowsky is silent).

Elegant beet borsch is served either hot or cold. An old-time recipe may involve beef bones, pork knuckles, various other meats, 15 or 20 other ingredients, and hours of preparation and watching.

However, Comet Brooks, a veteran *Chef*, understands a basic principle of borsch: If you begin with beets and end with sour cream, you have wide latitude on other ingredients.

2 cans (No. 1 *each*) shoestring beets
1 small head cabbage, shredded
1 onion, sliced
Small piece of bay leaf
Tops from 2 stalks celery
Juice of 1 lemon
2 cans (10½ oz. *each*) bouillon
2 soup cans water
Sour cream (approximately ½ pint)

Drain juice from beets and set aside. Place beets, cabbage, onion, bay leaf, celery tops, and lemon juice in a large saucepan along with bouillon and water. Bring to a boil and simmer ½ hour. Strain. Add reserved beet juice and heat but do not bring to a boil.

"Try putting the soup and the music together"

Serve at once with great gobs of sour cream. Serves 4 to 6.

Comet Brooks
Biochemist (retired)
Rolling Hills, Calif.

OLD-FASHIONED CHICKEN SOUP

In an age when cookery tends to get more and more sophisticated, we should all stand up and cheer a man who does a good job of reversing the field. Candidate Schuyler C. Hill brews an honest-to-goodness soup using nothing but common old-fashioned ingredients, no exotic imported seasonings, not even onion or garlic, nothing more frivolous than some parsley to top it with flecks of bright green.

In spite of the impressively solid phalanx of ingredients, it is not at all heavy like the usual cream soup. You could serve it in cups as a preface to dinner, or in man sized bowls as a main dish.

    1 cup minced cold chicken
    1 quart chicken stock
    1 cup table cream
    2 hard cooked egg yolks
    1 tablespoon flour
    1 tablespoon butter or margarine
    Salt and pepper to taste
    Minced parsley

Add chicken to broth and heat. Stir in the cream and, when it almost comes to a boil, thicken with the egg yolks, previously mashed together with the flour and butter. Continue to cook and stir until the mixture is creamy. Season with salt and pepper to taste. Serve while hot, sprinkled with minced parsley. Serves 6

"Nothing more frivolous than parsley"

to 8 as a first course for dinner, or 4 as a main dish.

Schuyler C. Hill

U.S. Army
Fairchild Air Force Base, Wash.

"A fishing guide introduced him to 'Pea Soup Sierra' back in 1912"

POTAGE POULET À LA PARME

6 onions
1/4 pound ham, minced
4 tablespoons butter
1/4 pound fresh bread crumbs (1/4 of a
    1-pound loaf)
3 pints rich chicken stock
    Salt and pepper to taste
    Blade of mace
1/4 pound Parmesan cheese, grated
2 egg yolks, slightly beaten

Peel, slice, and fry onions with minced ham and butter. Add bread crumbs, chicken stock (canned chicken broth may be used), and seasonings. Cook for 1/2 hour and then add grated cheese and egg yolks. Strain and serve at once. Approximately 10 servings.

ROBERT L. BALZER
*Purveyor of fine foods
Los Angeles, Calif.*

PEA SOUP SIERRA

O. E. Cook from Acton, California, says he has been husbanding this delectable recipe for over 40 years—ever since a fishing guide in the high Sierra introduced him to "Pea Soup Sierra" in 1912. It's still him to "Pea Soup Sierra" in 1912. It's still a weekly must in the Cook family.

Ingredients for pea soup are usually about the same the world around. This recipe follows the line on the basic ingredients—split peas, ham, and onions—but the proportions and seasonings show the imagination of a *Chef of the West* in action.

4 quarts water
1 medium sized onion
1/2 clove garlic
2 pounds ham hocks
1 teaspoon curry powder
2 tablespoons lemon juice
1 tablespoon brown sugar
1 teaspoon pepper
1/2 teaspoon Tabasco
1 pound dried split green peas

Put water in a large kettle, then add whole onion, garlic, ham hocks, curry powder, lemon juice, brown sugar, pepper, and the Tabasco. (The peas are late comers and won't be added until the preliminaries are completed.)

Simmer very, very slowly for about 2 hours. Remove the ham, discarding the bone, skin, and fat. Cut the meat into small pieces and set it aside. Add the dried peas to the liquid and let simmer slowly for 1 1/2 hours, stirring occasionally after the first hour to keep from sticking.

After the peas are cooked, beat the soup with a rotary or electric beater for about 5 minutes, or until you have a perfect blend of all the ingredients—with no lumps of any size or description. Heat for about 15 minutes, then toss in the ham you set aside earlier, and heat for about 10 minutes more. Serves 10 to 12.

O. E. Cook

Acton, Calif.

NAMELESS TOMATO SOUP

    8 ripe tomatoes, medium size
    4 cups water
    4 tablespoons butter
  ¼ cup diced, uncooked ham
  ½ cup each diced onion, celery, and carrot
    2 sprigs parsley, minced
    2 slices green pepper, minced
    1 can consommé or beef broth
    1 bay leaf
    4 whole cloves
    3 sprigs thyme
    2 teaspoons Worcestershire sauce
    1 pinch paprika
    1 teaspoon salt
       Pepper to taste

Cut up unpeeled tomatoes, add water and cook 10 minutes. Crush, then spoon out skin particles. Add butter to ham, vegetables and seasonings, and sauté for 5 minutes. Combine all ingredients and cook slowly for 1¼ hours, adding water—but not too much — if necessary to increase liquid. Serves 6 to 8.

A large can of tomatoes may be substituted for the raw ones.

Gary H. Travers

Oakland.

SOPA DE GARBANZOS

We thank Frank Dale Morgan of Los Angeles for this contribution. He writes: "In Tampa, Florida, I discovered that the best places to eat were the restaurants of Ybor City, a suburb of Tampa. According to local history, this suburb was the place selected to make the first Cuban cigars in the States. As the population includes about twenty thousand Spanish-Cuban Americans, this district naturally features Cuban dishes.

"My favorite is the Sopa de Garbanzos. This soup is delicious when newly made, but it always is better on the second day. You can heat it in a pot on the grill of the outdoor barbecue. And you'll find it excellent to store in your home freezer for future use."

Needless to say, this is soup of the hardiest character. Saffron and chorizo sausage introduce flavors new to many palates. We strongly advise that you watch the fat content carefully. We would go to some trouble to avoid having a floating lake of oil on top of the final product. If your beef or ham bones are quite fatty, you may need no lard. Or you may eliminate all the bacon drippings. Better experiment on this point a little, and, if necessary, skim off excess fat again just before you ladle it into the bowls.

  1½ cups garbanzos (chick peas)
  1½ quarts water (approximately)
    1 ham bone
    1 beef bone
  ¼ pound bacon, finely chopped
    1 large onion, finely chopped
  ½ tablespoon salt
       Pinch of saffron
    4 tablespoons lard or shortening
    1 large or 2 medium-sized potatoes, diced
    1 chorizo sausage

Soak garbanzos overnight in salted water. Drain. Add the 1½ quarts water, or enough to cover the garbanzos by at least 2 inches. Add the ham and beef bones and cook 1½ to 2 hours over slow heat or until garbanzos are done. Skim off the extra fat.

Next, lightly fry the finely-chopped bacon and onion. When golden brown, add them to the garbanzos along with the salt, saffron, lard, and diced potatoes. Continue cooking slowly until potatoes are done. Immediately before serving, slice chorizo as thin as you can manage and place 2 or 3 thin slices in each soup plate. Fill with hot soup and serve with plenty of garlic bread and hot Cuban coffee. Serves 8.

Frank Dale Morgan

Lawyer
Los Angeles, Calif.

ALBONDIGA SOUP

I onion, minced
I clove garlic, minced
I large or 2 small green chili peppers,
    minced (seeds removed)
¼ cup salad oil (preferably olive oil)
½ can (8 oz.) Spanish-style tomato sauce
12 beef bouillon cubes
3 quarts water

Sauté onion, garlic, and chili pepper in oil until onion is translucent. Add tomato sauce, bouillon cubes, and water; heat to boiling point. Prepare meat balls for soup as follows:

Meat Balls (albondigas)

¾ pound lean beef
¾ pound lean pork
⅓ cup raw rice
2 level teaspoons coriander seed
2 teaspoons dried mint leaves
1½ teaspoons salt
¼ teaspoon pepper
I egg, beaten

Put the meat, rice, coriander seed, and mint leaves through the meat grinder together, using finest blade. Add salt, pepper, and egg. Shape mixture into balls about the size of a walnut. Drop balls into boiling soup, cover kettle, and simmer gently for 45 minutes. Serve with crisp crackers. Serves 5.

Geo. C. Truman M.D.

Physician and surgeon
Mesa, Arizona

MARROW BALL SOUP

2 ounces beef marrow
2 eggs
I teaspoon salt
½ teaspoon pepper
    Pinch of sugar
4 ounces toasted, fine bread crumbs
    Chopped parsley
    Juice of ½ medium-sized onion

From a raw shin-bone of beef, extract the marrow; chop it and work in the eggs, salt, pepper, and sugar until the mixture is smooth. Add the bread crumbs, parsley, and onion juice, and stir until smooth again. Set aside for several hours to stiffen in a cool place or in the refrigerator. Bring your favorite soup stock to a good boil, divide the marrow mixture into marble-sized dumplings, and drop them into the soup. Let them cook slowly for 15 minutes. The marrow balls should then be light and porous—but good! Just remember that too much cooking causes them to fall apart.

W. G. Doss
Artist
Laguna Beach, Calif.

POT-AU-FEU

4½ or 5 pounds beef and bone (plate or brisket
    recommended—cut beef in cubes)
I large onion, sliced
6 or 7 stalks celery, diced
I bunch parsley
5 or 6 cloves
3 bay leaves
4 quarts cold water
I bunch turnips
2 bunches carrots
    Salt to taste

Put all ingredients in kettle except turnips, carrots, and salt. Bring to a boil, then simmer until the meat is done. Cool, and skim off fat.

Add whole turnips and carrots and salt to soup. Cook about 30 minutes, or until the vegetables are done. Remove meat, bones, and carrots. Reserve only the edible portion of the meat. Pour the soup through a large, fine colander or strainer. Reheat and serve.

With the broth serve the carrots, mashed and seasoned with French dressing, the hot meat, some French bread, and wine. Serves 6.

CHARLES SLOAN
Cook
Dinuba, Calif.

salads

LETTUCE IMPERIAL

From the garden land around San Diego, Merle F. Miller almost always can commandeer a green salad's most essential ingredient — superb quality lettuce. As he says appreciatively:

"When business takes us to Imperial Valley during the lettuce season along about the first of the year, we come home with at least two crates of this wonderful crop. Following is my recipe for enhancing it."

Place in a measuring cup ¼ cup sugar, 1 teaspoon Worcestershire sauce, 1 teaspoon salt, ¼ teaspoon pepper, ¼ teaspoon garlic salt, 1 teaspoon prepared mustard, 2 drops Tabasco sauce.

Measure the total contents of the cup with your eye, then add about an equal amount of cider vinegar. Stir, and let stand while you fry 3 strips of bacon in 4 tablespoons olive oil.

Break up 1 large head of lettuce in a large bowl. On top, drop ½ large onion, diced, and slivers of radish.

Now add to the contents of the cup enough water to fill it up. Stir, and combine with the fried bacon and oil. Heat (do not boil) and pour over bowl of lettuce. Cover immediately and rush it to the table. Serve in large, large helpings and watch it disappear.

This much salad will serve only two of us, but it can be stretched for four or more if their green salad appetites are not so healthy as ours.

Merle F. Miller

Vice President
National City, Calif.

MIXED GREEN SALAD

2 heads romaine
1 bunch watercress
4 stalks celery
1 clove garlic

Remove the salad greens from the refrigerator and proceed as follows:

Tear romaine in pieces. Remove large stems from watercress. Slice celery. Mix all together in a wooden salad bowl which has been well rubbed with garlic. Place bowl of greens in the refrigerator until needed. Dress salad just before serving with Sauce Eileen.

Sauce Eileen

¼ cup mayonnaise
¼ cup salad oil
2 tablespoons lime juice
2 tablespoons tarragon wine vinegar
1 tablespoon white table wine or sherry
½ teaspoon seasoned salt

Combine all ingredients in a bowl and beat with a rotary beater. Just before serving the salad, pour the sauce over the chilled greens, and turn greens with a wooden fork and spoon so that all are well coated.

ARTHUR STROCK
Attorney
Los Angeles, Calif.

HOLIDAY EGG SALAD

In many homes, a buffet supper is spread Christmas Eve or Christmas Night. For just such an occasion, *Chef* Paul de Sainte Columbe devised this feature dish.

1 can devilled ham
1 cup mayonnaise
½ cup tartar sauce
1 jigger *each* sherry and Bourbon
Juice of 2 lemons
2 tablespoons dried tarragon
Pinch *each* curry (imported is best), nutmeg, salt, and pepper
1 dozen hard-cooked eggs, sliced

Blend ham and mayonnaise; mix with remainder of ingredients. Garnish with halved stuffed olives, parsley, and paprika. Serve as buffet salad.

Paul de Sainte Columbe

Writer and columnist
Hollywood, Calif.

INSALADANG CAMATIS

(Tomatoes Stuffed with Pineapple)

This dish is an import from the Philippines; the name comes from the Tagalog dialect.

6 medium sized firm tomatoes
1½ cups shredded fresh pineapple, or 1 can (No. 2) drained, crushed pineapple
½ cup chopped salted peanuts
2 teaspoons anchovy paste
Salt to taste

Scald the tomatoes, plunge them into cold water, and remove their skins. Cut a slice from the top of each and remove the pulp and seeds. (You can always find some future use for this meat of the tomato.) Thoroughly chill the tomato jackets. Combine the pineapple, peanuts, and anchovy paste; and stuff each jacket with the mixture. Arrange the tomatoes on lettuce leaves and serve one to each guest. Serves 6.

Secretary
Seattle, Washington

APHRODITE VERDANT DRESSING

½ medium-sized avocado
⅔ cake (3 oz.) cream cheese
⅛ teaspoon dry mustard
1 teaspoon lemon juice or ½ teaspoon onion
   juice
  Salt
  Mere dash of white pepper
2 tablespoons mayonnaise

Cream avocado with fork until smooth. Add cream cheese, mustard, lemon or onion juice, and seasonings, beating until smooth. (Use lemon juice for fruit salads and onion juice for vegetable salads.) Then mix in mayonnaise.

This dressing is particularly delicious on salads of alternate slices of avocado and grapefruit segments.

Publicity
Fresno, Calif.

FANCY HOLLOW HEAD FRENCH DRESSING

There's a proper restraint in seasonings for this salad dressing, and some special legerdemain in the mixing of liquids. Why the name? *Chef* B. N. Prieth of Carmel Valley, California, says, "My small office sports a sign 'Hollow Head Acres'—five acres on which we have two more or less hollow heads, three kids, two dogs, a Siamese cat, three ducks, five chickens, and more gophers than the law allows." The dressing is *Chef* Prieth's variation on some he has found in books and seen made by chefs in large hotels. *Sunset* testers rated it "tart and tangy."

⅓ cup wine vinegar
1 teaspoon salt
¼ teaspoon freshly ground pepper
1 teaspoon dry mustard
1 teaspoon sugar
1 teaspoon paprika
  Garlic powder or chopped garlic to taste
    (very, very little)
⅛ teaspoon fines herbs
½ cup (¼ lb.) Roquefort or blue cheese
½ cube (4 tablespoons) butter
1 cup olive oil
2 tablespoons water

Mix together the vinegar, salt, pepper, mustard, sugar, paprika, garlic, and herbs. Blend cheese and butter together to make a paste, add to other ingredients, and mix well again. Add olive oil and blend well. Dilute with water. Makes enough dressing for a tossed green salad to serve 6.

Lumbering
Carmel Valley, Calif.

"Three kids, two dogs, a cat, three ducks, five chickens, more gophers than law allows"

FRUIT SALAD WITH HAM

Kenneth C. Yeazell is a Police Lieutenant in Tucson, Arizona. His off-duty hobby is "the intricate problem of putting together various basic foods so that they have a taste and sight appeal . . . Only when I hit the right combination do I consider the case closed on a particular culinary item."

For example, he combines the season's fruits in a salad to serve over hot baked ham, an excellent suggestion for a hot weather meal. If you like this salad sauce more tart, augment the lemon (or lime).

Dice and combine:
- 1 apple
- 1 banana
- 1 peach
- 2 stalks celery
- 1 orange
- 1 handful seedless grapes, cut in halves
- 2 tablespoons chopped nut meats

Prepare sauce:
- ½ cup boiling water
- ¼ cup orange juice
- 4 tablespoons honey
- 1½ tablespoons seedless raisins
- 1-inch piece stick cinnamon
- ½ dozen marshmallows
- About 15 red hot cinnamon candies
- ¼ cup date sugar
- ½ teaspoon lemon juice

Simmer sauce three minutes. Cool to lukewarm.

Stir in:
- ½ wedge pineapple cream cheese or 1 package (3 oz.) cream cheese

Just before serving, add about 1 cup of sauce to above fruit mix. Serve on top of hot sliced baked ham. Enough fruit salad sauce for 8 portions.

Kenneth C. Yeazell

Police lieutenant
Tucson, Arizona

COLD'N CRISP SALAD

"This salad is entirely unheard of outside my immediate family," says *Chef* Jim Murphy of Yakima, Washington. "Served cold and crisp, it is a wonderful addition to any barbecued dinner. With no oils or creams, only sugar to add calories, no one need be afraid of gaining much around the waistline. It can be tossed together in jig time. I enjoy it winter or summer."

"I enjoy it winter or summer"

- 2 oranges, peeled, sliced, and slices cut in half
- 2 tomatoes, sliced and slices cut in half
- 1 green pepper, cut in slivers
- 3 green onions, sliced
- 5 radishes, sliced
- 1 cucumber, sliced
- 2 stalks of celery, sliced diagonally

Dressing:
- ⅓ cup vinegar
- ½ cup sugar
- ⅔ cup water
- ½ teaspoon salt
- ¼ teaspoon pepper

Have oranges, vegetables, and dressing "refrigerator cold." Mix them together just before serving. Serve in side dishes— can be eaten with spoon if you want to enjoy dressing. Serves 4 to 6.

Jim Murphy

Yakima, Washington

ZUCCHINI SALAD

Select eight medium-sized, tender zucchini about 4-inches long. Do not peel. Boil in salted water until partially cooked (about 6 minutes). Let cool, cut in half lengthwise. Hollow out centers a bit and place in flat dish with hollow center up. Pour over a generous amount of French dressing. Lay sliced onion and garlic over the zucchini halves and let them stand, well covered, for the day in the refrigerator. At the same time, pour a can of tomato sauce in an ice tray to freeze.

When ready to serve, take off the onion and garlic. Place zucchini on crisp lettuce leaves. Fill the hollows with frozen tomato sauce. Top with mayonnaise, sprinkle with a generous amount of grated Parmesan cheese, and serve immediately.

A. R. Van Meter M.D.

Physician and surgeon
San Francisco, Calif.

OLD KENTUCKY BOILED DRESSING

    1 tablespoon salt
    1 teaspoon dry mustard
    1 tablespoon flour
    ½ cup sugar
    8 egg yolks
    1 cup cream or milk
    ½ cup vinegar

Chef Pulliam suggests that this dressing is a boon to those to whom oil is forbidden food.

Mix all dry ingredients. Place egg yolks in top of double boiler. Beat well with rotary beater, adding dry ingredients slowly. Stir in the cream. Place mixture over boiling water, and add vinegar slowly while stirring. Stir constantly until dressing is as thick as heavy cream..

A. G. Pulliam

Retired
Los Angeles, Calif.

THOUSAND ISLAND DRESSING

When you see a recipe with an arm-long list of ingredients, it isn't fair to jump to the conclusion that some *Chef* is trying for a new record.

We wouldn't guarantee that every ingredient in this recipe is absolutely indispensable, but we do know that the combination added something new to our experience with Thousand Island Dressing. It is light and nippy, without the usual heavy taste of such dressings. We can understand why *Chef* G. B. Graves says, "The response from men has been remarkable." He insists that "lemon thyme is a must."

We suggest you serve this dressing on greens alone or on some quite simple combination of vegetables or fruits; otherwise, you can't truly appreciate its delicacy of flavor.

    6 tablespoons chili sauce
    2 stuffed olives, chopped fine
    2 green peppers, seeded and chopped fine
    1 pimiento, sliced
    1 tablespoon chives (or green onion),
        chopped fine
    2 tablespoons (about 6 slices) sweet pickle
        chips, chopped fine
    1 tablespoon juice from sweet pickles
    3 tablespoons sugar
    1 teaspoon lemon juice
    ¼ teaspoon salt
    ⅛ teaspoon white pepper
    ¼ teaspoon dried lemon thyme, crumbled
    ⅛ teaspoon dried sweet basil, crumbled
    1/16 teaspoon (approximately) paprika
    1 cup mayonnaise

Mix all ingredients—be sure to add mayonnaise last—and let stand overnight before serving on salad. Makes 3 cups of dressing

G. B. Graves

Retired
Los Altos, Calif.

BEER-WITH-ROQUEFORT DRESSING

The sour cream, beer, and Roquefort seem to take the place of oil in this recipe. You can vary the amount of Roquefort as you wish, to thicken the dressing and to control the bitter flavor of the beer.

    ½ cup Roquefort or blue cheese
    1 cup beer
    1 cup sour cream
    1 tablespoon wine vinegar or garlic vinegar
    ⅛ teaspoon pepper
    1 teaspoon salt

Blend all ingredients, using as much Roquefort as necessary to make a good thick dressing. Makes 2 cups of dressing.

We like this dressing on a tossed salad of romaine, a few pieces of lettuce, sliced tomatoes or cucumbers, with a few pieces of cheese crackers, and some crab legs added to each portion.

Carl B. Jedin

Seattle

SHELTON'S SIMPLE SALAD DRESSING

"Upon the rash assumption that fruit salad, no matter how cleverly concocted, can be improved by any dressing, I submit for your consideration one that has the virtue of simplicity and which enlivens salad or fruit cup."

All might not agree that fruit always needs additional flavoring, but all our taste testers approved this addition. Almond flavoring lends an exotic touch to fruit. It is faintly reminiscent of maraschino, or even Kirsch, and is much less expensive than either.

"Almond flavoring lends an exotic touch"

For 6 servings of fruit salad, use the juice of 1 lemon and add 4 or 5 drops almond extract. Mix and pour over the fruit. What could be simpler?

£. a. Shelton
Lawyer
Claremont, Calif.

FIVE STAR DRESSING

Before making any comment on the long list of ingredients, be sure to note that actual preparation of this dish can be covered adequately in one word: "Mix!" In defense of the recipe, we can testify that the salad dressing is flavorful and also unusually light—not at all cloying.

    ½ cup salad oil
    ½ cup mayonnaise or salad dressing
    1 small (3 oz.) package Roquefort cheese
    1 tablespoon *each* tarragon, sweet basil,
        white wine vinegar, lemon juice,
        prepared mustard, and catsup
    1 egg yolk
    1 teaspoon capers
    1 medium sized onion, sliced or quartered
    2 cloves garlic, halved
    1 teaspoon *each* paprika, salt, and
        monosodium glutamate
    2 tablespoons sugar

Place all ingredients in blender. Blend for several minutes. Pour in bottle and store in refrigerator until ready for use. Makes about 1 pint of dressing. It is excellent to serve on any green salad, especially on hearts of lettuce or tossed greens.

Lieutenant, USN
Port Hueneme, Calif.

LOMI SALMON

Raw fish is no novelty in Hawaii. According to many, there's a piquancy to raw salmon, for example, that should not be cooked away. To these same hardy souls the juice from raw salted salmon is a delightful pre-dinner cocktail!

    2 pounds fresh or salted salmon
    6 large tomatoes
    4 green onions
    1 bunch green onions

Skin salmon, remove bones, and cut into small cubes. If the salmon is salted, soak it in cold water for 3 hours. Dice the tomatoes and the peppers; slice the onions, including tops. Combine all ingredients; add 1 cup cold water; mix well. Chill and serve as a salad.

Jac M. Benz
Honolulu, T.H.

fish

DALMATIAN FISH CIOPPINO

Dalmatian fishermen have been fishing in our California waters for almost a century, and the following modified recipe superbly suits California tastes.

    1 rock cod (2 to 2½ pounds)
    2 tablespoons olive oil
    1 large onion
    1 can (8 oz.) tomato sauce
    1 teaspoon black pepper
    2 cups water
      Salt to taste
      Dash of vinegar, if desired

Have your fish dealer remove the insides of a fresh rock cod, and scale it thoroughly. Have him leave the fins and head, after removing the gills. To prepare it for cooking, remove the head, split the fish in two, and cut in 1- or 1½-inch slices as if for frying.

Brown the onion slightly in olive oil in a small but deep kettle. Add the tomato sauce, heat, then add all the ingredients, except the fish. Boil vigorously, add fish, and boil for an additional 10 minutes without stirring, merely shaking to prevent scorching. Let stand for a minute or so and serve.

This may be served plain with sour dough French bread, and an endive-romaine salad with garlic-flavored French dressing, and perhaps a boiled or baked potato, or better still, with steamed rice to which is added the gravy from the cioppino. Serves 4.

Ivo H. Lopizich
Attorney
Los Angeles, Calif.

PETRALE SOLE SESAME

Here's a trick well worth knowing: *Chef Ellis G. Bovik* has devised a way to give a sesame seed coating to pan-fried fish.

The secret is to flour them first, then dip in egg, then dip in sesame seeds. He submits it here in the form of a recipe, but he says it is just as good for any other type of fish and also for chicken. The seeds do stick on evenly and give the fish a very interesting flavor.

"Wash sole and dry"

    4 medium sized soles, filleted
      Flour
      Salt
      Pepper
      Seasoning salt or garlic salt (optional)
    2 eggs
    ½ cup half-and-half (milk and cream)
      Sesame seeds
      Salad oil for frying

Wash sole and dry. Drop each fillet into paper bag in which you have put flour, salt, pepper, and seasoning or garlic salt. Shake gently. After fish is well floured, remove and dip into a mixture of the well beaten eggs and the half-and-half. (I also season this dip with salt.) Roll the fillets in a plate of sesame seeds so that they are well covered. Fry over high heat until they are golden brown on both sides. Serve immediately. I usually serve with a lemon-butter sauce. Serves 4.

Ellis G. Bovik
Dentist
Monterey, Calif.

PESCADO BALBOA

Chef Carroll O'Meara confesses "This fish casserole has drawn inspiration, frankly, from New Orleans cuisine which performs miracles with sluggish fish from the bayous.

- 2 pounds fish fillets
  (halibut, sole, or albacore)
- ½ cup fresh lemon juice
  Worcestershire sauce
- 1 teaspoon freshly ground pepper
  Minced parsley
- ½ cup mushrooms
- 2 tablespoons butter or margarine
- ½ cup water
- 2 tablespoons vinegar
- ½ teaspoon sugar
- 1 cup small San Francisco Bay shrimp
- ¾ cup grated Parmesan cheese
- 1 can mushroom soup
- ½ cup sherry wine
- ½ cup chopped chives

Wash fillets in cold water and blot dry with paper towels. Soak in lemon juice for 1 hour. Drain, blot dry, and place in casserole. Shake a few drops of Worcestershire sauce on each fillet. Then sprinkle with the teaspoon freshly ground pepper and minced parsley. Sauté mushrooms lightly in butter. Mix water with vinegar and sugar. Bring to a boil. Drop in small shrimp and simmer for 3 or 4 minutes. Spill shrimp and mushrooms over fillets. Dust lightly with part of the Parmesan cheese. Mix mushroom soup with sherry wine, pour into casserole, and spread over fillets like a mason using a trowel. Sprinkle with remaining cheese, chives, and additional parsley. Bake in a hot oven (400°) for 15 minutes. Serve with (or over) rice. Serves 6.

Carroll O'Meara

Television director
North Hollywood, Calif.

POACHED FILLET OF PETRALE
SOLE WITH SAFFRON SAUCE

- 1 tablespoon butter
- 4 large fillets of Petrale sole
  Milk and water

Butter a medium-sized shallow baking pan. Wipe the fillets well with a damp cloth, and place in the baking dish. Cover with equal parts of milk and water. Bake uncovered in a moderate oven (350° to 375°) about 25 to 30 minutes or until tender. While the sole is in the oven make the following sauce:

- 2 tablespoons butter
- 2 tablespoons flour
- 1 cup cream (half and half)
- 1 cup clam juice
- 1 teaspoon lemon juice
- ¼ cup dry Vermouth
  Salt to taste
- ¼ teaspoon powdered saffron
- 1 cup small cooked shrimp

Mix butter and flour well in the top double boiler with a wooden salad fork. Place over boiling water. Heat cream and clam juice to the boiling point and add gradually to butter and flour, stirring constantly. (Having liquids hot will prevent a lumpy sauce.) Keep stirring until sauce is well mixed. Add lemon juice and Vermouth and blend well. Salt to taste. Let this set for about 5 minutes over briskly boiling water. Turn the heat low. Add saffron and mix into the sauce, using rotary beater if necessary. Add shrimp; let stand over boiling water a few minutes longer. When fish is done, remove from the baking dish to a hot platter. Pour the sauce over the fillets and serve immediately. Serves 4.

Kenneth Melrose

Sales manager
Santa Cruz, Calif.

A WAY WITH MACKEREL

As soon as it is caught, break the fish's neck by twisting its head backwards and allowing it to bleed. Also, run a sharp knife down the dark line running from gills to tail.

On arriving home, clean, cut off the head, and remove all traces of blood and veins. Dry with a damp cloth; do not wash. Split open and flatten out. Soak in a solution of salt and water (plenty of salt) for 24 hours. Then wash off all traces of salt and paint liberally with liquid smoke. Grill lightly for five minutes to a side over oak bark coals. Serve hot or cold. These make a good snack, or even a meal with a salad and beer.

M. C. Cocksworth

Mechanical engineer
Arcadia, Calif.

SOLE IN DILL BECHAMEL SAUCE

- 1 medium-sized onion
- ½ carrot
- ½ stalk celery
- 1 bunch parsley
- 3 whole peppercorns
- ½ bay leaf
  Salt
- 1 teaspoon butter
- 2 pounds fillet of sole

Cut onion, carrot, and celery in pieces and place in kettle with other seasonings and butter. Add enough water to cover the fish when it is put in later. Boil water with vegetables for 10 minutes. Then add fish, reducing heat to simmer. Simmer for 20 minutes. Turn off heat and allow fish to remain in kettle for another 10 minutes. While fish is simmering, prepare this sauce.

Dill Bechamel Sauce
- 1½ tablespoons butter
- 2 tablespoons flour
- 3 tablespoons sour cream
- ½ cup fish stock from kettle
- 1 tablespoon chopped fresh dill
- 1 tablespoon chopped parsley
- ½ teaspoon lemon juice
  Pinch of salt
- 1 egg yolk (optional)

Melt butter in double boiler; add flour as for cream sauce. Blend with sour cream. Into this mixture, pour gradually the hot fish stock, stirring constantly to keep sauce smooth. More stock may be added if necessary. Add dill, parsley, lemon juice, and salt. For added richness, beat egg yolk in bowl and add hot sauce slowly to it, stirring constantly until blended. Pour over fish. Garnish with parsley and lemon.

Henry O Fuchs

Engineer
Los Angeles, Calif.

COD À LA O'CROTTY

- ¼ cup California olive oil
- 2 tablespoons tree-ripened fresh lime juice
- 1 onion
- 1 pound of rock cod fillets, skinned
  Salt, pepper, and a little mono sodium glutamate
- 1 tomato, quite ripe
  Chopped parsley

Mix the oil, lime juice, and 1 teaspoon of grated onion. Drench the fillets with this mixture. Place in a shallow pan, well-covered with bacon grease. Pour the rest of the oil mixture over the fillets and add salt, pepper, and mono sodium glutamate sparingly. Slice the rest of the onion and the tomato and place over the fish. Bake in a moderate oven for 25 minutes, then place under the broiler to brown for 5 minutes. Sprinkle parsley on top. Don't forget to serve the fish gravy which forms in the pan.

Peter O'Crotty

Writer
Santa Monica, Calif.

FILETS AUX CHAMPIGNONS SEC

- 1 Spanish onion, minced
- 1 ounce dried mushrooms
- ½ teaspoon marjoram
- ¼ teaspoon ground cloves
- 12 drops Tabasco sauce
- 1 wine glass dry red wine
- 1 pint fish stock, made from bones, etc., of the fish and seasoned with Cayenne, red peppers, and salt
- 6 fillets of sole or of any white fish

Prepare the following sauce: Sauté the onion in olive oil and add the other ingredients. Let the sauce simmer for 15 minutes; then add the fillets and let them cook 10–12 minutes.

Serve with rice, well dried, and watercress as an entrée before the main meat course. Serves 6.

W. MARTIN LATHROP
Aircraft equipment
Glendale, Calif.

TUNA LUAU

- 1 long fin tuna, about 25 pounds
- 1 stone lined pit, which has had a fire burning in it for at least 10 hours
- 12 large banana leaves. If not available, four clean, wet gunny sacks
- 2 big bulbs of garlic, ground in food chopper
- ½ bottle Tabasco sauce
- 1 cup sugar
- 1 bottle Worcestershire sauce
- ½ cup prepared mustard
- 2 bottles catsup
- ½ pint vinegar
- 1 quart olive oil
- ½ gallon sauterne
  Salt and pepper

Do not clean the fish. Wrap the tuna in dampened banana leaves or wet gunny sacks. Place in a pit of hot stones, cover with ashes a foot deep, then place a layer of earth six inches deep over the ashes. After about six hours, build a fire of oak charcoal on top of the pit and let it burn down for about three hours. Combine the sauce ingredients and simmer for about 10 minutes, stirring constantly. Now you are ready to dig out the tuna. With a shovel, place the steaming tuna on a big wooden plank, peel off the wrappings and skin. Feed the innards to the dog or to any guests unappreciative of your efforts. The pieces of tuna are eaten Polynesian style with the fingers, dipping the tuna into the bubbling sauce. Serve with dry white wine. Serves 15 normally hungry guests.

Peter O'Crotty

Writer
Santa Monica, Calif.

BAKED FISH NATIVE STYLE

1½ cups freshly grated coconut meat from an immature nut. (When grated, a medium-sized coconut usually yields 3 cups)
1½ to 2 pounds whole mullet, butterfish, kumu, moano, moi, or any other mild-flavored fish
1 teaspoon salt

This recipe for baked fish originated in the Pacific, but it has also been translated into a usable stateside version.

To prepare the coconut, pierce the eyes of the nut with a nail or ice pick. Drain off the milk. Crack with a hammer and take out the meat; grate enough to make 1½ cupfuls. Heat the coconut milk and pour over the grated meat. Allow mixture to stand 15 minutes and strain through a poi cloth, squeezing out as much milk as possible. Discard coconut pulp or reserve it for some other purpose. Scale and clean the fish, but do not remove the head or tail. Rub inside and outside with salt. Place fish in the center of two thicknesses of *ti* leaves. Pour coconut cream over fish; wrap up and tie securely with strips of *ti* leaves. Place in *imu* (underground oven) and bake for 1 to 1½ hours or until done. Serve hot in the *ti* leaves. Serves 6.

West Coast version:

1¼ cups packaged coconut
¾ cup coffee cream
1½ to 2 pounds any mild-flavored fish

Soak the packaged coconut in the cream for ½ hour. Simmer for 10 minutes and strain through several thicknesses of cheesecloth, squeezing out as much cream as possible. Young banana leaves or husks of fresh corn may be used instead of the *ti* leaves mentioned in the native recipe. (If corn husks are used, keep the stem and sheaves intact in removing from the ear of corn.) Cut the fish to size, wrap, place in a pan, and bake in a moderate oven (350°) about 1 to 1½ hours. Swab the husks with water from time to time, turning occasionally to prevent burning. Serves 6.

Don't use pepper or any other seasoning. To do so would destroy the delicate flavor entirely.

Lieut. E.C. Brauer, USN.

Lt. U.S. Navy (retired)
Los Angeles, Calif.

COUCH'S FISH EGGS

Couch's Fish Eggs ("and I don't mean caviar or roe") threw our taste testers into a fine state of confusion. Here are random reactions: "Deceitful but fine . . . crisp crust . . . an oddity . . . could use cream sauce . . . little more spice . . . try with lemon . . . just too cute for words . . . good combination." Nevertheless, the majority of the panel found the finished product surprisingly good.

We suggest it—after you give it your finishing touches, of course—as a main course for meatless dinners or as a somewhat esoteric addition to the buffet table.

½ pound steamed white fish, or 1 can (7 oz.) tuna or salmon
2 cups hot mashed potatoes
Salt and pepper to taste
4 hard cooked eggs
1 egg, beaten
Fine dry bread crumbs
Oil or shortening for frying

Free the fish from the skin and bones and pound it up. Mix with the freshly boiled and mashed potatoes. Add salt and pepper to taste. Shell the hard cooked eggs; divide the fish mixture into 4 equal portions. Take each portion, roll it into a rough ball, and press an egg gently into the center, molding the mixture around with the hands until the egg is evenly and completely covered. Dip in beaten egg, roll in bread crumbs, and fry in a deep saucepan or deep fat fryer, in plenty of hot fat, until nicely browned.

Drain on paper toweling. Serve whole or cut in halves, serving 2 halves to the plate, with a pile of green peas for them to lean against. Serves 4.

Frisco Bert

Investigator, Justice Department
San Anselmo, Calif.

BAKED BLENNY FISH

Chef Emerson Street of Oakland admits this recipe grew out of his fondness for seeking the blenny-eel among rocks and tidal pools along California's Sonoma County coast. It can be used also for almost any other fish that is good for baking, including the numerous and varied rockfish.

"Fish for him patiently and gently"

For the fisherman, *Chef* Street advises: "Fishing equipment is a plain, long bamboo pole with a No. 6 single-barbed straight hook affixed by only an inch or two of line. This minimizes snagging in the crannies and shelvings of reef rock where the eel lies, feeding solely on seaweed and drifting bits of marine life. The best bait is a piece of mussel taken right off the rocks at hand. Low tide and calm enable you to reach the crevices and recesses where he lives.

"An eel doesn't strike; he swallows bait. Fish for him patiently and gently."

    3 to 4 pound blenny-eel, ling cod, or rockfish
    2 cups water
    1 can (7 oz.) mushrooms, chopped
    1/3 cup chopped chives
    1/2 cup chopped parsley
        Salt and pepper to taste
    1/2 cup fish broth (boiled from trimmings)
    2 teaspoons flour
    1/2 cup dry white wine
    1 bay leaf
        Pinch, each, of thyme, tarragon, and oregano
    2 tablespoons butter or margarine
    2 cups uncooked rice
        Several sprigs parsley
    1 lime or lemon
    1 cup drained pineapple chunks

Behead fish, skin, then simmer the trimmings with water for broth. Sprinkle bottom of buttered baking dish with mushrooms, chives, and parsley. Lay in dressed fish. Salt and pepper to taste. Thicken fish broth with flour, add wine, then pour over fish. Cover with buttered butcher paper and bake in moderate oven (350°) until done through, about 20 minutes or more per pound.

Remove fish to heated platter. To remaining sauce add bay leaf, thyme, tarragon, and oregano, and gently stir in butter until melted. Pour back over fish and glaze by constant basting, either under broiler flame or back in oven.

Cook rice by any preferred method and arrange on serving platter. Serve fish on bed of cooked rice, garnished with parsley, lime or lemon wedges, and chunk pineapple. Serve with wilted lettuce and a good dry white wine. Serves 4 to 6.

Emerson Street

Oakland

WEST INDIES OVEN FISH

Clean and skin fish; remove head and tail. Rub fish with garlic; sprinkle with salt, pepper, and celery seed. Lay bacon strips close together across top of fish. Place fish in oven pre-heated to 250°. Cook at 250° for 20 minutes, then allow temperature to come down to 200° and cook for about 1 hour, depending on size of fish.

While the fish is cooking, baste occasionally with sauce made as follows: Mash some garlic and cover with boiling water; add salt, pepper, and butter to taste. Fish will come apart easily at the backbone and the two halves can be laid on the serving platter and garnished. Serves 10 or more.

FRANK R. WEST
Oil company foreman (retired)
El Cajon, Calif.

SOUSED HERRING

"Here is Soused Herring the way my grandmother used to prepare it for our savory Sunday suppers," says *Chef* E. P. Albord of Inverness, California.

Chef Alvord makes quite a point of keeping the roe intact. We know of some other *Chefs* who would enjoy the dish, but would rather skip the roe. Let your own conscience guide you.

The flavor is mild, but is likely to gain in character as you eat it with other food or drink.

    1 dozen fresh herring, with roe
    1 cup vinegar
    1 cup water
    2 teaspoons salt
    2 teaspoons whole black peppers
    4 bay leaves

Scale, behead, and clean fish—but guard the roe with your life. Place fish in baking pan, alternating head and tail so fish fit nicely. Barely cover with vinegar-water mixture to which salt has been added. Add whole peppers and bay leaves. Bake 15 to 20 minutes in slow oven (300°). Set aside to cool. Serve cold with hot buttered toast and tea, or whatever else goes to make up your Sunday supper.

Inverness, Calif.

GRILLED SEA BASS

Frank T. Thompson sends a tantalizing suggestion from Los Gatos, California.

It is bass, grilled over an open fire and stuffed with Mexican sausage. We presume he means the variety of sausage called *chorizo*.

Automobile refinisher
Los Gatos, Calif.

FRENCH FRIED SQUID

I have chosen to give you a recipe for perhaps the least-consumed fish in America, although it is one of the world's best known. This fish literally inhabits the seven seas; and it is relished by the most ancient peoples on earth for its distinctive flavor. Holding all the patents on the original smoke screen so extensively used by mankind in defensive warfare, it is known as the squid, more popularly called "ink fish." Squid can be broiled, boiled, or stuffed and baked. But it is the creed of every good chef that food should be prepared in its most palatable form, while still capturing its natural flavor. In this case, the most simple preparation and the surest way to bring back the flavor of the ocean's hidden depths is French Fried Squid.

    4 pounds of small squids
    1 cup flour
      Olive oil or cooking oil
      Salt
    1 lemon

Avoid buying the squids too large, as they are much less tender than small to medium-sized fish. Clean each squid by cutting off tentacles just above the eyes. Then grasp head and remove it from the body. Slit the body and remove all insides, including the transparent cartilage back bone. Slice fish in quarter-inch strips, clean well in cold water, and dry each piece between towels. Dip in flour and fry in hot oil until each piece is well browned and crisp. Drain on brown paper, sprinkle with salt, and garnish each serving with a quarter lemon. The tentacles are the choicest morsels. Figure on ½ pound squid per person.

Use caution in frying, as moisture in the fish will cause oil to pop.

Musical director
Denver, Colorado

ABALONE MENDOCINO

There's a special kind of fishing done along the coast of California. It involves wading deep in the surf or diving under the surface and searching the rocks with tire iron and gunny sack in hand.

"Wading deep or diving under the surface with tire iron and gunny sack in hand"

The reward is a celebrated delicacy. If you've been around folk singers much, you've probably heard its praises sung in the many verses of the "Abalone Song." Abalone is most often fried, but this recipe submitted by Bill Johansen of Fort Bragg, California, adds a finishing-off period in the oven.

    2 eggs
    1/3 cup milk, water, or beer
    2 abalones cut into thick steaks, or 12 slices
      Cracker meal, flour, or prepared coating mix
      Olive oil
    2 cloves garlic
    1 sprig fresh rosemary
    1 cup dry white table wine

Beat eggs and combine with the milk, water, or beer. Dip well pounded abalone steaks or slices into cracker meal or other coating. Heat 1/4 inch of olive oil in 2 large frying pans, one of which should have a tight fitting cover. Add a clove of garlic to each pan. Brown abalone quickly in the hot oil. Transfer all to the frying pan with the cover, adding crushed rosemary and 1/2 cup of the wine.

Cover, place in a 350° oven, and steam 30 minutes. Remove from oven, add remaining 1/2 cup of wine, then steam in oven again for about 1 hour, or until abalone is fork tender.

Serve with tossed green salad, French fried potatoes, lemon wedges, French bread, and peas or corn. Serves 6.

Bill Johansen
Truck driver
Fort Bragg, Calif.

DEEP-FRIED ABALONE

Take the abalone from the shell, clean, and trim as for steaks. Cut into half-inch slices and pound lightly with the side of a milk bottle until meat is limp, relaxed, and pliable. This does not cut the meat; and it is sufficient pounding for this method of cooking. After pounding, cut into strips about the same width as thickness. Have deep fat or oil heating on the stove, and prepare this batter:

    1 cup prepared biscuit or waffle mix
    3/4 cup milk or canned milk
    2 large eggs

Season with salt and garlic to taste. Mix well; be sure batter is quite stiff, as too thin a batter will fry off and splash grease all over the stove. Roll abalone strips in batter and gently lower into hot deep fat (about 375°). Turn them over when they fry to a golden palomino brown, and cook on the other side to same color. As they come out of the kettle, put them on absorbent paper in a warm oven until all are finished.

Hal Stanger
Burbank, Calif.

BAKED TROUT

If some of the trout in your creel are a little too large to meet the best flavor specifications for pan frying (about 6 to 9 inches), *Chef* A. E. Clamp can teach you some tricks on how to stuff a trout. In fact, his trout stuffing and the tart sauce that goes with it could be used with almost any white fish. Lemon, capers, and anchovy paste contribute a nice tangy edge to the flavor.

We give the proportions for two fair-sized trout. You can, of course, expand or—perish the thought—contract them according to your fishing luck.

    2 trout (about 10-inch length, or approximately
        ½ pound each)

Stuffing:

    4 tablespoons bread crumbs
    2 tablespoons suet or bacon, finely chopped
    1 tablespoon parsley, finely chopped
    ½ teaspoon thyme
    ¼ teaspoon grated lemon peel
    1 egg
    Milk
    Nutmeg, salt, and pepper to taste
    4 tablespoons butter, melted

Sauce:

    6 tablespoons (¾ cube) butter or margarine
    4 tablespoons (¼ cup) flour
    1 cup stock or consommé
    2 teaspoons capers
    1 teaspoon lemon juice
    ½ teaspoon anchovy paste
    Salt and pepper to taste

Clean, scale, and dry the trout.

Mix together bread crumbs, suet, parsley, thyme, and lemon peel. Add beaten egg and enough milk to make the stuffing thoroughly moist. Season to taste with nutmeg, salt, and pepper. Place stuffing inside trout and sew up.

Place fish in a baking dish with the 4 tablespoons melted butter, and bake, uncovered, in a moderate oven (350°) for 30 minutes, basting frequently with the melted butter.

*"Can teach you some tricks
on how to stuff a trout"*

Meanwhile, melt the 6 tablespoons butter in a frying pan and brown the flour in it.

When fish is baked, remove to a hot serving dish and strain liquor in the baking pan into the flour and butter. Add stock or consommé and stir until the mixture comes to a boil and becomes smooth. Then add capers, lemon juice, anchovy paste, salt, and pepper. Let the sauce simmer about 10 minutes. Pour on the fish and serve. Serves 2.

A. E. Clamp

*Chemical engineer
Sacramento, Calif.*

CRAB IMPERIAL

    1 pound crab meat
    Juice of ½ lemon
    1 egg
    1 heaping tablespoon *each* capers, minced
        parsley, and scraped onion
    Salt and pepper to taste
    Mayonnaise
    4 teaspoons dry bread crumbs
    2 teaspoons butter

Mix together crab meat, lemon juice, slightly beaten egg, capers, parsley, and onion. Add salt and pepper to taste, then just enough mayonnaise to bind the mixture together. Pile high in 4 ramekins, sprinkle bread crumbs on top, and dot with butter. Place under a slow broiler to heat and to brown—about 10 to 15 minutes. Serves 4.

Edward A. Block,

*Professor
Spring Valley, Calif.*

CURRIED SHRIMP DANIEL FROHMAN

"Some years ago I ran across a curried shrimp recipe which was supposed to be a favorite of theatrical producer Daniel Frohman. I tried it, liked it, and little by little altered and added, as *Chefs* of the West, South, North, or East will do, until I doubt that if Daniel returned he would recognize his shrimps at all. However, I have retained the name in his honor.

"Many people turn up their noses at the large Louisiana prawns and insist that only the small, tasty, tightly curled type should be used. I'm not sure that I don't agree with them, but either way makes a dish to my taste."

The littler the shrimp the better, say our trustworthy taste-testers. Best of all for this dish: the tiny San Francisco Bay shrimp, or the small pink "Alaska" found all along the Pacific Coast.

In saucepan, melt:
    3 tablespoons butter
Add:
    1½ small onions finely chopped
Cook for three or four minutes. Add:
    4 tablespoons flour
    1 teaspoon salt
    1½ tablespoons curry powder
Blend thoroughly and stir until smooth.
Add slowly:
    1¼ cups chicken stock
    1¼ cups tomato juice
Cook until thickened, stirring constantly.
Add:
    1½ tablespoons cream
Cook 2 minutes longer. Add:
    1 pound cooked small shrimp

Reheat and serve over boiled rice. This should serve 4 not-too-big eaters.

Weldon F. Heald
Writer
Tucson, Arizona

CAMARONES PACIFICO

    4 green (raw) shrimp
    French dressing
    8 slices of bread, ⅓ inch thick
        or 8 crackers
    ¼ pound cheese (your choice) grated
    ⅛ teaspoon garlic salt
    Tabasco sauce
    ½ teaspoon Worcestershire sauce
    1 large egg, separated
    ¼ teaspoon baking powder

Shell and clean shrimp, cut in half lengthwise, and marinate in French dressing for at least an hour in the refrigerator.

Cut bread into rounds or other shapes of your choice, at least 2 inches across. Toast one side. When cool, spread untoasted side with butter.

Combine grated cheese, garlic salt, Tabasco and Worcestershire sauce with beat-

en egg yolk. Blend thoroughly. Beat egg white with baking powder and fold in.

Lightly spread thin layer of this mixture on buttered side of toasted bread. Place one-half shrimp on each piece, then cover it with more of cheese mixture. Place on cooky sheet and place under preheated broiler to brown and puff up. Watch that they don't scorch.

Makes 8, but I feel a good trencherman won't be satisfied with just a sample.

A. B. Woodworth
Tacoma

CAMARONES CON ARROZ

This dish is substantial enough to be cheering, a bright yellow color from the curry, and enriched with cheese and mushrooms. *Chef* Clinton R. Vitous, whose experience in the dental profession may have sharpened his perception of a toothsome morsel, usually prescribes it "for a supper after cards, home movies, or colored slides during the holidays. This may be prepared ahead of time and then set at the lowest heat, since it really is better if allowed to 'mull' a bit. Serve the dish right at table."

(Shrimp with rice)
    ½ cube (4 tablespoons) butter
    ¼ cup flour
    1 egg
    1½ cups milk
    3 tablespoons grated Cheddar cheese
    1 can (4 oz.) mushrooms
    ⅛ teaspoon paprika
    2 teaspoons curry powder, or to taste
    ½ pound shelled cooked shrimp
    Salt and pepper to taste
    2 cups cooked rice (1 cup uncooked rice)

Put butter in sauce pan on medium heat and stir in flour to make a smooth paste. Mix slightly beaten egg and milk. Stir into flour mixture gradually. Then add other ingredients in the order given. When shrimp is thoroughly heated, keep on low heat until ready to bring to table. Serve on small mounds of hot rice. Will serve at least 8 for a supper, with vegetables and salad, but serves about 4 as a "piece de resistance."

Clinton R. Vitous
Dentist
Seattle, Washington

SHRIMP TEMPURA

Chef H. W. B. (Hod) White of Honolulu reveals a trade secret in presenting for our approval a second distinguished contribution to win his *Chef's* apron. "Tempura" is shrimp or prawns dipped in batter and fried, a Japanese dish which has a justly deserved popularity. To discover the particular secret of this dish, *Chef* White and his agents had to act as food detectives.

"Shrimp tempura is one of our local Island favorites, both for a luncheon dish and as an hors d'oeuvre. It is generally served with a dip: a mixture of mustard and either tomato sauce or soya *(shoyu)*.

"For years, people here have been envious of one local Japanese restaurant that put out a delicious tempura, crinkly and crisp on the outside—in fact, fabulously so. Everyone tried for years to duplicate this crinkly crust by varied batters, but all to no avail.

"The little chap who served this type had in his kitchen a special cubbyhole stall with a curtain behind which he always cooked his tempura."

"... special cubbyhole stall with curtain"

We shall not lift that curtain here before everybody. Suffice it to say that *Chef* White discovered the secret. He declares it so good that it should not be withheld from the waiting world.

3 cups flour
2 cups corn starch
2 teaspoons baking powder
2 well-beaten eggs
Salt to taste
Water
2 pounds large green prawns (20 to 25 count)
Oil or shortening for deep fat frying

Mix flour, cornstarch, baking powder, eggs, and salt with sufficient water to make a fairly thick batter. Then take out part of this batter and mix with more water to make an additional thin batter about the consistency of table cream.

Shell, clean and butterfly your shrimp, leaving a piece of the tail to hold onto (this is finger food).

Use a frying pan about 2 inches deep and 12 inches in diameter, filled up about 1 to 1½ inches deep with cooking oil, or use your deep fat fryer with temperature control set at about 375° to 400°.

Drop shrimp into the *thick* batter, about half a dozen at a time.

Now here's the secret! Just before you drop the shrimp into the hot oil with your right hand, dip your left hand into the *thin* batter, take a handful and sprinkle it quickly over the top of the fat. (Watch out for burns as the hot fat splatters.) The more fat you use, the more crinkly the shrimps will be. Quickly lay the batter-dipped shrimp onto this sprinkled batter before it has had time to cook on the top side.

The shrimp will fry quite quickly, and as soon as they are browned on one side, turn them over, and brown the other side. Serves 6 to 8 as a main dish.

You will have to use a scoop or slotted spoon to remove the excess sprinkled thin batter from the oil before starting the next round. But if you don't agree with me that it is the best looking and tasting shrimp you ever had, I'll eat them.

[signature]

Executive vice president
Honolulu, T.H.

We'll eat them, too, *Chef* White. We'd welcome another chance to practice the technique of launching those "shrimp boats" on a sea of hot oil.

CRAB Á LA SELLECK

Chef George A. Selleck contributes a crab sauce which is one of the most delicate we have ever tasted. Unlike most other dressings, it blends with the crab so completely that it leaves almost no traces of its own flavor. One ingredient which probably contributes to this result is the crab fat, sometimes called crab butter, which you get from the inner surface of the shell.

"I have used this sauce for more than 25 years," says *Chef* Selleck. "At one time it was on the menus in two of our San Francisco restaurants."

    Crab fat from one large crab (approxi-
      mately 4 tablespoons crab butter)
    I egg yolk
    4 tablespoons (¼ cup) olive oil
    2 tablespoons Riesling or Chablis wine
    2 teaspoons lemon juice
    ¼ teaspoon salt
      White pepper to taste
      Mayonnaise

Remove the crab fat from the inner corners and surface of the crab shell, discarding all the brown membrane. Whip to a creamy consistency in a blender or push through a fine sieve. Add egg yolk and whip until light; gradually beat in the olive oil, then the wine, lemon juice, salt and pepper to taste. Use the mayonnaise as a liaison. To marinate cracked crab, use less mayonnaise. To serve over crab as a sauce, add more mayonnaise to make it thicker. Be sure to use a good dry white wine; wine with a little SO_2 is likely to bring out a slightly bitter taste in the delicate crab sauce.

George A. Selleck

Dentist
San Francisco, Calif.

OYSTER SURPRISE

    2 tablespoons cream, or rich milk
    I tablespoon butter
    ½ teaspoon salt
    I tablespoon chopped parsley
      Few grains pepper
      Grated nutmeg
    2 cups mashed potatoes
    I dozen oysters, or more if desired
    2 eggs, beaten
      Fine bread crumbs

Add cream, butter, salt, parsley, pepper, and a dusting of grated nutmeg to the mashed potatoes. Whip with a wire beater until fluffy. With as little handling as possible, form mixture into oval pats, placing 2 oysters in each. Dip pats into beaten egg, and then roll in fine bread crumbs. Arrange on a greased cooky sheet and bake in a hot oven (425°) until brown, basting twice with melted butter. Makes 6 pats.

Lieut. E. C. Brauer, USN.

Lt. U.S. Navy (retired)
Los Angeles, Calif.

OYSTERS ABSTRACT

"Excellent opponent for fog or chill"— *Chef* Donald S. Fairchild describes his oyster creation better than we can.

We would serve it without a qualm both to friends who like oysters and to those who ordinarily do not.

    3 tablepoons butter or margarine
    I pint fresh oysters and their liquid
    I can cream of chicken soup
    ¼ teaspoon salt
      Pepper to taste
      Worcestershire sauce
    I teaspoon finely chopped chives
    I teaspoon finely chopped parsley
    ⅛ teaspoon oregano
    I cup half-and-half
    3 tablespoons sour cream

Melt butter or margarine in a saucepan. Pour in oysters and their liquid. Cook gently until liquid bubbles and oysters frill around the edges. Add salt, pepper, Worcestershire sauce—two dashes at least —chives, parsley, and oregano. Wait a

"Serves four elegantly, two hungry"

moment before stirring in the half-and-half, so the seasonings begin to work.

When the milk mixture is steaming—do NOT boil—blend in sour cream, and simmer for 10 minutes. Remove from heat and cool at least 1 hour. Overnight is best.

Reheat till steam rises, and serve. Add a dollop of sour cream, a small sprig of parsley, and a dash of paprika to each portion, with rye bread or melba toast on the side. Serves four elegantly, two hungry.

Donald Fairchild

Editor, public relations
Los Angeles, Calif.

CREAMED LOBSTER GASTRONOME

    2 pounds fresh or frozen lobster or
        lobster tails
    4 shallots or 1 bunch green onions
    ¼ pound white onions (1 medium onion)
    1 pint (2 cups) dry sherry
    ¾ cup dry sauterne
    2 small bay leaves
    ¼ teaspoon thyme
    1 celery stalk
    ½ cup parsley stems (not leaves)
    1 quart table cream
    ¼ pound butter
    ¼ cup sherry
    ¼ cup cognac or brandy (100 proof)
        Salt and pepper to taste
    2 egg yolks

Cook lobster in salted water for 25 minutes. Let cool.

The sauce: Chop shallots and white onions; put in saucepan with the 1 pint sherry and the sauterne, bay leaves, thyme, celery stalk, and parsley stems. Let reduce over fast fire until almost dry (about 15 minutes) then add table cream and simmer until thickened (a light cream sauce). Strain through a cheesecloth.

Take lobster from shell and cut into large dice. Sauté in butter for 5 minutes. Add remaining ¼ cup sherry and boil. Add cognac and flamb (set it afire).

Add sautéed lobster and its sauce to the first sauce and boil 2 minutes. Remove from fire and add egg yolks; blend well and season to taste. Bring to table in casserole and serve with buttered toast or French rolls. Serves 4.

If you want the sauce to have the proper consistency, not runny, do take *Chef* Pierre Coste seriously when he says, "Let reduce . . . until thickened."

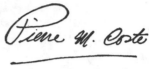

San Francisco

CRAWFISH LOMA MAR

     2 outside stalks celery
     1 clove garlic, sliced
     1 onion, quartered
     2 bay leaves
     3 tablespoons salt
     1 cup white wine
    40 live crawfish

Bring a gallon of water to a boil; add the celery, garlic, onion, bay leaves, and salt. At the rolling boiling point, add the wine and the live crawfish, and cook until the crawfish redden, about 15 minutes. Remove the crawfish to cool. Break off the claws which are large enough to hold meat, and cut off the tails with a butcher knife. Place the claws on their edges, break the shells by striking with a piece of wood, and remove the meat. To clean, hold a tail in your left hand, with the thumb of the right hand over the belly side of the tail, and press with your left fingers to break the crawfish shell. Remove and wash the meat, and place it in a bowl with the leg meat.

Serve the meat in this manner: Place two slices of buttered white bread on a dinner plate, cover with crisp lettuce leaves (to prevent the open-faced sandwich from becoming soggy), cover with crawfish meat, and top with a Louis dressing made to your taste with mayonnaise, catsup, sugar, salt, lemon juice, Worcestershire sauce, and chopped parsley. Serve with your favorite beer. Serves 4.

W. A. HEIMANN
Hardware merchant
Loma Mar, Calif.

PRAWNS NAN TA SSU

Chef Kenneth B. Fry of Sacramento, an old "China hand," has fond memories of the "*Pei Tai Ho* and *Nan Ta Ssu* days" and the "nightly chant of the fishermen laboriously dragging their nets across the bottom of the Gulf of Pechili and onto the beach."

He continues, "Then it is that thoughts wander to Liu, our houseboy, and the prawns he would occasionally manage to wangle from the head man to serve us as we finished our swim. He would never relinquish the secret of how he prepared them, but through devious ways I have been able to work out a substitute that might easily pass for the originals."

No dish was never harmed by such a graceful preliminary.

24 uncooked jumbo prawns
2 tablespoons lemon juice
2 teaspoons Worcestershire
2 tablespoons milk
½ cup fine bread crumbs
    Salad oil or melted butter or margarine

Peel, devein, (splitting them from top to bottom) and wash the prawns. Place them close together in a shallow bowl and sprinkle with lemon juice and Worcestershire. Allow to marinate for several hours, turning once or twice.

Add milk a few drops at a time and toss the prawns like a salad. Continue tossing until all the milk has been absorbed. Roll in fine bread crumbs and place close together on a broiler rack. Drip oil or melted butter over the prawns and broil until they are pink and tender on top. Turn them over and repeat the process. Serve hot. Serves 4 persons of average appetite, or 3 heavy eaters.

*Bureau chief, state fair
Sacramento, Calif.*

ASPARAGUS SHRIMP

In the "Asparagus Shrimp" promulgated by Charles Butters, of Los Angeles, you may note a rather smoky flavor that is hard to account for directly when you scan the ingredients. In general, the method of cooking is somewhat like the Chinese "steam-fry" technique, but you should watch the asparagus closely to see that it doesn't cook too long. A light browning seems desirable; just don't carry the process too far.

      1 pound raw shrimp (fresh or frozen)
      2 tablespoons salad oil
      ½ cup beer or water
      2 pounds fresh asparagus
      ½ cup water
      4 tablespoons soy
      1 tablespoon brown sugar
      2 teaspoons cornstarch

Shell shrimp and remove sand vein. Sauté lightly in 1 tablespoon of the salad oil until light brown. Add ½ cup beer or water and poach for 5 minutes.

Trim tough ends off asparagus and cut diagonally into 1-inch slices. Sauté in the other tablespoon of oil until slices are light brown.

Combine shrimp and asparagus, add ¼ cup of the water, cover and steam 5 minutes. If you prefer crisp vegetables, reduce cooking time to 2 or 3 minutes. Push shrimp and asparagus to outer edges of pan. In the center, stir into the liquid the soy, brown sugar, and cornstarch, previously mixed with the other ¼ cup water. Stir all together and allow it to cook an additional 5 minutes.

Serve with rice and green salad. Serves 6 to 8.

Charles Butters
Produce dealer
Los Angeles, Calif.

STUFFED JUMBO PRAWNS

Be prepared for a double twist in this preparation of the prawn. First, you leave the tail on each one as a handle for eating as an hors d'oeuvre. Second, you stuff the prawn—but no sewing—as if it were a bird.

Some of our testing tasters looked askance at the tails. And we had trouble keeping the stuffing in because a prawn curls when it fries. But, to tell the truth, the combination tastes so good that we'd recommend it even if you had to eat prawn and stuffing in separate spoonfuls.

      2 pounds large raw prawns (15 to 20 count)
      ½ pound ground lean pork, browned
      1 tablespoon chopped parsley
      1 teaspoon onion
      2 tablespoons chopped shrimp
         (about 2 prawns)
      ½ teaspoon salt
        Garlic salt
        Coarse ground pepper

Split each prawn almost through on curved side, but not all the way down to the end of the tail. Remove black vein. Stuff each slit with some of the mixture of pork, shrimp, and seasonings. Fry prawns-plus-stuffing in 1 tablespoon soy sauce and 1 cube butter—slowly. They do not get golden brown, but they are excellent for a lunch dish or pre-dinner appetizer.

Chester V Emmons
Reno, Nev.

CLAM FRITTERS A LA BAINBRIDGE

      6 cups finely chopped clams
      1 medium-sized onion, grated
         (or minced in blender)
        Juice of 1 lemon
      ½ cup finely chopped green pepper
      1 cup finely chopped parsley
      ½ cup finely rolled bread crumbs
      2 large eggs, lightly beaten

Mix all ingredients together in order listed above. Drop batter into a buttered frying pan, in patties slightly larger than a silver dollar and about ¼ inch thick. Flatten with pancake turner. Salt and pepper generously on both sides while cooking. Cook until brown. Serve with wedge of lemon on half of clam shell.

Emphasis must be placed on the rapidity of cooking in butter, which turns brown as a batch is cooked. The griddle must be cleaned at intervals in the course of cooking. Makes about 6 dozen patties.

WH Branchflower
Port Blakely, Wash.

PENGUIN CLAM PIE

If you were puzzled not to find a penguin in the list of ingredients, be assured that this bird appears in the name of the recipe only because *Chef* Brauer happened to be cruising Antarctic waters at the time he created this dish.

    2 dozen clams
    3 medium-sized onions, sliced
    2 potatoes, peeled and sliced ¼ inch thick
    3 tablespoons butter
    2 tablespoons flour
    2 cups evaporated milk
      Salt and pepper
      Pastry for 2-crust pie
    1 teaspoon minced parsley
      Paprika

Scrub clams thoroughly, removing all traces of sand. Place clams in pan and add one cup hot water; simmer until the shells open slightly. Remove clams from shells, saving the broth in which they steamed. Chop clams fine. Strain clam broth carefully, avoiding any sediment in the bottom of the pan. Add onion and potatoes to this broth and cook until tender, but unbroken.

To make sauce: Melt 2 tablespoons of the butter in a saucepan, then stir in flour. Add milk gradually, and stir until thickened. Add clams, potatoes, onions, and the liquid in which they were cooked. Season with salt and pepper, simmer for a few minutes to blend flavors, and pour into pan which has been lined with pastry. Sprinkle with minced parsley. Cover with top pastry. Slash top in several places to permit the steam to escape during baking. Dot top with remaining 1 tablespoon butter and sprinkle with paprika. Bake in a moderately hot oven (425°) about 30 minutes.

Lieut. E. C. Brauer, USN.

Lt. U.S. Navy (retired)
Los Angeles, Calif.

STEAMED CLAMS

Take the number of clams you wish to serve and scrub the shells with a stiff brush to remove all silt and sand. Place in a pressure cooker and bring pressure to 15 pounds for 10 minutes.

If you have no pressure cooker, use a saucepan and cover as tightly as possible. A flat lid with a weight on it works fine.

When steaming is completed, uncover the container and the clams will be open so the meat can be removed easily from the shells. The clam nectar can be served as an appetizer. Serve the clams while hot, with the following sauce:

Sequim Sauce

Mash together:
    1 clove garlic
    ½ teaspoon salt
    1 tablespoon sugar

Stir in:
    1 can (8 oz.) tomato sauce
    3 tablespoons olive or salad oil
    3 tablespoons horseradish
    1 teaspoon prepared mustard
    3 ounces (6 tablespoons) sherry
      or sauterne wine
      Juice of 1 small lemon
    ¼ teaspoon Tabasco sauce (more if you
      like it hot!)
    3 dashes Angostura bitters

Blend well. Serve with hot clams. Enough sauce for about 12 dozen clams. A bottle of sauterne wine is recommended.

Archie R. Hill
San Diego

CLAMS AND RICE

This recipe is strictly for clam lovers; there's just no point in wasting it on unfeeling souls who wouldn't appreciate such a tender blending of other flavors with the potency of clam. The dish is neither a chowder nor a bouillabaisse. It is just what Bennett K. Campbell calls it, "Clams and Rice," so good you'll lick the shells—if you like clams.

    6 pounds clams
    ½ cup olive oil
    1 medium sized onion
    2 cloves garlic
    1 can (8 oz.) tomato sauce
    1 cup boiling water
    1 tablespoon Worcestershire
    2 cups uncooked rice
    2 cups boiling water

Clams should be the size best for steaming (cockles or Washington clams). Thor-

"This recipe is strictly for clam lovers"

oughly scrub them with a brush under running water. Then let stand in cold water 2 or 3 hours. Pour olive oil into a large stew pot or Dutch oven and add onion and garlic, cut into very small pieces. Let simmer over low heat for about 15 minutes, or until vegetables are glossy. Then add tomato sauce, the 1 cup boiling water, Worcestershire, and the scrubbed clams (still in the shell).

Put cover on pot, turn heat to low, and let clams steam in this mixture until shells open. Add rice and the 2 cups boiling water; cover and steam 45 minutes, or until rice is cooked. Stir often to avoid burning any ingredients, and add more boiling water if necessary to cook the rice. It's better to take a longer time to cook this (at lower heat) than to risk burning the mixture. Serves 8 generously.

Bennett K. Campbell

Branch manager, insurance
Seattle, Washington

SALMON STEAKS WITH GREEN TOMATO

Melt in iron skillet a generous amount of butter. Remove from heat and put in as many steaks as needed, smearing butter on top and salting lightly. Next, slice very thinly one small and quite green tomato per steak. Place these slices on and around the steaks. Take a large pinch of oregano and scatter over steaks and tomatoes. Salt tomatoes lightly. Finally, dust with a very small amount of curry powder.

Put the skillet in the oven with the temperature set at 400° and bake for 30 min-

utes, or until the tomatoes are tender and translucent, but not mushy. Serve.

Ben R. Hager

Capistrano Beach, Calif.

BROILED OR BARBECUED SALMON

Those who like their salmon without sauce will be especially enthusiastic about William Felse's treatment of it—suitable for either broiler or barbecue. It heightens the innate salmon flavor rather than smothering it with the glorified stuffing or sauce.

"... those who like salmon without sauce"

Use a salmon of about 6-pound size which has been carefully filleted. Chop ½ clove garlic very fine and press into fillets. Place them skin down on the grill and sprinkle with a mixture of salt and pepper which has been blended with ¼ clove garlic in a mortar. Also sprinkle with ½ teaspoon monosodium glutamate—or a little more if the fish is larger.

The cooking takes about 15 minutes under broiler flame, longer in the barbecue. Baste with a mixture of 1½ cubes melted butter or margarine, pepper and onion salt to taste, 1 tablespoon Worcestershire sauce, and ½ cup finely chopped parsley. Before the cooking starts, be sure to oil the grill well with olive oil or the salmon may stick.

Serve with small artichokes, and baked potatoes topped with sour cream and chives, to 12 to 14 persons.

San Jose, Calif.

CHARCOAL-BROILED SALMON

"This is the way some Italian fishermen charcoal-broil fresh salmon on the boats they fish and live on," says Phil Burch of Sausalito, California. "Properly prepared, few fish dishes on earth are more fit to eat than broiled salmon."

> 1 cup olive oil
> ½ cup wine vinegar
> 1 clove garlic, chopped fine
> 1 tablespoon fresh basil or 1 teaspoon dry basil
> 1 tablespoon fresh rosemary or 1 teaspoon dry rosemary
> ½ teaspoon thyme
> ⅛ teaspoon pepper
> 1 teaspoon salt
> 8-pound salmon, cut into steaks 1 inch thick
> Lemon wedges

Mix all ingredients except salmon and lemon wedges to make the basting sauce. Let stand for an hour or more, stirring occasionally. Place fish steaks in a hinged (toaster-type) grill. This grill is absolutely necessary, so you can turn the fish steaks all together without their falling into 101 pieces.

Baste fish on one side and place on fire, basted side down. (If possible, tie some rosemary sprigs together and use as a baster; otherwise, do the best you can with a brush or mop.) Now baste the top side, letting some of the sauce drip down on the fire to add a little smoke flavor. Cook for 2 to 2½ minutes, or until underside of fish begins to brown well. Baste top side again and turn fish. Baste side already cooked. Grill for another 2 minutes. Squeeze lemon over pieces of fish just before serving. Will serve 10 to 12 persons.

Serve with green salad, red table wine, and sourdough French bread.

Private detective
Sausalito, Calif.

SHRIMP A LA NEWBERG VIA TEXAS

Chef Tidwell introduces himself as a "transplanted Texan . . . strictly from the pinch, dash, smidgen, chunk, and spill measurement school of cookery."

"Properly prepared . . . broiled salmon"

shrimp a la newburg

"We use it for a quick dish when guests pop in unexpectedly"

"We use it for a quick dish, one plate dinner, or when guests pop in unexpectedly. Would you believe it that some of these hammer-headed friends even call and invite themselves to dinner *IF* we are having shrimp."

2 quarts water
1 large onion
1 clove garlic
1 lemon
1 tablespoon salt
1 teaspoon thyme
15 peppercorns (whole black peppers)
Dash of cayenne
1½ pounds green shrimp (20 to 25 count)
1 cup uncooked rice
2½ cups water
½ teaspoon salt
½ pound processed Cheddar cheese
⅔ cup light table cream
¼ cup very dry cooking sherry
1 egg
Paprika
Green pepper rings
Lime slices

Place the ½ gallon water in a saucepan sufficiently large that the shrimp may be added later without any spilling over. To the water, add the onion quartered, the garlic minced, the lemon quartered and squeezed and then dropped in rind and all, and the salt, thyme, peppercorns, and cayenne. Bring this conglomeration to a boil, then drop in the unpeeled shrimp or prawns.

Meanwhile, cover the rice with 2½ cups of water, add the ½ teaspoon salt, and allow to boil vigorously.

Then the sauce: In upper half of double boiler, break up the cheese into pieces the size of a pecan; add the cream and allow cheese to melt, stirring occasionally to keep blended. As soon as cheese is melted thoroughly, add the sherry gradually, at the same time stirring the mixture vigorously. As soon as the sherry has blended, add the egg which should be well, but not stiffly, beaten. Stir in very carefully.

By now, the shrimp should have boiled their allotted 10 minutes. Remove from the fire, run cold water into the pan to cool them quickly. Then peel, remove the sand tract, rinse, dry and add to the sauce, which should continue cooking until slightly thickened.

Serve the sauce over the rice, which should be fluff-cooked by this time. Slap the top of the dish with a dash of paprika, garnish with green pepper rings, lime slices, and serve immediately. Serves 4 to 6.

Once you get the knack of it, this is a 30-minute job from start to finish.

Seattle

FRIED SMOKED SALMON 'N EGGS

If your guests aren't the fish-for-breakfast type, save this dish for a lunch. If you are looking for possible variations or improvements, try a sprinkling of paprika for color, a dash of Worcestershire sauce, some Cheddar (less stringy) instead of Swiss cheese.

"If your guests aren't the fish-for-breakfast type"

    1 medium onion, sliced in very thin rings
    4 to 6 tablespoons butter
    ½ pound smoked salmon, sliced thin
    6 eggs, well beaten
    4 slices Swiss cheese

Slowly sauté onion rings in butter until soft but not brown. Add slices of smoked salmon, shredding them with two forks as they turn a pink color in the frying pan. (At about this point, it may be necessary to add a bit more butter.) Turn up heat and add well beaten eggs, scrambling all ingredients well together. Top with slices of Swiss cheese and brown under broiler until bubbly.

Cut in wedges like pie and serve to 4 to 6 hungry people, along with thin slices of pumpernickel bread spread with lots of cream cheese.

Ella Mathias
Physician
San Carlos, Calif.

SALMON LOVERS' SALMON

If you were to ask any questions about Chinese ovens in the East Bay area around Orinda, California, someone would sooner or later mention the name of Dr. Roger Stark. His enthusiasm for smoke oven cooking is contagious; he has been known to forego a night's sleep just to finish the brick laying job on a friend's oven.

"There aren't many things we haven't smoked in one of these ovens," says Dr. Stark. His favorite involves fish—fresh salmon. "This simple recipe was developed and refined by a select group of salmon lovers to which I belong."

"A select group of salmon lovers"

Dr. Stark suggests this method for determining when the fish is cooked: "Take a fork and carefully separate two layers of the meat. At first you'll notice a pink line of demarcation between the cooked and uncooked portions. As soon as this line disappears, the fish is ready to eat—wait any longer and it will begin to dry out."

    Whole salmon, 6 to 8 pounds
    1 cup lemon juice
    1 cup dry white table wine
    2 teaspoons salt
    ½ teaspoon pepper
    1 medium sized onion, chopped fine

Have the salmon cleaned and filleted with the skin left intact. Marinate both fillets in the lemon juice, wine, salt, and pepper mixture for at least 30 minutes. Lay the salmon, skin side down, on a piece of hardware cloth and sprinkle on the chopped onions. Bake in a very slow Chinese oven (200 to 250°) about 45 minutes.

Roger A. Stark
Orinda, California

poultry

game

rabbits

STUFFED FRYERS FOR FOUR

    2 frying chickens (about 3 pounds each)
1½ cups dry white wine
    1 large bunch chard
    2 tablespoons olive oil
    2 tablespoons finely chopped onion
    1 cup dry French bread crumbs
    1 tablespoon grated Italian cheese
    2 eggs
    1 good pinch *fines herbes* (mixed herbs)
      Salt and pepper to taste
    2 tablespoons butter, melted

Have chickens cut in half. Clean well; wipe dry with a towel. Lay in a baking pan and pour the wine over them. Leave in the wine, turning once or twice, while making the dressing. Cook chard in small amount of boiling water until tender, or about 15 minutes. Chop well, but not too fine. Heat olive oil in large frying pan, sauté onions in oil, add chard, and mix well. Mix bread crumbs and grated cheese, and add to onions and chard. Beat eggs well with a fork; add to dressing. Add herbs, and season to taste with salt and pepper. Fill halves of chickens with dressing, put halves together, and tie loosely with string. Use marinating wine and butter as a sauce for basting. Bake in a moderately slow oven (325°) until tender, then turn up heat for a few minutes to brown thoroughly. Cut string, and serve each person a half chicken with the dressing side up. If you like, mix 2 tablespoons of finely chopped parsley with 1 teaspoon grated cheese, and sprinkle a little over each serving. This doesn't need gravy, but you can make it with the remainder of the basting sauce, the pan drippings, some mushrooms, and a little flour and water. This dressing is as good as it is unusual, and the chicken is tender and moist. Serves 4.

Hayward, Calif.

ARROZ CON POLLO PANAMA

"Arroz con Pollo," which always sounds much more impressive than the English equivalent, "Rice with Chicken," is a specialty with Frederick W. Hopkins of San Francisco. On its throne of rice, the chicken is surrounded by such a colorful retinue and reigns in such Oriental splendor that we would be tempted to reverse the order of their names.

"On its throne of rice, the chicken reigns in Oriental splendor"

    1 stewing hen of 3 or 4-pound size
    1 medium can (No. 2) tomatoes
    1 large dry onion
    1 medium-sized green pepper
    1 tablespoon vinegar
¼ cup sherry
¼ cup raisins or currants
    1 teaspoon Tabasco
    2 teaspoons salt
½ teaspoon pepper
    2 quarts (8 cups) water
    2 or 3 tablespoons shortening or salad oil
    2 cups rice
    5 cups stock from chicken
    1 small can (10½ oz.) peas (not fresh or
      frozen)
    3 slices canned or very ripe, fresh pineapple
¼ cup fine bread crumbs
    1 small can (4 oz.) pimiento, cut in strips; or
      1 small orange and about 1 tablespoon
      guava jelly

Cut up the chicken and simmer with the tomatoes, onion, pepper, vinegar, wine, raisins, and seasonings in the 2 quarts water. When chicken is tender, remove from the pot and allow to cool a little; then remove the meat from the bones. Keep the meat warm.

Put the shortening in a large skillet and add the washed rice. Fry and stir until rice is nicely browned; then add the 5 cups of stock to rice, cover, and cook carefully until nearly dry, about 20 minutes.

Meanwhile, heat up the peas. Also cut the drained pineapple into 1-inch wedges, coat with the bread crumbs and brown over low heat for about 5 minutes. Use none of the pineapple juice.

Turn the cooked rice out onto a large platter, mounded up with a valley in the middle. Arrange the boned chicken on top to cover, surround by the drained hot peas and the breaded pineapple. Garnish with strips of pimiento. Or cut a small, peeled orange into thin slices, put a large drop of guava jelly in the center of each, and use these to garnish.

Serves 6 so bountifully that it should normally serve 8.

San Francisco

ROAST CHICKEN WITH FILBERTS

    1 roasting chicken (5 pounds)
    1 teaspoon salt
    3 strips bacon
    1 tablespoon Worcestershire
    ¾ pound (3 cups) shelled filberts (or as many
        as chicken will hold)
    ⅛ teaspoon curry powder
    1 cup sauterne or sherry
        Water

Rinse chicken thoroughly, inside and out, in cold water. Dust lightly with salt. With toothpicks, pin one strip of bacon across breast and another between thighs. Place third strip of bacon in cavity. Spoon Worcestershire into cavity. Put giblets in cavity, pushing them as far forward as possible. Fill rest of cavity with filbert meats. Sprinkle curry powder over chicken. Use self-basting roaster (or Dutch oven), with rack.

Pour wine in bottom of roaster and then fill with water to top of rack. Put top of roaster in place and roast chicken in moderate (350°) oven for about 2 hours, or until done. Serves 6 to 8.

When warmed, the liquid in the bottom of the roaster makes an excellent bouillon. When chilled in the refrigerator, it makes an aspic that is worth any trouble involved. You can eat it straight, or mixed with remnants of meat scraped off the chicken bones.

Wallace S. Wharton

*Farmer and Civil Defense Director
Turner, Oregon*

CHICKEN BIJOU

Not every chef has the time for several hours of preparation before serving a meal. Because he likes to entertain at dinner after a day's work, Roy Pohlmann of Millbrae, California, developed and perfected the following recipe for a rich chicken and noodle casserole that can be partially prepared the evening before.

Before his guests arrive, *Chef* Pohlmann assembles all the pre-prepared elements of the casserole, makes a sauce, then slips *Chicken Bijou* into the oven one-half hour before his *E. T. E.* (Estimated Time of Eating).

A tossed salad, rolls, a dry white wine, and a simple dessert complete his menu.

    2 fricassee chickens (3½ to 4 pounds each)
        Salt and seasonings to taste
    1 small package (8 oz.) noodles
    4 tablespoons chicken fat
    4 tablespoons flour
    1 quart chicken stock
        Juice of 1 lemon
    ¼ pound (1 cube) butter
    ½ pint (1 cup) table cream
        Salt and nutmeg to taste
    2 tablespoons butter or margarine
    1 pound fresh mushrooms, sliced
        Grated Italian cheese (Parmesan or
            Romano)
        Paprika

One day before you plan to serve *Chicken Bijou,* simmer whole chickens in water to cover until tender (about 2½ to 3 hours). Remove chickens from the kettle; then reduce stock to about 1 quart. Strain stock and place in refrigerator. At the same time, cook noodles until tender; drain and rinse.

When chickens are cool enough to handle, cut into serving pieces and set aside. Place drained noodles in a large, flat casserole or baking dish, and carefully lay separate pieces of chicken over the bed of noodles. Place casserole in the refrigerator.

Next day, remove enough solidified fat from the chicken stock to make 4 tablespoons; blend with the flour to make a *roux.* Reheat the stock and as soon as it simmers, add lemon juice and the cube of butter. When butter has melted, add cream, salt, and nutmeg. Thicken sauce with the *roux* and cook until smooth and creamy.

In a separate pan, melt the 2 tablespoons of butter and sauté mushrooms lightly.

Remove already prepared casserole from refrigerator and spoon over it first the mushrooms, then the sauce. Top with grated cheese and paprika. Place casserole in a cold oven and bring the heat up to 400°. Cook for about ½ hour, and bring to the table hot and bubbly. Serves 6 to 8 persons.

Roy F. Pohlmann
Photoengraver
Millbrae, Calif.

POULET ABBAYE

    1 young broiler
    Sweet butter
    Salt and pepper to taste
    ½ cup rich cream
    2 tablespoons Benedictine or sherry
    Toast

Sauté chicken in a heavy iron skillet, in butter, until it's a light golden color. Then season lightly with salt and pepper. Flow cream over the chicken and simmer, covered, over the lowest possible flame, so that the cream doesn't curdle. Then, 7 or 8 minutes before removing from flame, add Benedictine or sherry. Stir gently and serve very hot on toast. Serves 2 to 3.

ROD LA ROCQUE
Actor
Ventura, Calif.

AGANA CHICKEN CURRY

    1 stewing chicken (4 pounds)
    1 ripe coconut
    1 onion, sliced
    2 tablespoons butter
    3 tablespoons flour
    2 cups chicken broth
    2 heaping tablespoons curry powder
    1½ cups coconut milk
    ½ teaspoon salt
    ⅓ teaspoon pepper

Boil chicken until tender, then remove all skin, bones, and gristle. Cut meat into small pieces.

Drain milk from coconut and reserve. Grate the coconut meat, saving ½ cup

for a condiment. Add enough water to the coconut milk to make 2 cups, and pour over the remainder of the coconut meat. Let stand while chicken is cooking, then strain through cheesecloth. (This is the coconut milk.)

Sauté onion in butter until slightly browned. Add flour and stir until mixture is smooth. Pour in 2 cups chicken broth slowly, stirring constantly. Mix the curry powder with just enough chicken broth to make a thin mixture and stir in slowly. Add the chicken a little at a time, then the coconut milk, and season with salt and pepper. More curry powder may be added if the curry flavor is not strong enough. Do not cook long after the coconut milk has been added.

The mixture should have the consistency of a medium-thick gravy. If too thick, add more chicken broth. If too thin, mix a little flour with broth and stir in slowly.

Serve hot with rice molded in small cups. On a separate tray, at the table, serve the following condiments: 3 tablespoons finely chopped, crisp bacon; 3 hard-cooked egg yolks, grated; ½ cup grated coconut; 4 tablespoons, or more, chutney.

Shrimp, crabmeat, or veal may be used instead of chicken.

WILLIAM G. JOHNSTON
Agana, Guam

BARBECUED CHICKEN PAPRIKA

    2 (about 1½ to 2 pounds) fryers or **broilers**
    2 cups olive oil
    2 or 3 cloves garlic, well minced
    4 heaping tablespoons paprika
    Salt and pepper

Quarter, wash quickly, and dry chicken well; place in shallow pan. Mix together the oil, garlic, and paprika, then pour over chicken. Marinate for 3 to 4 hours, turning the chicken every half hour. Season with salt and pepper just before barbecuing over hot coals, basting frequently with the marinade. Serves 4.

Dr. Charles R. Cassidy

Physician
Oakland, Calif.

"Experiments with sour cream cookery"

CHICKEN WITH SOUR CREAM AND WINE

From his experiments with sour cream cookery, *Chef* R. W. Winskill of Tacoma has evolved a recipe which seems much more complicated than it really is.

Now this dish may satisfy you so well that you won't want to do anything that might spoil it. However, we would suggest one variation to avoid any chance that the sour cream might curdle with long cooking. Simply omit the sour cream from the sauce that the chicken cooks in. When the chicken is done, pour gravy into saucepan and add sour cream, previously scalded to keep it from curdling. Stir over flame until smooth and boiling, then mix with chicken pieces and serve.

   1 large fryer or capon
   1 teaspoon salt
   ½ teaspoon pepper
   1 cup flour
   ¼ pound (1 cube) butter or margarine
   1 pint cultured sour cream
   Pinch of oregano or tarragon
   1 clove garlic
   1 pint (2 cups) sauterne wine

Cut up chicken, sprinkle with salt and pepper, flour well, and brown in butter in frying pan. Arrange in casserole.

Sauce:

Mix sour cream with oregano, mash garlic and add. Pour wine into frying pan and stir around. (After chicken is browned, there will be some flour, drippings, and delicious whatnot in the pan; be sure they all go into the sauce.) Combine sour cream mixture with wine and drippings. Pour sauce over chicken in casserole. Cover casserole and cook in slow oven (300°) for 1 hour or more or until tender. Serves 6.

R. W. Winskill
Tacoma

CHICKEN IN SURFLODE SAUCE WITH HERBS

   1 large fryer, disjointed
   ¾ cup flour
   1 teaspoon salt
   ¼ teaspoon freshly ground pepper
   ⅛ teaspoon grated nutmeg
   5 tablespoons olive oil
   ½ cup milk
   1 sprig each: savory, thyme, marjoram, and sage
   1 tablespoon paprika
   1 cup sour cream
   12 cooked, small white onions

Clean chicken with a damp cloth and then place in paper bag with flour, salt, pepper, and nutmeg. Shake the ingredients in bag first, then toss chicken about in it until each piece is well covered. Heat olive oil in a large frying pan. Brown chicken in it, then turn down the heat, cover, and cook for about 20 minutes.

Place fried chicken in a covered casserole and set in very slow oven (275°) while you prepare the following sauce, using the pan in which you fried the chicken:

Add the milk, herbs, and paprika. Over low heat, stir until well blended. Add the sour cream, and when well mixed pour this warm sauce over the chicken in the casserole. Put casserole back in the oven for 30 minutes. Before bringing to table, top with cooked onions. Serves 4.

Paul B Davidson
Draftsman
Los Angeles, Calif.

SMOKY CHICKEN

5-pound fricassee chicken
Flour
1 teaspoon salt
Pepper
Olive oil or salad oil
1 can or bottle of beer
1 chicken bouillon cube
2 tablespoons honey
1 cup undiluted frozen orange juice
⅛ teaspoon liquid smoke
¼ teaspoon hickory seasoning salt
¼ teaspoon garlic salt

Cut and disjoint chicken. Shake with flour, salt, and pepper in a paper bag. Brown in oil in a large frying pan. After chicken is browned on all sides, pour off all the oil and add the beer.

In a separate pan, heat chicken bouillon cube, honey, and orange juice together until cube is dissolved. Then pour over chicken. Add liquid smoke, hickory seasoning, and garlic salt. Cover the frying pan and cook chicken over low heat for about 2 hours, or until done. Serves 6 to 8.

Kennett Richardson

Real estate consultant
Walnut Creek, Calif.

CAPON A LA NELSON

2 capons or roasting chickens (about 4 pounds each)
2 cups white vinegar
½ teaspoon salt
¼ teaspoon pepper
2 cloves garlic, minced or pressed
1 cup olive oil or salad oil
2 cans (10¾ oz. each) cream of mushroom soup
1 can (10½ oz.) chicken and rice soup
Flour
Paprika
4 tablespoons shortening or salad oil
2 cups chopped almond meats
½ cup finely chopped green onions
Parsley

Cut capons into serving size pieces. Prepare a marinating liquid by combining vinegar, salt, pepper, garlic, and oil. Place capon in deep bowl or pan, cover with marinating liquid, and let stand for at least 2 hours.

Put the mushroom soup and chicken and rice soup in a small pan and blend over low heat to make a gravy.

Remove capons from marinating liquid and sprinkle lightly with flour. Melt shortening in heavy skillet, add capon pieces, and sprinkle generously with paprika. Brown quickly but lightly on all sides. Place browned pieces in roaster or large baking dish, with chopped almonds and onions sprinkled between each layer. Cover with heated gravy. Place in cold oven, turn on heat to 250°, and bake for 3 hours.

Serve in a baking dish or roaster. Garnish with sprigs of parsley and top with some toasted almonds. Serves 10 to 12.

Woody Nelson

Weiser, Idaho

CHICKEN SAUTÉ MONTROSE

1 (2-pound) broiler, cut in 8 pieces
Salt and pepper
Butter, clarified
2 small onions, finely chopped
1 wineglass Sauterne
1 cup minced mushrooms
1 tablespoon each: finely chopped chives, tarragon, and parsley

Season the chicken with salt and pepper and place in a pan with enough melted butter to cover bottom of pan; add the chopped onions. Cook for a few moments over a moderate fire without browning. Turn pieces frequently. Then add wine, mushrooms, and chopped herbs. Cover pan and simmer for 25 minutes. While the chicken is cooking prepare the following sauce:

Sauce Supreme

2 tablespoons butter
1 heaping tablespoon flour
½ pint warm milk
½ cup cream or top milk
2 egg yolks
Paprika, salt, and pepper

Melt butter in a pan and work in the flour, taking great care not to scorch it. Add the milk and then the cream. Boil up once, remove from fire, and thicken with the beaten egg yolks. Dust with a little paprika and stir well to blend thoroughly. Season with salt and pepper to taste.

*"His recipe arises from a diffusion of many memories, and
a personal vision of how a particular dish should taste"*

Pour the sauce over the chicken and
serve. Serves 2 to 3.

CHARLES A. POST
Business education
San Francisco, Calif.

PAJARO ENCANTO

Sometimes the *Chef* tries consciously to
reconstruct a particular food experience
still vivid in his memory. More often, perhaps, his recipe arises from a diffusion of
many memories, and a personal vision of
how a particular dish could or should
taste.

"The epicurean delight I describe is guar-
anteed to equal or surpass what the
swank Manhattan cafes might designate
as something like *Pheasant grand prix
avec goo de vin a la Francois de Reuben
Bleu.* It tastes as good but doesn't bother
the pheasant population or household
budget nearly so much."

    1 cup white port wine
    ½ cup white wine vinegar
    1 medium sized onion, minced
    1 clove garlic, minced
    3 tablespoons soy
    1 tablespoon Worcestershire
    2 teaspoons salt
      Freshly ground pepper to taste

    ¼ teaspoon celery salt
    1 bay leaf
    ⅛ teaspoon cloves
    3 pounds fryer chicken parts, preferably legs
      and thighs or bisected breasts
    1 small can (6 oz.) mushroom sauce
    1 sprig parsley, finely chopped

Mix together a marinade of the white
port, vinegar, onion, garlic, soy, and
Worcestershire. Add seasoning of salt,
pepper, celery salt, bay leaf, and cloves.
Place chicken in a crock or bowl, add
marinade with seasonings, and marinate
overnight. Turn fowl parts 2 or 3 times·
to assure proper exposure to elixir.

When ready to prepare dinner on the following day, place chicken parts in a baking dish and pour marinade over. Place,
uncovered, in a moderately slow oven
(325°) and bake about 1½ hours, or until
tender, basting once or twice. Then turn
off heat but leave in oven until ready to
serve.

Remove chicken and place on a hot platter. Combine mushroom sauce and remaining marinade in a saucepan, heat,
and pour over chicken. Sprinkle some
chopped parsley on the top. Serves 6.

Carroll O'Meara
Television director
North Hollywood, Calif.

CHICKEN IN WINE

Disappointed in the chicken cooked with wine that he was served in several Paris restaurants, J. H. Kindelberger of Pacific Palisades, California, came right back to his kitchen and made up his own version of how he thought that celebrated dish should taste.

"The formula is simple"

The results are smooth. The formula is simple. The magic ingredients: three thoughtfully chosen cans of soup.

> 2 large fryers cut up for frying (or the equivalent in chicken parts)
> ½ cup flour
> 2 teaspoons salt
> 1 tablespoon seasoning salt
> ¼ teaspoon pepper
> 1 cup chicken stock, or 1 chicken bouillon cube dissolved in 1 cup of water
> 1 can *each* mushroom, cream of celery, and cream of chicken soup
> 1 bottle dry white wine
> 4 tablespoons flour, including any seasoned flour left in paper bag

Shake chicken in a paper bag with flour, salt, and seasonings. Fry in a large hot skillet with a minimum of fat until brown all over, turning frequently. Transfer to a large casserole. Pour excess fat out of skillet, stir in the 4 tablespoons flour to make a *roux*, and pour in chicken stock or bouillon. Then add the canned soups and wine.

The addition of the entire bottle of wine seems like a lot, and the taste of the sauce at this particular moment will be very disappointing. However, do not worry about it. As soon as it has simmered smooth, pour over the chicken, cover the casserole, and put in a moderate oven (350°) for approximately an hour. Serve with rice. This will serve 8 people, or 6 who are really hungry.

Pacific Palisades, California

COQ AU VIN

"This dish has much to recommend it: (1) It is remarkably simple to prepare. (2) It can be either subtle or hearty. (3) It is inexpensive in comparison to the end result. (4) It has delightful taste, eye, and olfactory appeal. (5) It lends itself to endless variety, limited only by your imagination."

There are times when the recipe, so neat and so pat, is a lie. All really good *Chefs* play by ear to a certain extent. They fol-

low the recipe up to a point. Then, in midstream, with half the ingredients bubbling or sizzling, they pause, weigh one delicious possibility against another, and finally conclude the dish with the flourish or variation that suits their mood of the moment.

We're going to start this recipe with the usual list of ingredients, but we're going to follow with the originator's full and rich commentary on what goes through his head as he puts them together.

(to serve 4 to 6)
    1 chicken (1½ to 2½ pounds)
    ½ cup flour
    1½ teaspoons salt
        Coarse ground pepper to taste
    4 tablespoons butter (or more if necessary)
    4 to 6 tablespoons brandy
    1 cup dry red table wine
        Onions, mushrooms, garlic, herbs as desired

For a party occasion, I select broilers or plump young fryers. I cut them into convenient serving size pieces, split them in half, or, occasionally, cook them whole.

I shake the chicken in a paper bag containing flour, salt, and pepper. After removing the chicken, I shake it heartily to remove all of the flour except that which tenaciously hangs on.

There is only one ingredient on which I refuse to stint. That is butter. A tender fryer cooked in anything but butter is a culinary monstrosity. I cook it in an iron skillet until it is a delicate, golden brown. Do not overcook; cook just enough to sear in the juices. Then I remove the pieces to the slightly pre-heated casserole.

Coq au Vin can be prepared in a heavy skillet over a slow fire. I prefer mine cooked in a casserole. For this purpose I use one of earthenware, glazed inside.

If I am cooking for 6 to 8 people, which is average, I prepare enough for 12. As each pan of chicken is properly browned, I place the pieces in the casserole until I have completed the searing operation. Then I put them all back in the skillet again. At this point I take a bottle of brandy and sprinkle the chicken liberally. For those who like exact measurements, 2 to 3 ounces is about right. Light the brandy. There is a tendency to become so entranced by the resulting aroma and fascination of the flame that one forgets to put out the fire. I count five slowly, then snuff out the flame.

The chicken is then piled in neat layers in the casserole. Pour over it the essence from the skillet, scraping it for every last tidbit. Pour over the chicken 1 cup of dry red wine. I use any red wine we have in the house.

From here on, it is up to you. I like onions and generally put in a dozen of the small white ones, about the size of a golf ball. The tips of fresh green onions do nicely, or thick slices of any onion at hand. Add mushrooms, either the dried chips, a can (including the liquid), or a few fresh buttons with the stems. Then a clove of garlic (sliced), a spray of parsley, a pinch of thyme—but add any herb or combination of herbs you prefer.

The casserole then goes into a 250° oven to bubble gently until the chicken is tender and the vegetables are cooked. (With fryers this takes almost no time at all.)

We serve Coq au Vin with oven-warmed garlic French bread and a crisp tossed green salad with a simple oil and vinegar dressing. Cheese and fruit, or an ice, is most complementary for dessert. With this meal I ignore the experts and serve almost any kind of dry white or red wine.

I have tried this recipe with the toughest of roosters and stewing hens with equally excellent results. In this case, I suggest cooking with a heavier red wine, perhaps a lusty Burgundy. Cooking longer, the chicken will take on the color of the wine. When it is almost tender, I put into the casserole any vegetables that happen to be at hand, a few carrots, the peas left over from the night before, chopped chard leaves—take your choice.

Incidentally, I like the sauce not too thick. It can be sopped up better with crusts of French bread. But if the sauce is too thin, you can thicken it easily with tiny balls of flour and butter roux.

Coq au Vin is even better a day or two later when the flavors have thoroughly married. It also seems to me to improve with freezing.

Edward Lawrence —

Public relations
Los Angeles, Calif.

"Any newcomer is welcome to throw in almost anything that might improve flavor"

CHICKEN JAMBALAYA

Some would insist that a "Chicken Jambalaya" (or "Jambolaya") should always contain some ham (from the French: *jambon*). However, there seems to be no complete agreement on this point in the rather loose traditions of Creole cookery. In fact, you get the slight impression that any newcomer is welcome to throw in the pot almost anything he thinks might improve the flavor.

This recipe is a favorite with Russ Taylor, of Los Angeles, because "It is comparatively easy to prepare, can be made the night before except for the final addition of rice, and you just can't go wrong with it. It bakes while the host is relaxing with his guests. I occasionally vary it by using shrimp or pork chops instead of chicken. Preparation is the same. The shrimps should first be cooked; the chops should be well browned."

It is full of flavors, but they are well mixed; a little on the hot side, but not too much for most tastes.

1 large onion, finely chopped
1 clove garlic, minced
2 tablespoons butter
1 package *each* frozen chicken breasts, thighs, and drumsticks
1 cup flour
4 to 6 tablespoons bacon drippings or shortening
3 bouillon cubes
1¼ cups sherry wine
1 cup water
3½ cups (No. 2½ can) canned tomatoes
3 tablespoons crushed dried parsley
½ teaspoon powdered cloves
½ teaspoon powdered marjoram
1 teaspoon chili powder
Dash of cayenne
1½ teaspoons salt
⅛ teaspoon pepper
½ cup sliced pimiento-stuffed olives
½ cup sliced canned mushrooms
1 cup uncooked rice

Brown onion and garlic in butter and set aside. Shake chicken in paper bag with enough flour to coat evenly; brown well in drippings or shortening you have added to pan in which you browned onion and garlic. Place browned chicken in 4-quart casserole or roaster. Dissolve bouillon cubes in the wine and water that has been brought to a boil in the pan in which chicken was fried. Add tomatoes, onion and garlic, and all remaining ingredients. Stir well to distribute rice. Pour over chicken, cover tightly, and bake 1½ hours at 350°, or until rice absorbs all liquid. Serve with a crisp mixed greens salad and almost any fresh vegetable. Serves 6 to 8 hungry people.

Russ Taylor

Advertising executive
Los Angeles, Calif.

NORWEGIAN CHICKEN
WITH CARAWAY SEEDS

Chef R. R. Engelbrecht writes, "A dish that is especially enjoyed by all my guests is one based on an old recipe used by my grandmother, which we call Norwegian chicken. Be sure not to diminish the quantity of caraway seeds called for, for they are its secret 'something.' Have a second helping with my compliments."

Our compliments to you, *Chef* Engelbrecht. You are ready for our select company.

      1 large young hen
        Flour
        Potato flour
        Salt
        Pepper
        Shortening
      2 tablespoons caraway seeds
      ½ cup chicken stock or bouillon
      2 cups sour cream

Select a good-sized fowl that can be cut into meaty pieces. Cut it up, flour well with equal parts of flour and potato flour, and season with salt and pepper. Then brown in hot shortening. You will find that potato flour gives an especially rich brown color. Now add caraway seeds which have been crushed with a pestle to release more of their flavor. Add the chicken stock, or bouillon if stock is unavailable, and one cup of the sour cream. Be sure cream is at room temperature, or it will curdle when added to hot chicken. Put in covered casserole and bake in

slow oven (300°) for 1½ hours. Just before serving, add remaining cup of sour cream. Serves four.

R R Engelbrecht

Mortgage banker
Santa Monica, Calif.

BOISE BASIN CHICKEN

      1 (about 3 to 4 pound) fricasseeing **chicken**
      1½ cups white wine vinegar
      1 cup chicken broth
      2 cloves garlic, peeled
      ¼ teaspoon freshly ground black pepper
      1 pinch each of cayenne, cloves, allspice

Disjoint chicken and wash quickly; place in a large kettle. Cover with boiling, salted water and simmer slowly 2½ to 3 hours, or until tender. Cool slightly; remove meat from bones and pack in a bowl. Combine vinegar, chicken broth, garlic, and seasonings. Pour over chicken meat. Let stand two days before using. Serves 3 to 4.

Mining
Boise, Idaho

SESAME CHICKEN

Ali Baba said "Open Sesame!" and got the treasure. Ellis G. Bovik of Monterey, California, says "Sesame," and you get it, this time in the form of *Sesame Chicken*. Make a paste of 1½ cups of olive oil, a cup of sesame seeds, a minced clove of garlic, and salt and pepper. Roll a cut-up frying chicken in the paste, arrange it in a flat baking dish, and pour ½ cup of sesame seeds over the top. Bake for an hour in a moderate oven. This is another knack learned from the Orient. It's a terrific trick, but take a tip from Ali Baba and look out for those thieves!

Ellis G. Bovik

Dentist
Monterey, Calif.

CHICKEN CURRY

Chef Richard K. Freeman contributes a recipe for Chicken Curry which you may star for service when you wish to honor some special guests with special favors.

```
3 tablespoons butter or margarine
12 onions, sliced thin
 2 tablespoons ground onion
¼ teaspoon ground garlic
 1 teaspoon powdered saffron
 1 teaspoon curry powder
 1 teaspoon ground chilies
¼ teaspoon ground ginger
½ teaspoon ground coriander seed
 1 stewing chicken, cut in pieces for serving
1½ teaspoons salt
 1 cup water
```

Melt butter and fry sliced onions until crisp. Remove onions and add ground onion, garlic, and spices. Cook until mixture turns brown. Place chicken in the curry mixture, add salt, and fry until chicken is brown. Add water and fried onions. Place cover on pan and simmer slowly until the gravy is reduced and the meat is tender. Serve with boiled rice and at least three different condiments.

RICHARD K. FREEMAN
Roscoe, Calif.

ARABIAN CHICKEN

Down in Santa Cruz, California, Jack Angel has developed a way of cooking chicken with oranges and honey as well as the traditional seasonings. The results are distinctly unusual, but good. The delicate flavorings remind you faintly of the "perfumes of Araby."

Says *Chef* Angel, "The creation I am submitting is dedicated to the exclusive use of all masculine chefs who cook for the joy of the thing." As you might suspect, he "builds" this dish, step-by-step, as follows:

Get a fat young chicken, figuring at least one pound per person—a four-pound bird may be stretched to feed four persons, but if you plan for five or more, better play safe and buy another bird. Prepare chicken for roasting.

arabian chicken

"Chicken with oranges and honey"

Mix together the following:

Seasoning Mixture

```
2 teaspoons salt
2 teaspoons powdered cloves
½ teaspoon pepper
1 teaspoon poultry seasoning
```

Rub this mixture thoroughly over the walls of the inside cavity of the chicken.

Over a low flame, combine 1 cube of butter with 1 pint of honey. Rub 4 to 6 tablespoons of this sauce all over the inside area of the chicken.

Stuff the bird with slices of unpeeled orange about ½-inch thick. When the cavity is crammed full, set the bird on its neck and pour in several more tablespoons of the butter and honey mixture. Now sew up the slit and, if necessary, the neck skin in order to confine all the flavoring materials.

Set the bird on its back in a roaster and rub more of the seasoning mixture over the outer skin. Then coat the skin very thoroughly with the honey and butter sauce and place three strips of bacon over the breast. Cover the roaster and slip in an oven with temperature set at 325°.

Allow at least 30 minutes cooking time per pound for birds weighing over four pounds, 35 minutes per pound for smaller birds. Baste every 20 minutes with the remainder of the honey and butter mixture; and, when this is exhausted, use the fluid from the bottom of the roaster. The chicken can be cooked for a longer time at an even lower heat, but not for a shorter time at a higher heat or the succulent natural juices will evaporate.

Keep the roaster covered except for the final 20 minutes, then remove the lid so that the chicken can brown to a golden hue. Watch closely to see that the honey does not darken the skin too much. Make sure the chicken is well done before removing from the oven. Stick a fork in the leg and twist slightly to see that the meat separates easily.

Remove from oven and put chicken on a pre-heated platter. Discard the bacon strips. Serve immediately.

Avoid serving another "special dish" with Arabian Chicken. Excellent accompaniments are baked potato, green peas, and a fresh vegetable salad.

Jack Angel

Santa Cruz, Calif.

POULET SAUTÉ MARENGO

Tradition surrounds a favorite way of cooking chicken known as Poulet Marengo. The name is said to derive from the Battle of Marengo, when, to save time, Napoleon's chef contrived the original recipe that serves, in addition to chicken, eggs, prawns, tomato sauce, and mushrooms!

    1 frying chicken, disjointed
    3 tablespoons butter
    2 tablespoons olive oil
    3 small onions, finely sliced
    2 tablespoons flour
    1½ cups dry white table wine
    2 tablespoons tomato paste
       Salt and pepper
    ½ pound mushrooms, cut in thick slices

Sauté chicken in butter and olive oil, using heavy iron skillet or Dutch oven. Remove chicken, and sauté onions until tender and light gold in color. Sprinkle with flour and stir well; add wine, stirring constantly. When blended, add tomato paste and replace chicken. Cook for 30 minutes, then add mushrooms. Cover and allow to simmer for another 15 minutes. Correct seasonings and serve. Serves 2 to 3.

Gene Van Antwerp

Landlord
Santa Cruz, Calif.

CHICKEN LUZON

There is unusual simplicity, altogether commendable, in the recipe submitted by Commander J. W. LeCompte, USN, and introduced thus:

"While in the boondocks of northern Luzon, just before the war, our Philippine boys prepared chicken for us in the following manner. While the original recipe calls for wild limes, which were available from the nearest tree, I have found that ordinary limes are satisfactory."

"Original recipe calls for wild limes, available from the nearest trees"

    1 frying chicken (about 3 lbs.)
       Salt and pepper to taste
    3 tablespoons soy
    3 limes
    ⅓ cup salad oil
    1½ cups brown rice
    3 cups water

Cut fryer into serving pieces; salt and pepper and rub with 2 tablespoons of the soy. Slice one lime into thin slices, discarding the end slices. Fry chicken and lime slices in hot salad oil, squeezing the juice of another lime over the chicken as it cooks 40 minutes or so, until done.

Meanwhile, steam brown rice in 3 cups water for about 40 minutes. Pour the third tablespoon soy and juice of the other lime over rice. Serve with chicken. Serves 4.

J. W. LeCompte

U. S. Naval Air Station
Alameda, Calif.

PILAU

According to Chef Rooksby, the Northern India preference for *pilau* rather than curry, as we know it, shows the historical Persian influence. The curry powder, in this case, goes right into the rice as it cooks, to add flavor and color.

> 2 large onions, chopped
> 1 green pepper, chopped
> ½ cup salad oil
> 2 fricassee chickens
> ½ cup flour
> 1 teaspoon salt
> 1 teaspoon pepper
> 1 cup water
> 1 pound package rice
> 3 teaspoons curry powder
> 1 cup white raisins
> 1 cup cashews (or almonds or walnuts)
> 1 medium-sized onion, finely chopped

After eating *pilau* in the palace of the Mayor of Sind, Mr. Rooksby asked for a kitchen demonstration and got it. This is the recipe, adapted for Western markets:

In a Dutch oven, sauté the onions and green pepper in the oil until soft; then remove from oil and set aside. Cut up the chickens and shake pieces in paper bag containing the flour, salt, and pepper. Brown chicken in the oil, then return the sautéed onion and green pepper to the kettle, add the water and simmer about 2 hours.

Wash the rice and dump into boiling salted water to which you have added the curry powder. You want a fair amount of curry powder, as the product made in this country isn't as strong as that made in India. That amount of Madras curry powder would bring tears to your eyes. Cook the rice until tender (the only way to tell this is to chew on a few pieces), then pour it into a colander and give it a quick wash with warm water. The rice will be golden. Add the raisins and the whole or broken cashews.

Remove chicken from bones, add rice, and mix with the chicken stock. They do this with their hands in India, so why not here. Taste, and add more salt if necessary. Make it into a mound in a casserole and cover with finely chopped onion. Put it in the oven to keep hot until ready to serve, but not too long or you will ruin the rice. The secret of this dish is the rice. This will serve 10. Serve with mango chutney.

> DENIS A. ROOKSBY
> *Author*
> *San Francisco, Calif.*

CROQUETTES MODERNE

> 2 cups ground, cooked chicken or turkey
> 1 cup homemade or canned cream of potato soup (should be good and thick)
> ½ teaspoon salt
> ¼ teaspoon pepper
> Dash of paprika
> 16 soda crackers, finely crumbed
> 1 egg, well beaten

Mix chicken, soup, and seasonings together thoroughly. Mold mixture in cone shapes, roll in cracker crumbs, dip in beaten egg, and roll in cracker crumbs again. Let the croquettes chill for an hour, then fry in ¼-inch hot salad oil. Keep turning so that all sides will be golden brown. Serve with creamed green peas. Serves 2 to 3.

> FRED G. HARLEY
> *North Hollywood, Calif.*

CHICKEN GRITS GERLACK

Recipes originated by *Chefs of the West* often may owe their invention to a gastronomic whim of the moment, particularly in regard to seasonings. Nowhere is this more evident than in rib-sticking mixtures for which there is no definite recipe. Alvin Gerlack, San Francisco, substantiates this in his logically indefinite formula for Chicken Grits Gerlack.

Take an old fat hen — the older and tougher and fatter the better. Cut it up and put it in a large kettle with lots of water and simmer for several hours, or until meat is separated from the bones. Remove the bones, leaving the meat and the stock in the kettle. Gradually add hominy grits and cook until it has the consistency of mush. Flavor with copious quantities of ripe olives, chopped onion, green peppers, and just enough garlic mashed up fine to give it a good flavor without saying definitely there is garlic. Stir in some Spanish pepper, both the chili con carne and the tamale varieties, and a little monosodium glutamate. Use other condiments as desired. You'll have to stir this mixture constantly to keep it from burning. The amount this will serve depends on the hen and the amount of hominy grits used, but you can bank on its taking care of eight guests, even with two or three servings apiece.

Attorney
San Anselmo, Calif.

"Chicken with sausage—
ever hear of such a thing?"

CHICKEN WITH SAUSAGE

Chicken with sausage—ever hear of such a thing?

Chef H. W. B. (Hod) White, reporting from his look-out post in Honolulu:

"I have discovered a dish used extensively by the Portuguese here, a great number of whom are living around the slopes of Punchbowl.

"Whether for this reason or because the dish is usually served in a large punch-bowl-like casserole, I don't know, but it is always called 'Chicken Punchbowl.' It can be used for any large supper party, lends itself beautifully to preparation the day before, and for a one-dish meal accompanied here in the Islands always with rice, it is in a class by itself.

"The only unusual ingredient is Gouvea sausage, but you can use Redondos or any other good Portuguese sausage—not blood sausage, but the usual ham and garlic type. I have also found that a stewing hen or certainly a large fryer lends much more taste and interest than the small eight-week-old fryers."

The dish is very colorful. The vegetable "sauce" is a dish in itself. Some of the Italian sausages are eligible for this use if you can't find the Portuguese ones in your local markets.

1 stewing hen (about 5 to 6 lbs.) or 2 fryers (about 3 lbs. *each*), disjointed
Flour, salt, pepper, garlic salt to taste
Cooking oil or shortening
1 cup celery, sliced
1 large onion, chopped
1 bay leaf
1 large green pepper, sliced
4 tomatoes, peeled and cut in pieces
1 can (7 or 8 oz.) mushrooms
2 Gouvea (Portuguese) sausages
2 cups water

If stewing hen is used, cover with water and simmer for 1 to 1½ hours, or until half cooked, then fry as described below.

Coat chicken pieces with flour, salt, pepper, and garlic salt; then fry until golden brown. Arrange chicken in a large casserole.

In the skillet in which the chicken was fried, lightly sauté all the vegetables. Cook sausage 15 minutes in 2 cups water; cut in 2-inch lengths. Arrange with chicken in casserole. Pour vegetable mixture over chicken, pour liquid from sausage over all, cover, and bake in moderate oven (350°) for about 1 hour. If desired, do all early preparation the day before, then bake just before serving. Serves 6 to 8.

Executive vice president
Honolulu, T. H.

GIBLETS LYMAN

In many households chicken giblets have a way of collecting in the refrigerator, especially in the chicken barbecuing season when the giblet is not the pièce de résistance. John H. Lyman suggests a good solution, a dish that is quite easy to prepare for a buffet, luncheon, or a particularly hearty breakfast. We would recommend it also for hors d'œuvres, kept hot in a chafing dish.

    1 pound chicken giblets
    1 can (10½ oz.) consommé
    1 small onion, diced (optional)
      Salt and pepper to taste
    4 tablespoons butter
    2 tablespoons flour

Wash giblets and remove excess fat from gizzards. Simmer in consommé with diced onion, if desired, until tender, about 45 minutes. Add salt and pepper, if necessary. Remove giblets and reserve liquid. Grind giblets through coarse blade of a meat grinder or in a blender using the slowest speed. Combine butter, flour, and the liquid to make a sauce. Add ground giblets and reheat. Serve plain, or on toast, rice, noodles, or spaghetti. Serves 2 to 3 as luncheon dish.

John H. Lyman

Palo Alto, California

CHICKEN GIZZARDS
À LA ARCHULETTA

In submitting his original recipe for chicken gizzards, Joseph Archuletta of San Francisco says it serves four persons. Maybe his guests aren't very hungry, or maybe we're guilty of gluttony, but by doubling the recipe we managed to produce enough for four.

    1 small onion, chopped
    1 small clove garlic, chopped
    2 tablespoons butter
    ⅔ to 1 cup sherry
    ½ pound chicken gizzards,
      boiled until tender
    1 small can mushrooms
      or ¼ pound fresh mushrooms
    2 cups chicken stock
    2 tablespoons flour
    2 tablespoons chili sauce
    1 tablespoon Kitchen Bouquet
      Salt
      Pepper

Sauté chopped onion and garlic in butter until brown. Add sherry and simmer until the mixture has been reduced to about half the original amount. Add sliced gizzards and mushrooms and sauté. Add stock, flour, and seasonings to taste, and bring to a boil. Serve on toast points to two persons.

Joseph Archuletta

San Francisco

SAUTÉED CHICKEN LIVERS
AND MUSHROOMS

It's that much-neglected spice, coriander, which makes this such a superb dish. Coriander, brought to Europe by the Romans, can add distinction to many dishes —pea soup, apple sauce, gingerbread, and roast pork to name just a few. Even a rice pudding can be transformed by its touch.

    1 pound chicken livers
    ¼ pound fresh mushrooms
    4 tablespoons butter
    1 teaspoon chopped green pepper
    1 teaspoon chopped green onion
    1 teaspoon chopped parsley
    1 tablespoon flour
    ½ cup dry, white wine
    ½ cup rich chicken broth
    ½ bay leaf
    ¼ teaspoon ground coriander
      Pinch of thyme
    ¼ teaspoon nutmeg
      Salt and pepper
    ⅓ cup chopped almonds

Cut livers in about 4 pieces each, and slice mushrooms. Sauté in butter, along with green pepper, onion, and parsley, for 4 minutes, stirring constantly. Sprinkle with flour. When slightly browned, add wine and broth, stirring constantly. Add bay leaf, coriander, and thyme. Cover, and simmer gently for 10 to 15 minutes, stirring occasionally. Fish out bay leaf. Add nutmeg, and season to taste with salt and pepper. Just before serving, stir in the chopped almonds. Serve at once with boiled, buttered rice or on triangles of hot buttered toast. Serves 4.

Public relations consultant
Long Beach, Calif.

CHICKEN LIVERS MARIPOSA

½ pound chicken livers
1 cup sweet vermouth
1 tablespoon smoked mustard, or 1 table-
    spoon prepared mustard plus a pinch
    of smoke salt
1 teaspoon garlic salt
2 dashes Worcestershire sauce
2 dashes Angostura bitters
¼ teaspoon black pepper
    Juice of ½ lemon
    Dash paprika
½ cube butter

Use fresh chicken livers and do not wash or drain them. Place in a shallow bowl. In a separate bowl combine the rest of the ingredients. Pour marinade over chicken livers and mix well. Marinate overnight, or for at least 12 hours, at usual room temperature.

Brown butter in frying pan. Add chicken livers and all of the marinade. Simmer under cover for approximately 15 minutes. Remove cover and continue cooking over medium flame until liquid has become very thick. At this last stage turn livers frequently until well browned.

Serve on hot plates. Excellent with toasted garlic-buttered French bread. Serves 2.

Los Angeles

GIZZARDS JYOU JIN SHAN

The three supporting ingredients are used extensively in Chinese cookery.

1 pound chicken gizzards
½ teaspoon monosodium glutamate
¼ cup soy sauce
2 tablespoons sesame oil

Clean gizzards *thoroughly* and cut each one into 3 pieces. Boil in unsalted and otherwise unseasoned water for about 3½ hours or until gizzards are very tender. (If you use a pressure cooker, cooking time is about 45 minutes at 15 pounds pressure.) Add monosodium glutamate about 5 or 10 minutes before the gizzards are done.

"The supporting ingredients are used extensively in Chinese cookery"

While gizzards are cooking, mix in a shallow dish the soy sauce and sesame oil. Add hot cooked and drained gizzards to this sauce and mix thoroughly. Allow to marinate for about 45 minutes; then skewer each piece with a toothpick and serve as small chow for a party. This dish may be served either hot or cold. Serves 8 to 10 as appetizers.

Territory manager
Oakland, Calif.

DUTCH OVEN DUCK

Chef Vernon McDonald offers a good workmanlike recipe for domesticated duck—or, as he puts it, "a good deal in dux." In its simplicity (3 vegetables, 3 liquids), in its use of the Dutch oven, and in its use of beer, the recipe has special appeal for the man who doesn't like cooking too fussy.

> 2 ducks
> 3 large stalks celery, thinly sliced
> 3 large carrots, thinly sliced
> 1 large white onion, quartered
>   Salt and pepper to taste
> ¾ cup soy sauce
> 1½ cups tomato juice
> 1 can (12 oz.) beer

Stuff the ducks with the celery, carrots, and onion, seasoned well with salt and pepper. Pour half of the soy sauce into 1 duck and skewer tightly to keep in as much of the soy as possible. Do the same with the other duck. Put the ducks in a large Dutch oven or covered roaster and add tomato juice and beer. Cover and bake at 350° for 2 hours, basting occasionally with liquid in pan. Turn off heat and leave in oven for 30 minutes longer before serving. Serves 6 to 8.

Vernon McDonald
Retired
Long Beach, Calif.

WELL BARBECUED WILD DUCK

Most people like the combined flavors of garlic and soy sauce. Some might enjoy their duck even more if the basting sauce were used also for a preliminary marinating.

> 1 cup olive oil
> ½ cup vinegar
> ¼ cup soy
> 6 cloves garlic, mashed
> 1 sprig rosemary
> 1 tablespoon celery seeds
> 1 teaspoon salt
> ¼ teaspoon pepper (or to taste)
> 4 pintails (or other wild ducks)

Combine all sauce ingredients and simmer 10 minutes to blend flavors. Cut duck into halves and barbecue, turning several times and swabbing sauce on generously. Forty-five minutes over a rather hot fire should do the trick if you like yours "medium." Cut the time for those characters who want their birds still kicking. Serves 8.

Loyd R. Miller
Santa Cruz, Calif.

BROILED WILD MALLARD DUCK

> 1 mallard duck (2 to 3½ pounds)
> 1 cup prepared French dressing
> 1 teaspoon dry mustard
> 2 teaspoons Worcestershire
> 2 teaspoons grated orange peel
> 1 teaspoon grated lemon peel

"A good deal in dux—with 3 vegetables, 3 liquids"

Split duck up backbone with poultry shears. Place breast side down on meat cutting board and break down breast bones by pressing with another board or by pounding gently with a meat tenderizing mallet.

Mix the sauce ingredients together and use it to baste the duck liberally. Insert the duck in a hinged wire grill and broil over hot coals until done to taste, basting it at least once more while cooking. We recommend not over 10 minutes a side; most duck fanciers prefer 5 minutes a side. Divide duck at breastbone into two portions and serve. Serves two.

Seattle

WILD DUCKS, BROILED

Wild ducks
Salt and pepper
Olive oil
Drawn butter
Lemon juice
Minced parsley

Clean the ducks thoroughly, wipe well, and split down the back. Season with salt and pepper, rub with fine olive oil, and place on the broiler. Let them cook from 7 to 10 minutes on each side, turning them over at least twice. Place on a very hot dish and pour over them drawn butter which has been mixed with lemon juice and minced parsley. Garnish with watercress or parsley sprigs.

ROD LA ROCQUE
Actor
Ventura, Calif.

JUGGED HARE

1 rabbit, disjointed
1 onion, thinly sliced
1 cup Burgundy
3 ounces salt pork or bacon
Flour
Salt and pepper
Bag of mixed herbs: thyme, parsley, bay
    leaf, and a clove of garlic

Place the disjointed rabbit in a deep dish containing the sliced onion and wine; cover and marinate for several hours. Remove the rabbit and save the marinade for the gravy. Using a Dutch oven or any deep, heavy kettle, fry the salt pork or bacon until crisp, then remove it. Dust the pieces of rabbit with flour seasoned with salt and pepper, and sauté in the hot drippings to a golden brown. Add the salt pork or bacon, the onion-wine mixture, and the herb bag to the rabbit; cover tightly and cook over low heat for 2 to 3 hours or until the rabbit is tender. Remove the rabbit to a hot serving dish and keep it warm while preparing the gravy.

Skim the fat from the cooking liquor and blend 6 tablespoons of this fat with 6 tablespoons flour. Add enough water to the skimmed cooking liquor to make $2\frac{1}{2}$ cups liquid; stir this slowly into the flour-fat mixture and cook over low heat until gravy is thickened and smooth. Pour gravy over the rabbit or serve in a separate bowl. Serves 6.

Professor
Eugene, Oregon

OVEN BARBECUED RABBIT

2 rabbits, cut in serving size pieces
Salt and pepper
Tabasco sauce
1/8 teaspoon each cinnamon, allspice, and
    garlic salt
1/2 teaspoon paprika
3 small mint leaves, minced
3 tablespoons chopped parsley or
    1 tablespoon parsley flakes
2 cups water
2 tablespoons melted butter
Juice of one lemon

Season rabbit with salt and pepper and place in one layer, meaty side up, in uncovered baking pan. Shake 1 or 2 drops of Tabasco on each piece. Mix together the cinnamon, allspice, garlic salt, and paprika, and sprinkle over rabbit, along with minced mint leaves and parsley. Add water. Bake in a hot oven (400°), basting frequently with the melted butter mixed with the lemon juice. Baste with juice in the pan when lemon butter runs out. Cook for 1 hour, or until tender. The liquor in the pan may be thickened for gravy. Serves 8 hungry persons.

Louis Mandros
Klamath Falls, Ore.

RABBIT ALLA ROMANO

The Italian character of this recipe for rabbit is evident in its use of olive oil, garlic, thyme, mushrooms, and wine. The oil, in particular, gives it a distinctive flavor and probably contributes much to its attractive, well browned color. Since wine tenderizes rabbit very quickly, be careful not to overcook. The meat can become mushy in texture if left over the heat too long.

    ½ pound fresh mushrooms
    2 tablespoons olive oil
    I rabbit, cut in serving pieces
    2 cloves garlic
      Salt and pepper to taste
    ¼ cup flour
    2 tablespoons olive oil
    ¼ cup chopped parsley
    I pinch thyme
    ½ pound fresh mushrooms
    I cup white table wine
    I tablespoon flour

Cut mushrooms in half lengthwise and sauté in the olive oil; remove mushrooms and set aside to use later.

Rub the pieces of rabbit with cut cloves of garlic, salt, and pepper. Dust with the ¼ cup flour, and brown in the same olive oil. Arrange pieces in a casserole and sprinkle with freshly chopped parsley and a generous pinch of thyme. Add sautéed mushrooms and wine; cover tightly, and cook over slow heat for 1 hour. Stir in 1 tablespoon of flour, then return to range for 30 minutes additional cooking. Serves 4.

Douglas North
Seattle

DEAN'S HOSENFEFFER

Friends need little coaxing to stay to dinner when W. B. Dean announces he is cooking up some of his special "Hosenfeffer." It is really his form of *Hasen-*

pfeffer, the famous German Sour Rabbit dish—rabbit with a *Sauerbraten* flavor. ("Ach, ja!" said our taste testers.)

Chef Dean specifies jack rabbit but adds that beef or venison can also be given this treatment. Incidentally, this dish may remind you that rabbit is highly eligible for an occasional appearance at your dinner table.

Vinegar is a powerful tenderizing agent. Watch carefully that you don't overcook the rabbit and give it a mushy texture.

And so with the usual preamble, "First catch your rabbit," we are now ready to proceed:

    I jack rabbit or 2 domestic rabbits
      Salt
    I large onion
      Hot peppers (approximately 4)
    I quart distilled vinegar
    I tablespoon pickling spices
    I bay leaf
      Flour
    ¼ cup shortening or salad oil

Cut up the rabbit into serving pieces and soak in salted water (2 quarts water, 2 tablespoons salt) for about 3 hours. (If using domestic rabbit, eliminate salted water procedure.) Place pieces in a deep crock (a cooky jar works well). Slice onion and place slices between pieces of rabbit. Also add hot peppers to taste and other spices if desired. Pour over vinegar to cover rabbit. Add bay leaf. Then cover crock and place in refrigerator for about 2 days.

Drain rabbit, dust with flour, place in hot frying pan, and brown each side in shortening. (Add salt and pepper to flour when using domestic rabbit which has not been brined.) When rabbit is browned, remove, place in casserole, and add ½ cup water. Cover and place in moderate oven (350°) and steam for about 1 hour, or until rabbit is tender. Remove rabbit while you make rich gravy from the stock. Then serve with mashed potatoes and a vegetable. Serves 2 to 4.

William B. Dean, Jr.
Los Angeles

TURKEY A L'ABSINTHE

J. D. Zellerbach of San Francisco cooks this turkey over a bed of coals and smoking wood, "preferably pieces of oak, alternating with manzanita. If the wood catches fire, spray water on the flame so the wood will continue to smoulder. Suggested weapon: the bulb type spray that florists use to spray flowers." The turkey comes out well browned, slightly smoky-tasting, and very moist.

Sauce:

    1 tablespoon dried tarragon leaves
    1 teaspoon celery salt
    1 teaspoon onion salt
    1½ teaspoons Worcestershire
    ½ teaspoon freshly ground black pepper
    1 jigger (4 tablespoons) Pernod
    2 cups olive oil

Bird:

    12 to 14-pound young turkey

Stuffing:

    2 pieces milk bread
    1 small onion, quartered
    1 small apple, quartered
    2 stalks celery

Final seasoning:

    2 tablespoons smoked hickory salt
    1 jigger (4 tablespoons) Aquavit

Combine all ingredients for sauce. Before stuffing the turkey, put the 2 pieces of bread in the sauce to soak up some of it; then place inside turkey next to breast. Complete the stuffing of the bird with the onion, apple, and celery. Sew up and paint with sauce. Place on a spit and allow to cook about 20 to 30 minutes per pound. After the first hour, baste occasionally with sauce.

Half an hour before cooking is completed, add final seasonings to sauce and continue to baste thoroughly until turkey is ready to serve. Then place on platter or carving board and pour remainder of *warmed* sauce over it. Serves 12.

San Francisco

BARBECUED TURKEY STEAKS

Buy a large, hard frozen, eviscerated tom turkey—the bigger the better. Have your butcher cut it on his power saw, into 1-inch transverse slices, starting at the front of the breast bone, and working back to about where the thighs join the body. If you're serving a large number of people, have him cut more slices—one slice will make two good servings. The two ends that are left can be kept frozen until you need them. Now lay the frozen slices out in a large flat pan, sprinkle with mono-sodium glutamate, and drizzle on enough cooking oil to coat each one. As they thaw, the oil and the turkey juices will make a fine marinade in the pan. This should be brushed back over the slices from time to time. When they are completely thawed, divide each slice into two steaks with a sharp, heavy knife. (You'll find that the cross sections of breast and backbone will split easily.)

Have a good, hot bed of coals going in the barbecue. Arrange the steaks in toasting racks, brush with basting sauce (¼ pound butter, ½ cup dry white wine, salt, and pepper). Broil about eight inches from the fire for around 10 minutes on each side. Turn them a couple of times during the cooking, and brush with more butter-wine mixture.

Serve them up, one to a customer, with the remainder of the basting sauce heated and spooned over each serving, and have the guests guess what they're eating. You'll get quite a variety of answers—pork, veal, even swordfish were guessed, when I asked the question. It doesn't taste like the customary roast turkey, but you'll agree that it is some of the best turkey you ever sank a tooth into. Once again, not too much cooking. Don't let them dry out.

Rare book dealer
Pasadena, Calif.

OREGON TURKEY TAMALE PIE

This type of tamale pie probably traces its origin back to Chile, where both the turkey and maize, or Indian corn, grew wild. However, Italian cooks are the ones most likely to add raisins to such a dish. It's the kind of trick practiced by cooks all over the world, although they may use quite different ingredients. The one thing you observe in every nation's cookery is the striving for a sweet-sour balance.

The raisins are the unique feature of this recipe, but if you prefer the more usual combination, you can omit them and still have a good tamale pie. We recommend cutting the turkey into bit-size chunks.

    6½ cups turkey stock
    1 cup yellow cornmeal
    2 teaspoons salt
    1 medium to large onion
    2 tablespoons margarine or butter
    2 cups cold turkey chunks
    1 teaspoon chili powder
    1 can (8 oz.) Spanish style tomato sauce
    1 tablespoon catsup
    ¼ teaspoon pepper
    ½ cup raisins
    ½ cup pitted ripe olives
    1 tablespoon vinegar

To make stock, cover turkey bones with water and desired seasonings and simmer an hour or more; strain. Bring 4½ cups of the turkey stock to a boil, add cornmeal and salt, and cook into mush. When mush is of medium thick consistency, remove and set aside to cool.

Chop onion fine and fry in margarine until golden brown, using low heat and taking care not to scorch. Add turkey, chili powder, tomato sauce, catsup, pepper, and the other 2 cups turkey stock. Cook until mixture thickens. Add raisins, olives, and vinegar.

Line baking dish with half of the cornmeal mush, add meat mixture, and cover with remainder of mush. Bake one hour in moderate (350°) oven. Serves 8 to 10.

Chas. G. Cole

Horticulturist
Salem, Oregon

BOMBAY CURRY

    1 can (12 oz.) yellow split pea soup
    2 teaspoons good strong curry powder
    Juice of ½ lemon
    ¼ teaspoon nutmeg
    6 drops Tabasco sauce
    ½ cup seedless raisins
    1 medium-sized green apple (unpeeled),
       finely chopped
    2½ cups cubed cooked turkey, or any other
       meat leftover
    1½ cups light cream

Combine all ingredients except turkey and cream; cook slowly 45 minutes, until apple becomes tender and flavors blend. Stir frequently to avoid sticking to the pan. Add cream and turkey. Cook slightly and serve hot. Serves 4 to 6 persons.

Serve with steamed rice. In individual dishes on a tray, provide any or all of the following condiments to be eaten with the curry: chutney, candied ginger, grated coconut, tiny slivers of grapefruit and orange peel, crumbled roasted peanuts (roll with a rolling pin or bottle). For the beverage, serve claret at room temperature, chilled Chablis, or cold beer.

Luis Jubrias

Laguna Beach, Calif.

Chef Jubrias has a trick in preparing his slivered citrus peel. Remove rind from fruit in sections. Scrape off all the white membrane, leaving the peel. Slice the peel in 1/16-inch strips, lengthwise. Slice again crosswise, making minute squares of peel.

TURKEY CACCIATORA À LA SAM PEPE

Lieutenant Commander Sam Pepe decides not to try his inventive powers on the usual 20 to 25-pound Thanksgiving turkey. Instead he studies one of the junior-size birds. He looks at the size of these 4 to 8-pound birds and realizes how satisfactorily they could be cut into pieces just right for individual servings.

He considers how moist cookery would be an absolute guarantee against any possible tendency towards dryness on the part of the turkey. The flavor of turkey—stronger than that of chicken—can easily compete with a rich, highly seasoned sauce. Then he reasons that the Italian "cacciatora" approach, common with chicken, would be even better with turkey.

The colorful, flavorful, definitely juicy result is:

    1 junior size turkey (4 to 8 pounds)
    2 teaspoons salt
    ½ cup flour
    ¾ cup olive oil or salad oil
    2 cloves garlic, minced or mashed
    2 large onions, chopped
    3 small red chili peppers, very finely minced
    ½ cup sherry
    2 green peppers, chopped
    2 cups solid pack tomatoes

"He studies one of the junior-size birds"

Cut turkey into serving pieces (about 10 to 12 pieces, depending on size of bird). Wash, then dry thoroughly, and roll lightly in salt-seasoned flour.

Heat oil in a large (12-inch), heavy skillet then add turkey, and brown lightly on all sides in the hot oil. Add garlic, onions, chili peppers, and sherry. Transfer to a covered casserole and place in a moderate oven (350°), or simmer on top of the stove for about 1½ hours.

Cover turkey with chopped green peppers and tomatoes, and cook for 1 more hour. If liquid doesn't evaporate enough to suit your taste, uncover until the sauce is the right consistency. Serves 10 to 12.

Commander Sam Pepe

Pacific Grove, Calif.

POTATO STUFFING FOR GOOSE

Chef Bradley T. Scheer of Eugene, Oregon, is in a sense talking shop when he talks of food for he was professor of biochemistry and nutrition at the University of Southern California School of Medicine.

"Our Christmas festivities are basically Teutonic in origin, and it seems only fitting that the feast be ordered according to German culinary principles."

He admits the responsibility for preparing the goose, "the great feast bird of Central Europe," at his home, and stuffs it with potato filling which is served at the famous Shartlesville Hotel in the heart of the Pennsylvania Dutch country, a sort of naturalized German recipe, right for the feast.

Cook 6 medium-sized potatoes in boiling salted water; drain and mash. Chop 2 onions and cook in 6 tablespoons butter in a covered pan until tender. Add the mashed potatoes, 3 slices of dry bread, cubed, ½ cup milk, 2 beaten eggs, 1 teaspoon parsley, and 1½ teaspoons salt. Mix thoroughly. This is enough stuffing for a 7- to 9-pound bird. Before stuffing the bird, rub inside and out with a mixture of ginger, salt, and pepper. Baste during roasting with drippings and a light red wine.

Bradley Scheer

Professor
Eugene, Oregon

ITALIAN DUCK DRESSING

2 medium-sized onions, chopped fine
1 clove garlic, minced
¼ green pepper, chopped fine
  giblets, put through meat grinder
¼ pound butter
2 stalks celery, finely sliced
4 sprigs parsley, minced
2 or 3 cups very dry French bread crumbs
1 cup drained cooked spinach, chopped
1 teaspoon poultry seasoning
  Salt and pepper to taste
2 eggs, well beaten
1 cup grated Parmesan cheese

Sauté chopped onions, garlic, pepper, and giblets in butter. Mix with remaining ingredients in order listed, and lightly stuff into the fowl.

Charles Frein

San Francisco.

STUFFING SUPREME

1 clove garlic
1 onion
1 or 2 bay leaves
  Neck, heart, liver, and gizzard of turkey

Cover garlic, whole onion, bay leaves, neck and giblets with water and simmer until meat is easily removed from neck. (Do not trim fat from gizzard.) Grind all except bay leaves, saving the liquid in which these were cooked.

Now, get together equal amounts of dry white bread and cornbread. You'll need approximately 1 large loaf of bread and 1 large recipe cornbread to stuff a 16 to 20-pound bird. And take out your shortening or margarine. Ready? Here's the list of other ingredients.

3 cups coarsely chopped onion
2 cups sliced celery
2 flat cans water chestnuts
2 large cans (6 oz. each) mushrooms
1 small jar stuffed green olives
1 small can pitted ripe olives
2 cups walnut meats, slightly broken
6 hard cooked eggs, sliced
  Salt, pepper, poultry seasoning, sage,
    thyme, and savory to taste
2 No. 1 cans small cove oysters, halved

Soak dry bread, 1 slice at a time, in water. squeeze dry as possible and sauté in hot fat until well browned. Break it into chunks and turn into a large bowl. Crum-ble cornbread *without soaking* into same skillet with additional fat and sauté a few minutes. Frying breads is very important! It keeps dressing from being soggy.

Sauté onions and celery in more fat until yellow. Drain water chestnuts, mushrooms, and olives. Thinly slice water chestnuts, coarsely chop mushrooms, and halve olives.

Add walnuts, eggs, seasonings, and all other ingredients to fried bread, saving oysters and ground giblets, both in liquid, until last. Mix thoroughly. Dressing should be soft and moist. If it seems too dry, add water. Use plenty of salt.

Unless your bird is unusually large, you will have dressing left over. Put it in a shallow baking pan, spoon grease from the roaster over it, and bake.

Stuart B. Moseley

Locomotive fireman
Eugene, Oregon

BARLEY-GREEN PEPPER-ONION STUFFING

"Those meals between turkey and turkey"

Chef Ralph Richard Rosso of Livermore, California, uses barley of the cooking variety often used in soups. This gives a good moist stuffing. Undercook the barley as *Chef* Rosso directs. You want individual grains—not a mush—in the final result.

Turkey giblets
1 cup pearl barley
2 or 3 large onions
2 medium-sized green peppers
  Poultry seasoning or individual seasonings
    to taste
  Salt, pepper, paprika to taste

Cover turkey giblets with lightly salted water and simmer until tender. Grind giblets in the food chopper, saving the

"Equipped for an almost unlimited range of cooking operations"

broth to moisten stuffing. Cook barley in 3 cups boiling water until *nearly* done (if cooked until tender, the stuffing will be pastelike and unsatisfactory). Drain.

In the meantime, shred onion and green pepper (the stuffing is much lighter if you shred rather than cut fine or chop); fry in bacon grease until limp. Combine ground giblets, barley, onion, and green pepper. Season to taste. Pour in enough giblet broth to barely moisten and mix thoroughly.

This recipe makes enough stuffing for a roasting hen, with a little left over to put in the baking dish and serve for second helpings. Increase or decrease amounts as necessary to conform to size of the bird.

Ralph Richard Rosso

Nursing education
Livermore, Calif.

SURPRISED SQUAB

Ernest Kai of Honolulu has an indoor barbecue equipped for an almost unlimited range of cooking operations—with a barbecue grill, a built-in electric burner for use with a Chinese wak, and a Chinese oven.

The recipe that he developed for squab is a natural for the Chinese oven. It utilizes traditional Chinese ingredients to develop a dish that is unusual and tantalizing, but not too exotic for most tastes. Serve it on the patio and your guests can feel more free about wresting the succulent meat from this bird's multitude of tiny bones.

        4 tender, fat squabs
        3 tablespoons soy
    1/4 teaspoon monosodium glutamate
        1 tablespoon brown sugar
        3 tablespoons Scotch whiskey
          Salt and pepper to taste
        1 medium sized onion, chopped
        4 squab gizzards, sliced
        3 tablespoons butter
        2 cups diced white bread
        3 medium sized cooked shrimp or 6 dried
            Chinese shrimp, broken in small pieces
        6 water chestnuts, sliced
        1 cup milk
        1 teaspoon salt
    1/4 teaspoon pepper
          Salad oil

Marinate the squabs in a mixture of the soy, monosodium glutamate, brown sugar, whiskey, salt and pepper for about 1 hour. Brush the inside and outside of each bird with this mixture several times during the hour.

Fry the onion and gizzards in 1 tablespoon of the butter until brown. Add the remaining two tablespoons of melted butter and mix with the diced bread, shrimps, water chestnuts, milk, salt, and pepper.

Fit this stuffing inside each bird, and sew up the openings. Skewer together each pair of legs or tie with light wire. Brush skins with oil and hang in a moderate (300° to 400°) Chinese oven for about 1 hour and 15 minutes. Brush the skins with salad oil once again during the cooking process. Serve one juicy squab per person.

Ernest Z. Foi
Honolulu

SQUAB ROBERT

There is acknowledged luxury in the following recipe devised by Fred Benrath of Los Angeles, but good sound eating, too. For the squab he wisely allows a short roasting time under cover, which, with the succulent dressing, preserves every ounce of moisture.

        4 1-pound squabs
           Monosodium glutamate
        4 tablespoons butter
        1 clove garlic, mashed
        1 tablespoon chopped onion
        ¼ teaspoon freshly ground black pepper
        2 cups wild rice
    4½ ounce tin Pate de Fois Gras
        ½ can clear chicken broth
        2 tablespoons butter
        ½ teaspoon nutmeg
           Salt to taste
        ¼ pound salt pork, sliced thin
        2 ounces port (¼ cup)

Rub squabs well with monosodium glutamate. Let stand for 15 minutes. Melt butter in heavy frying pan and stir in mashed garlic, onion, and pepper. Add squabs and brown all over evenly, using low heat.

Pour boiling water over wild rice, let stand 5 minutes. Drain and repeat process two more times. Add remaining ingredients, except salt pork and port, to drained rice and mix lightly but thoroughly. Stuff squabs with mixture. Serve remaining rice with squabs.

Arrange squabs in baking dish. Cover breasts of birds with thin slices of salt pork. Pour a tablespoon of port over each bird. Cover and bake 20 minutes in a very hot oven (550°).

Sauce

        1 tablespoon flour, rounded
        ½ can clear chicken broth
        2 tablespoons red currant jelly
        ½ cup port

Add flour to the drippings in the pan in which the squabs were sautéed. Stir well and add the remaining half can of chicken broth, scraping the pan well to mix in the gelatinous products that stick to the pan. If too thick, add a little water. When smooth, add jelly and port wine. Simmer briefly to desired thickness.

Fred Benrath
Wine salesman
Los Angeles, Calif.

QUAIL SUPREME

Skin 4 quail and soak overnight in a bowl of salt water.

Prepare a frying pan with the drippings from about 3 slices of bacon. Get it hot and have a cover ready. It really pops the grease around when you drop the quail in for browning.

Meanwhile, put a covered casserole dish in the oven at a temperature of 300°. Have about ¼ cup of water in the dish.

As your quail become browned, put them into the casserole. After they have been in the oven about 15 minutes, salt and pepper them and put ¼ cup of cream in the casserole. After another 15 minutes, add ½ cup of sherry, then allow quail to cook another 30 minutes.

About 5 minutes before time to take the quail out, start making your gravy. To the bacon grease, which has now acquired a little of the quail juice, add about 1 tablespoon flour. Brown this mixture, then add grated peel from half a lemon, a couple of dashes of Angostura, and the cream and sherry juice from the casserole. Stir to eliminate lumps. You're ready to serve.

Jackson R. Arnold
Commander, USN
San Diego, Calif.

DOVE, OR WHITE WING Á LA ARIZONA

In the wild game division, we have a recipe for the dove, or white wing, that hunters seek in the Southwest. Martin Gentry, of Bisbee, Arizona, observes that many people do not like dove, as it is ordinarily cooked, because it tends to be very dry and is also very dark meat. "This recipe does not eliminate the darkness," says he, "but it does eliminate the dryness. I have found that persons who ordinarily do not care for dove become very enthusiastic about it when cooked in this manner."

All the additives contribute toward keeping these birds moist and tender. Some may prefer to leave the vegetables in the gravy. If you haven't any wild doves to try this on, squab will do very nicely.

6 doves or white wings
2 teaspoons seasoned salt
½ cup flour
1 teaspoon salt
½ teaspoon pepper
4 slices bacon
½ cup chopped onions
¾ cup diced carrots
½ cup sliced celery
1 can (10½ oz.) beef bouillon
2 cups dry white table wine

For best results and tenderer birds, keep birds in refrigerator 3 to 4 days after killing and cleaning.

Sprinkle birds with half of the seasoned salt and dredge in the flour seasoned with salt and pepper. Cut bacon into small squares, fry, and remove from bacon fat. Sauté birds in bacon fat; then place in casserole and sprinkle with the other teaspoon of seasoned salt. Add small pieces of bacon. In remaining bacon fat, sauté onions, carrots, and celery for about 3 minutes, stirring constantly. Pour whole mixture over birds. Add beef bouillon, previously brought to a boil.

Cover casserole and place in a moderate oven (350°) and bake for 1½ hours, adding 1 cup wine after the first 30 minutes, the other cup of wine at the end of an hour. When birds are done, remove them and strain the liquid. Make gravy from the remaining liquid, adding chopped chives and Kitchen Bouquet if desired. Serves 2 or 3.

Lawyer
Bisbee, Arizona

ROAST WILD GOOSE

This recipe is for hunters who heed the call of the wild goose, or others who share their good fortune. It is submitted by Arthur Hargrave, who often hunts this bird—commonly called a snow goose or a Canadian goose—on the Stanwood Flats along Puget Sound, about half way between Seattle and Bellingham. You will note by the plentiful addition of bacon fat that this is quite a different bird from the domesticated goose often served for Christmas dinner.

If you're lucky at hunting, *Chef* Hargrave suggests that you roast 2 wild geese together (they run about 5 pounds each) because they are so delicious served cold or as leftovers.

Here is his tried-and-true cooking method:

Since this bird is hard to pluck, skin all but the breast, and then pluck it by hand. If the bird is old or tough, or if you have had bad luck in handling it, you may sometimes have to skin the breast, too. In that case make a rich pie crust-like paste of butter, flour, and just a touch of water; coat the breast with this paste to keep it moist.

Rub the cavity and the outside liberally with bacon drippings. Then put the bird, breast down, in a hot oven (425°) until the back is browned. When it looks the right shade of brown, take it out of the oven, flip it on its back, and stuff it with your favorite dressing. (I use a regular bread dressing that contains more onion than usual; one large tart apple, chopped; several stalks of celery, chopped; and plenty of sage.)

Put 3 strips of bacon across the bird's chest and return it to the oven, still at 425°. When it is nicely browned, put ½ cup water in the bottom of the roaster, put on the lid, and roast at 375° for approximately 3 hours, basting at least 3 times. One goose will serve 3 to 4 persons.

Commercial artist
Kirkland, Washington

FRUIT STUFFING FOR GOOSE

Chop goose liver. Plump 1 cup prunes and 1 cup raisins; remove seeds and chop. Do not grind any of the ingredients. Add to liver. Take 1½ to 2 cups stale corn bread, depending on size of goose, and crumble into the mixture. Add 2 well-beaten eggs, ½ cup parsley, ½ cup chopped onion, and ½ cup chopped apricots. Add salt and pepper to taste. Mix all together and stuff goose. This will be a dry, fluffy dressing, but the fat of the goose will cook into the stuffing, making it delicious.

Reno, Nevada

ROAST DUCK COLBY

    2 frozen ducks, 4½ pounds each
    6 large or 10 small day-old French rolls
    1 can (10 oz.) Pacific oysters (8 to a can)
    1 can mixed nuts, coarsely chopped
    ½ teaspoon thyme
    ¼ teaspoon garlic powder
    ¼ teaspoon onion powder
    8 stalks celery, strings removed, and
        very thinly sliced
    ¼ teaspoon black pepper

Let the ducks thaw; then dry them thoroughly inside and out.

To prepare stuffing, cut rolls into cubes and pour liquid from oysters over them. Cut oysters into small pieces and add them and also all the remaining ingredients, working all together with the hands. Stuff the ducks with this mixture, sew them up, and place them on a revolving spit or in an oven which has been pre-heated and set at 250°. Cook for 4½ hours. (NOTE: *If you cook them over a barbecue fire, the time, naturally, may vary with the heat of the coals.*) Just before serving the ducks, make brown gravy from the pan drippings and add the sliced cooked giblets. Serve Burgundy wine with the dinner. Serves 8.

Oahu, T. H.

ROAST WILD DUCK WITH SAUERKRAUT

Rub 2 mallard ducks on the inside with a clove of garlic. Season lightly with salt and pepper and stuff with wild rice dressing. Truss and place, breast up, in a small roasting pan. Cover top and sides with sauerkraut (homemade or No. 2½ can) cover, and roast in a slow oven (300°) for 2½ hours, or until done. Serves 4.

Wild rice and mushroom dressing

Soak 1 cup of wild rice overnight, or boil until soft. Mince 2 medium-sized onions and 1 celery heart, and sauté in 2 to 3 tablespoons of butter until golden brown. Add 2 cups of small, toasted bread cubes (about 4 slices of bread), the wild rice, and 1 medium (3½ ounce) can chopped mushrooms, including liquid. Season with ¼ teaspoon sage, 1 teaspoon salt, pepper, and a pinch of oregano. Add ⅓ cup melted butter. Either boiled chicken livers or sausage meat may be added if desired.

Homemade sauerkraut

For best flavor, cabbage should be placed in the crock within an hour after cutting. Cabbage purchased at the market after being cut only a day or two previously never measures up in quality.

For a six-gallon crock, weigh out 70 pounds of cabbage. Remove outer leaves, halve or quarter cabbage as you go along, and shred into medium-fine strips.

When you have shredded enough to make a layer about 2 inches deep, place in the crock and sprinkle with approximately 3 teaspoons salt. Sprinkle with ¼ teaspoon caraway seed. (This will give great flavor and does wonders for the digestibility of this cabbage dish.) Then repeat until within an inch of top.

Store in a moderately warm location. Place a dish that almost covers the top of the cabbage over the crock, and weight it down with a six-pound (more or less) rock. Let stand for 11 days, no less. Process in jars (water bath for 30 minutes), or store crock in cool place.

Caution: Because the fermenting kraut will run over the sides for a day or two, place the crock where the runoff will not damage anything.

This will give you kraut for wild game, spare ribs, sausage, and roast fowl through the winter.

Yakima, Wash.

meats

CARBONNADE

4 ounces beef suet
2 pounds round steak or sliced sirloin tips
5 medium-sized onions
1 bottle beer
1½ tablespoons butter
Salt
Pepper

Render fat from beef suet. In this hot fat, brown steak or sirloin tips which have been cut in 2- or 3-inch squares. Take out meat and brown onions in the same fat. Remove onions and pour beer into the drippings and stir until both are well mixed. Then add butter.

Place a layer of browned meat in a casserole, then a layer of browned onions over the meat, repeating with alternate layers of meat and onions until all are used. Season with salt and pepper to taste. Pour the mixture of drippings, beer, and butter from the skillet over the meat and onions.

Cover the casserole and bake slowly in a slow oven (300° F.) for about 3 hours. If you use sirloin tips, about 2 hours is enough. Serve with hot boiled potatoes cooked separately. Serves 4.

George Ayrault

Oakland, Calif.

STEAK WOHLFORD

For the marinade:

Juice of 3 or 4 lemons
½ cup salt
⅛ cup pepper (or more)
6 to 8 cloves garlic
Good-sized pinch of thyme
Small pinch of oregano
½ cup olive oil or salad oil
3 or 4 large sirloin steaks, 1½ inches thick

Blend all ingredients (mash garlic in a pestle with salt, or put in a liquidizer with some of the oil). The finished mixture should be about the consistency of library paste, thicker than the usual marinade. Spread on steaks at least 4 to 8 hours ahead of cooking time.

Use all the marinade mixture, pile one steak on top of the other, and let them stand—the longer the better. Do not forget to coat both sides of the bottom steak.

Make a strong tea of bay leaves, letting the leaves steep in hot water half an hour. Start an outside fire of lemon wood and let it burn until practically no flame remains. Just before putting steak on the grill, scrape off practically all vestiges of marinade. Grease the grill well with chunks of beef suet. Coat the steaks lightly with melted beef suet, if you have it, otherwise bacon grease.

Sear steak on both sides and then allow to cook slowly on one side without turning until cooking is half-way through, then turn and complete cooking to guests' preference. Continue to baste with melted suet to keep from drying.

Whenever the fat dripping from the meat causes the fire to flame, sprinkle the flame lightly with the bay leaf mixture, using a spray of white sage as a brush. Also, at intervals, place several sprays of white sage on the coals. Maybe it is imagination, but we feel the resultant smoky aroma adds to the taste of the finished product.

NOTE: While almost all the marinade should be scraped off, experience has taught me that a little left on makes a thin delicious crust.

Burnett Wohlford

Farmer
Escondido, Calif.

STEAK ON THE COALS

Use any good steak cut 1 to 1½ inches thick. Build up your fire until you have about 2 to 3 inches of coals. Have steak at room temperature and throw it directly on the coals. Turn it when the juices show on top and place on an area of coals not previously covered by steak. The cooking process should take about 10 to 15 minutes. Season to taste and serve from the fireplace.

In our testing we found it advisable to use a hard charcoal or hard wood that gives off a very fine ash after it burns. Also, it's a good idea to whisk any surplus ash off the top of the coals with a fireplace broom or blow it off with a bellows. Actually, the steak doesn't burn; it damps down the fire a bit, unless you get your bed of coals too thick and too hot.

However, this method of cooking steak cannot be done altogether satisfactorily by rote. You have to practice it a time or two before you can count on reasonably consistent results. It's so much fun,

"Actually, the steak doesn't burn"

though, that you'll probably consider it worth the risk.

Production manager
Menlo Park, Calif.

GARLIC STEAK

When fried potatoes are cooking in one pot, steak should be cooking in another. In this version of a Swiss steak, Dr. Banner R. Brooke uses an unusual amount of garlic. But when it is cooked in this manner, the steak gets only the kiss of garlic.

"The steak gets only the kiss of garlic"

```
  1 flank steak, scored
    Flour
    Bacon drippings or lard
  2 tablespoons vinegar
  1 teaspoon dry mustard
  8 small or 4 large cloves garlic (or less,
      if you prefer)
    Salt and pepper to taste
```

Cut steak in 3-inch squares, pound in all the flour that meat will hold, brown in suet or bacon fat. Cover with water and add remaining ingredients. Simmer with lid on for an hour and a half, making up any loss of water to create sauce (gravy) of right consistency. Serve (with mashed potatoes) to 4.

Physican (retired)
Portland, Oregon

BRANDY-BROILED STEAKS

About 15 minutes before you get ready to barbecue steaks, sprinkle both sides of the steaks generously with California brandy. Then let them stand in a crock or on an enamel plate. Grease the broiler, and broil the steaks. When nearly done, salt both sides to taste.

State chamber of
commerce executive
Palo Alto, Calif.

MUSTARD STEAK

Let's clear up one point right away. Stuart Moseley's recipe for "Mustard Steak" is not intended, or needed, for "real steaks" —rare enough (in one sense, only) in some households these days.

"I've tried other cuts of steak with this recipe, but none works out like flank steak," says *Chef* Moseley. Fortunately, flank steak is near the low end of the steak social and economic scale. But its coarser fibers are softened and permeated with good flavors by this treatment which includes "steam frying" in a slow oven. Make sure that each guest gets a fair portion of any of the rich coating which may have dropped off during the cooking or serving.

```
    Flank steak
  1 tablespoon dry mustard (approximately)
  1 tablespoon paprika (approximately)
    Salt and pepper
  1 egg, well beaten
  1 tablespoon water
    Bread crumbs, rolled fine
    Fat for frying
```

Have a flank steak scored by the butcher when you buy it. Rub on both sides with all the mustard that the meat will absorb. Repeat this process with the paprika. Salt and pepper to taste. Cut into serving-size portions, dip in beaten egg mixed with water, dredge in crumbs. Brown lightly in plenty of hot fat. Put in roaster, adding about ½ cup of the fat in which the meat was browned (add more shortening to the pan to make up this amount if necessary), and ½ cup water, and cover tightly. Steam fry in very slow oven (250°) until tender—about 1½ hours. Serves 6.

Gravy may be made from the drippings, of course, but it is rather too tangy to suit my taste. We usually serve this with baked potatoes and skip the gravy.

Stuart B. Moseley

Locomotive fireman
Klamath Falls, Oregon

STEAK MARCHAND DE VINS

    2 tablespoons chopped shallots
    1 cup dry red wine
 ¼ pound butter
    1 teaspoon chopped parsley
    3 tablespoons very thick soup stock
      A few drops of lemon juice
      Salt and pepper
      Beef marrow
    4 porterhouse steaks, 1½ inches thick

Put the chopped shallots and the wine in a wide saucepan and cook until the total volume has been reduced by more than one-half; let cool. Then cream this wine and shallot mixture into the butter, along with the parsley, soup stock, lemon juice, salt, and pepper. The marrow should be poked from two-inch sections of beef leg bone and poached in salted water for 1 minute before slicing. If you share my passion for marrow, you'll spread some on a piece of toast, salt it lightly, and slip it under the broiler for a minute, which produces a delicacy to munch on while you're completing the sauce. Grill the steaks over a wood fire (use dried grape shoots if possible). At the moment of serving, strew small pieces of beef marrow over the steak and pour the sauce over all. Enough sauce for four good sized steaks. This is a true Bordelaise sauce. It's also excellent on broiled lamb, or mutton chops, and on grilled mushrooms, or liver.

Frank Schoonmaker

Writer
San Francisco, Calif.

STUFFED HAMBURGER TURNOVERS

You will need:

Bowls of the following, all *finely* chopped:

onions	toasted almonds
garlic (red)	sweet red peppers
parsley	sweet green peppers
olives	celery leaves
carrots	

Chopped beef—6 oz. for each turnover
Heavy waxed paper
Cracker crumbs seasoned with curry
Butter
Monosodium glutamate
Salt and pepper
Burgundy

You prepare:

All the chopped and grated things. Store in covered containers in refrigerator. Add curry (your taste, but go easy) to crumbs. Leave some plain, just in case.

Put previously weighed-out portion of chopped beef (a scale or a cooperative butcher is essential!) on sizable sheet of strong waxed paper. Pat beef with fingers. Make it big. Make it flat. Make it thin. Result should be reasonably round and about 10 inches in diameter. Score lightly across center with knife-back for easy folding. Leave on waxed paper. Beef can all be prepared ahead of use, stacked and stored in refrigerator.

Guest participates in (or you carry on alone!):

Sprinkle crumbs over each turnover, leaving margin. Drop dot of butter on one side. Load one half with liberal pinches (or guest's choice) of *all* the chopped and grated things. Dust well with monosodium glutamate, salt, pepper. Lift empty side over "stuffings," leaving paper stuck to meat for support while you pinch edges together. Carefully lift paper from upper side. Loosen meat from paper around all edges so you can remove it easily at will. Strive for no "leaks." Repair same, if any. Spread top-side with butter.

On the fire:

"To all those who have suffered the repercussions of a too-rich Beef Stroganoff"

A large spider holds two. Have it hot. Drop turnovers (careful!) off paper, butter-side down. Reduce heat. When ready to turn add gob of butter, 3 tablespoons Burgundy for each pair and hold heat medium. You're not trying to cook the stuffings; just heat 'em. Do the hamburger the way you like it. The innards will take care of themselves. Don't miss all the fine goo in the pan. "Wipe" it out with a small portion of that steamed rice the missus has ready (well, didn't she *know?*) or a bit of bread, but be sure each guest receives his share. After all, you shouldn't get all the gravy—even if you like it that way!

James Henry O'Brien
Los Angeles, Calif.

HAMBURGER STROGANOFF

"To all those who have suffered the repercussions of a too-rich Beef Stroganoff, I offer a modification," says William Idelson, of Encino, California. "This dish makes a simple and delicious dinner or supper. The recipe below serves 4 hungry people, but I have served it to as many as 35 by multiplying the measures. It is foolproof and improves with age. If you make a big batch, you can freeze it with great success."

Our only suggestion is: Adjust amount of A-1 sauce to suit your own taste. You may want more than specified—or you might even prefer to substitute Worcestershire. If you like a little more color, sprinkle in some chopped parsley, or green pepper, or pimiento.

1½ pounds lean ground beef
3 tablespoons salad oil
1 large onion, chopped
1 clove garlic, minced
1½ teaspoons salt
¼ teaspoon pepper

Sauce:

1 cup evaporated milk
1 can (10½ oz.) consommé
3 tablespoons tomato paste
1 tablespoon A-1 sauce (or more to taste)
3 tablespoons flour
¼ cup sherry

Crumble the hamburger, then fry in oil together with onion, garlic, salt, and pepper until very brown. Meanwhile, combine evaporated milk, consommé, tomato paste, and A-1 sauce.

When the meat mixture is brown, sprinkle flour over it and mix in well. Then add the consommé mixture. Cook slowly until it thickens, stirring constantly. Then let it bubble at lowest heat for 15 to 20 minutes, stirring occasionally. Just before serving, add the sherry—if your hand trembles at this point, don't worry; a little more won't harm the dish. Serve over rice or buckwheat groats cooked according to package directions. Some may prefer over noodles. Serves 4.

William Idelson
Actor and writer
Encino, Calif.

ROUND GROUND ROUND

1 pound good beef
1 clove garlic
1 teaspoon cumin
3 teaspoons salt
½ teaspoon black pepper

Cut beef into strips. Crush clove of garlic and spread juice over strips of beef. Put cumin, salt, and pepper into an empty saltcellar and sprinkle contents over strips of beef. Grind meat fine, just once, catching it in a No. 2 tin can which has both ends cut out by a rotary can opener. Press ground meat into can gently. When full, take one of the ends previously cut from the can and use it to push meat out to desired thickness. Cut off with a sharp knife and place on hot griddle. Turn only once to retain the tenderness of the meat. Do not pat the meat, of course.

Chas. J. Dingeson

Aircraft inspector
Van Nuys, Calif.

BEEF AND GRASS

1 egg
1 pound ground beef
1 handful each of finely-chopped spinach
    and watercress
1 tablespoon chopped onion
½ teaspoon paprika
    Salt and freshly ground pepper

Break the egg over the meat, add the spinach and watercress, chopped onion and seasonings and work together until well blended. Then broil. Chopped oysters can also be added to the formula: parsley substituted for watercress.

L. B. WILLIAMS
Research director
Berkeley, Calif.

CHEF'S GROUND BEEF

Most men who appreciate the subtle flavor of beef prefer their steaks and roasts on the rare side. But the same men will often incinerate a hamburger until the tempting color and beef flavor are merely a memory. Not so Paul Murphy of Manhattan Beach, California, who offers this contribution to lovers of rare beef.

"Prefer steaks and roasts on the rare side"

1½ pounds ground lean beef
1 teaspoon salt
¼ teaspoon pepper
½ teaspoon monosodium glutamate
2 tablespoons butter or margarine

Sauce

1 tablespoon butter or margarine
1 tablespoon chopped parsley
1 tablespoon lemon juice
⅛ teaspoon salt
    Pepper and paprika

Blend the ground beef, salt, pepper, and monosodium glutamate and form into a loaf about 3 inches wide and 1½ inches thick. Spread the butter over the loaf.

For the sauce melt butter and add parsley and lemon juice. Mix thoroughly and add salt and a sprinkling of paprika and pepper.

If you broil the meat in the oven, be sure that the broiler is turned to the highest heat at least 5 minutes ahead of time. If you broil meat over coals, lower your grill so that the meat is close to the coals. (Extinguish serious conflagrations immediately.) Count on 5 or 6 minutes for each side, carefully turning the meat only once with a broad spatula. The result should be a loaf crusty brown on the outside, deliciously rare inside.

Place the loaf on a sizzling hot platter the instant it comes from the fire, and pour over it the lemon-butter sauce. Slice into individual servings and serve on warm plates without further delay. Serves 3 or 4, depending on individual appetites.

Architect
Manhattan Beach, Calif.

GROUND ROUND WITH ROQUEFORT CHEESE

1½ pounds ground lean steer meat
1 egg
  Salt and pepper
¼ pound Roquefort cheese, crumbled
1 teaspoon dry mustard
2 tablespoons mayonnaise
2 tablespoons Worcestershire sauce

Mix well and form into 8 uniform, thin patties 1½ pounds of ground, lean steer meat, 1 egg, salt and pepper to taste. In a small mixing bowl, combine Roquefort cheese, crumbled, dry mustard, mayonnaise, and Worcestershire sauce. Divide cheese mixture into 4 equal parts. Place 1 part cheese in the center of each of 4 patties. Place remaining patties over the cheese; press the edges together to hold in the mixture. Broil or fry as desired for the individual taste. The melted cheese mixture inside remains soft and gives what I think is an excellent flavor.

Physician
Phoenix, Arizona

POTATO HAMBURGER

1½ pounds ground beef
3 medium-sized unpeeled raw potatoes, diced
1 small onion, chopped
2 tablespoons chopped parsley
  Salt and pepper

Mix together the meat and the potatoes, run through the food grinder, skins and all. Add the chopped onion and parsley; salt and pepper to taste. Shape into medium-sized patties and broil. Serve without sauce.

For variety, fry in skillet. Brown flour in the pan juices after frying the patties, add milk, and season with salt and pepper, making a thick milk gravy. Pour the gravy over the patty and serve. A delicious quick gravy can be made by emptying a can of condensed mushroom soup in the cooking pan and thinning slightly with milk.

Life insurance
Palo Alto, Calif.

HAMBURGER ON THE LEAN SIDE

I pound ground beef
  Salt and freshly ground pepper
  A dash of meat sauce
½ teaspoon curry powder
½ jigger cognac
I egg
I small can chopped mushrooms
  Chopped onions
  Olive oil

Trim every trace of fat from the meat before putting it through the grinder. Season with salt, pepper, meat sauce, curry powder, and cognac. Add the raw egg, mushrooms, and the chopped onions that have been fried to a delicate golden brown in olive oil. Form meat into generous cakes and broil.

GEORGE WILSON
Ojai, Calif.

MINIATURE MEAT BALLS

2 pounds lean ground beef
I pound bulk pork sausage
I cup dry bread crumbs
2 tablespoons grated or chopped onion
I teaspoon salt
¼ teaspoon pepper
2 eggs
½ cup dry red wine
  Flour
2 tablespoons bacon drippings
I large can (7 oz.) button mushrooms
  (either stems and pieces, or whole)

Mix meat, bread crumbs, onion, salt and pepper, eggs, and about half of the wine in a large bowl. Form into small balls about the size of a medium-sized walnut. Roll in flour and brown in the bacon drippings in a heavy frying pan. Remove, place in a roaster (or casserole) with a tight fitting cover. Pour fat from frying pan over the meat balls and add the remainder of the wine and the juice from the can of mushrooms. Cover tightly and cook 2 hours in moderate oven (350°).

One hour before serving, add mushrooms. Just before serving, remove meat balls and thicken gravy with flour, adding water as necessary to make enough gravy to go around. Will serve 6 or 8 generously.

I serve the meat balls on a large platter; pile riced potatoes around the edge and fill the center with the meat. Pour a small amount of the gravy over the meat balls and use the rest with the potatoes. Serve with buttered green peas and new carrots, French or home-made bread, and a light dessert.

Gilbert A Pelling
Seattle

RUSSIAN MEAT ROLLS

Rolling up ground meat in a green leaf is a cooking technique practiced in a number of foreign countries. Russian, Polish, and Armenian menus are all known for meat rolls—some wrapped in grape leaves, some in cabbage leaves.

2 cabbages
I pound ground lean pork
I pound sausage
I pound ground lean beef chuck
3 large onions, finely chopped
3 tablespoons Worcestershire
I teaspoon freshly grated nutmeg
3 teaspoons salt
2 cups (I pint) sour cream
I can (10½ oz.) tomato soup
2 teaspoons curry

Core cabbages and pull off the tough outer leaves. Steam cabbages for about 10 minutes, or until leaves are pliable. Carefully pull off leaves, cutting out the heavy portion of the center rib on the larger leaves. While the cabbage is steaming, mix ground meats (ground twice if possible) with onions, Worcestershire, nutmeg, and salt.

Gently roll small egg-sized portions of the meat into cylindrical shapes. Place each one of these rolls on one cabbage leaf, tuck in the ends, and roll loosely. Arrange the cabbage and ground meat rolls in a large baking pan.

Combine sour cream, tomato soup, and curry powder; then pour over the meat rolls. Cover and bake in a very slow (250°) oven for 1 hour. Remove cover and bake 2 hours longer. Serves 8 to 10.

Kenneth Bristol
Salt Lake City

MEAT BALLS AU RAIFORT

    1 pound lean beef, ground
    ½ cup potato meal (or flour)
    1 medium-sized onion, minced
    ¼ cup butter
    1 cup beef stock or bouillon
    1 teaspoon paprika
    ½ teaspoon mustard
    ¼ teaspoon allspice
    1 tablespoon sugar
    1 tablespoon chopped parsley
    1 tablespoon dry sherry
    5 tablespoons bottled horseradish
    ½ teaspoon salt
    2 tablespoons potato meal (or flour)

Form meat into small balls about the size of marbles and dip in potato meal until well coated. Sauté onion in butter until golden brown. Add meat balls to pan and keep turning them until they are nicely browned. Remove meat balls from pan, taking care not to remove too much of the butter.

To the butter left in the pan, add the remaining ingredients in the order given. (If flour is used instead of potato meal, add it to the butter first.) Stir until the mixture is smooth and has the consistency of medium white sauce. Return meat balls to sauce and simmer 15 minutes.

Serve garnished with slices of hard-cooked egg and sprinkled with paprika or grated American cheese. Serves 4.

KENNETH KNIGHT
School administrator
Los Angeles, Calif.

FRIKADELLER (DANISH MEATBALLS)

Fars (Forcemeat):
    1⅔ pounds ground lean beef
    ⅓ pound ground pork
    1 small onion
    2 or 3 eggs
    4½ tablespoons flour
    1½ teaspoons salt
    ¼ teaspoon pepper
    2½ to 3 cups milk
       Hot shortening or bacon drippings

Ask your meat man to grind the meat twice, fine grind. At home, grind meat and onion together in a meat grinder 2 times. Mix in eggs, flour, salt, and pepper. Add milk, a little at a time, until

the mixture is of the right consistency to shape with a spoon into soft balls the size of a small egg. Scoop up meatballs one by one with a tablespoon dipped in the hot shortening, and drop into hot shortening to brown (dip the spoon in the shortening again before picking up each ball). Fry meatballs until done and well browned. Set aside and prepare the following sauce:

Sauce:
    1 large jar (10 oz.) large green olives
    2 cups water
    1 cup dry sherry
    1 tablespoon grated onion
    3 bouillon cubes
    6 tablespoons butter
    6 tablespoons flour

Drain liquid from olives and save to use in sauce. Slice green olives into slivers and set aside. Combine olive juice, water, sherry, grated onion, and bouillon cubes in a saucepan. Boil until bouillon cubes are dissolved. Melt butter in pan; blend in flour. Slowly add hot liquid mixture, stirring continually—otherwise it will lump. When this is thick and of gravy consistency, stir in previously sliced olives. Add salt and pepper to taste, if desired (remember that green olives are salty). This should make about 3 cups gravy.

(Amount of sherry can be varied to suit your preference. If you like a darker gravy, color with gravy concentrate.) Place meatballs in gravy and reheat slowly. Serve with either boiled or mashed potatoes, or with rice, and, of course, a green salad. Makes about 60 meatballs, enough to serve about 12.

Holger J. Jeppesen.

Mechanical engineer
Menlo Park, Calif.

MACLENNAN HAM

    1 center-cut slice ham, 1 inch thick
    1 pint ginger ale
    1 cup coarse bread crumbs
    2 tablespoons butter or margarine, melted
    3 bananas

Place ham in a medium-sized baking pan. Pour ginger ale over it, and cover with bread crumbs which have been mixed with melted butter. Cover and bake in moderately hot oven (400°) for about 50 minutes, or until tender. Uncover to

"While visiting at Len Turner's sheep ranch in New Zealand"

brown. Just before ham is done, cover with bananas which have been sliced in half lengthwise. Let bake about 15 minutes longer, or until bananas are soft. Frequent basting will give the ham a gentle infusion of ginger flavor and keep it moist. Serves 2 to 3.

Alexander Bruce MacLennon

Electrician
Seattle, Washington

HAM AND MUSHROOMS NEW ZEALAND

"While visiting at Len Turner's sheep ranch in New Zealand, I learned first hand of a popular country recipe which should find favor in this country," says Ken Morrish, of Orinda, California. "First, Len brought in a bucket of fresh mushrooms. After washing and trimming, he put them into his largest covered heavy frying pan with a great lump of home churned butter. . . . Next he went to the cool house and cut several slices from a shoulder of cured pork, which he laid on top of the mushrooms, and then covered the frying pan. . . ."

1½ pounds fresh mushrooms
¼ pound butter
3 small slices ham, ¼ inch thick

Wash and trim mushrooms and place with butter in a heavy frying pan. Put over low heat. Cut each ham slice into 4 to 6 pieces; lay on top of mushrooms. Cover pan and allow to simmer for 20 minutes. Remove cover, stir ham to bottom, replace cover, and simmer for 10 minutes.

Serve in soup bowls, with fresh homemade bread available for dunking up the juice. Or, if desired, the juice may be thickened with butter and flour and a bit of milk, and the gravy poured over bread or toast. Either way is a new taste treat straight from the New Zealand "bush." Serves 6 to 8.

Kendrick B Murrah

Banker and writer
Orinda, Calif.

HAM ROLL-UPS

2 medium-sized sweet potatoes
3 tablespoons butter, melted
½ cup crushed pineapple
¼ cup chopped pecans
½ cup cracker crumbs
3 tablespoons brown sugar
2 slices boiled ham, ¼ inch thick
¼ cup pineapple juice

Cook sweet potatoes in boiling water until tender; then skin, drain, and mash. Add melted butter, pineapple, pecans, cracker crumbs, and brown sugar. Mix well. Spread thick layer of filling on each slice of ham.

Roll up as for jelly roll and fasten with toothpicks. Place both rolls in a baking dish and pour pineapple juice over them. Bake in moderate oven (350°) for about 40 minutes, basting frequently with liquid in pan. Cut each roll in thirds. Serves 6.

Charles E. Collier, Jr.

Berkeley, Calif.

POOR MAN'S BARBECUED HAM SLICES

    1 tablespoon dry mustard
    ½ tablespoon powdered ginger
    1 cup spiced peach syrup (or any spiced
        fruit syrup)
    Ham slices, cut ¼ to ⅜-inch thick
        (as many as you want)

Make a paste of the dry mustard and ginger by adding the syrup slowly. Stir until a smooth sauce results.

Trim most of the fat from the ham slices and paint on one side with the sauce. Place on the grate, sauce side down, about 12 inches above a slow charcoal fire. Paint the top side of the ham. Turn the ham often and keep moist with the sauce.

Don't be in a hurry! Keep over slow fire for at least 30 to 40 minutes. Don't let it rest on one side too long. Turn it often, let it brown, not burn, and use all of the sauce.

Wallace Jones

Pharmacist
Menlo Park, Calif.

SOUTHERN PORK BARBECUE

    1 quart cider vinegar
    5 tablespoons Worcestershire sauce
    2 tablespoons A-1 sauce
    2 teaspoons salt
    1 tablespoon sugar
    6 whole mint leaves
    ¼ teaspoon paprika
    4 shakes Tabasco
    ½ teaspoon black pepper
    1½ tablespoons mixed whole pickling spices
    1 bouillon cube
    3 large slices unpeeled orange
    2 large slices unpeeled lemon
    1 cup water
    1 tablespoon catsup
        Sweet Basil and oregano to taste
    2 feet of the kitchen sink

Put on the stove in an enamel or glass container, and simmer until the orange and lemon peel are pretty well cooked.

Use this sauce on either pork or lamb. To barbecue spareribs, first cook them over coals until the fat begins to run out. The fire must not be too hot, or the ribs will char before they are thoroughly cooked. When the juices start to sizzle on the hot coals, start daubing the spareribs frequently with the sauce. These are excellent appetizers.

To barbecue a leg of pork, use the same low heat. Place the leg on a grate which is about 14 inches from the firebed. Cover with a good sized pan so that you keep in all the heat. Turn the meat every 20 minutes. Cook the leg of pork for 6 to 7 hours before basting with the sauce, then continue cooking for about 2 hours longer, basting frequently. A 14 to 16 pound leg of pork will require 8 to 9 hours' cooking time in all. Cooked this way, the meat will be very tender. It should be sliced *with* the grain, parallel to the bone, not across the grain, as is customary.

W. M. Blackburn

San Francisco

BUTTERMILK SKY SAUSAGE

A true chef hates to waste food, which is why George W. Phillips, of Portland, finding a soupçon of buttermilk left from his batch of hotcakes, decided to stretch his sausage patties in this original manner.

    ½ pound pork sausage
    2 slices dry bread, crumbled
    ½ cup buttermilk
    ½ teaspoon salt
    ¼ teaspoon pepper
    ½ teaspoon sage
        Pinch of thyme and cloves (optional)

Mix all ingredients, form into patties, and roll in more bread crumbs. Fry slowly until done. Don't cook too long, or you'll dry out moisture. Makes 6 patties.

George Phillips

Insurance and real estate
Portland, Oregon

ORCAS ISLAND SCRAPPLE

2 pounds pork odds and ends (knuckles, jowls, hocks, etc.)
½ clove garlic
2 stalks celery with leaves
  Bunch of parsley
  Pinch of sage
  Salt and pepper to taste
2 cups medium-grind cornmeal

Put all ingredients except the cornmeal in a 3-quart kettle; cover with cold water and simmer for about 2 hours, or until the pork falls off the bones. Remove bones, celery, and parsley, and gradually stir in the cornmeal. Cook slowly, stirring constantly and watching the mixture carefully to prevent burning. When it is about the consistency of thick mush, pour it into bread pans and let it stand for 2 to 3 hours to cool. Then cut into ⅛- or ¼-inch slices and sauté in bacon drippings over low to medium heat until crisp and golden brown. Serve with currant jelly, fried apples, or apple butter.

CAPT. HAL FERRIS
Master mariner
Eastsound, Washington

ROAST PORK WITH GLAZED APPLES

Here is a modification of the suckling pig with an apple in its mouth. *Chef* Abe Zwillinger uses four apples and makes them so good that they almost overshadow the pork.

"Apples so good they overshadow the pork"

Roast Pork:
½ loin of pork (4 to 5 pounds)
  Salt to taste
1 clove of garlic
½ pound bulk sausage
1 Spanish onion, finely chopped
2 hard cooked eggs, finely chopped
2 tablespoons chopped parsley
½ cup white table wine

Have roast boned so you have one long piece of solid meat; rub outside with salt and garlic. Cook sausage and onion over brisk fire for 2 minutes. Combine with eggs and the parsley, spread in the inside curve of the boned roast, then fold over and tie. Put into roasting pan, sprinkle with wine; roast in moderate oven (350°) until meat is tender (figure on 35 minutes to the pound). Remove from the pan, slice; arrange overlapping slices on serving dish. Pour pan juices over the meat and garnish with glazed apples. Serves 8 to 12.

Glazed Apples:
4 apples
¾ cup sugar
¾ cup water
  Juice and grated peel of 1 orange
  Juice of ½ lemon

Peel apples, cut in half crosswise, remove the cores; cook in syrup made of sugar, water, orange and lemon juice, and grated orange peel. Cook apples until soft but not mushy, about 10 minutes.

Abe Zwillinger

North Hollywood, California

CHAR SIU, COOKED IN AN OVEN

"For a very long time I have been nagging my many good Chinese friends to give with the recipe for Char Siu, the famous $2.00 a pound, barbecued, boneless pork meat. They hang onto that recipe jealously. And if you don't think so, just wander up on Grant Avenue, San Francisco, and start asking for the exact details. I've been after it for months. I even managed to have one Chinese friend get me into a basement where it was being cooked professionally, but nary a recipe nor pointer did I get on the seasoning. I met the Great Wall of China right here in dear old San Francisco. But I have not been an investigator for 32 years for Uncle Sam, Department of Justice, for nothing . . . here it is!"

1 pound boneless pork, cut in
　strips 1 inch in diameter
2 cloves garlic
3 tablespoons salt
1 teaspoon paprika
1 tablespoon catsup
5 tablespoons sugar or honey
1 teaspoon soy sauce
1 teaspoon Jamaica rum or white wine
2 cakes Chinese bean cake (this is obligatory
　with Chinese but can be omitted)
½ cup water
½ teaspoon monosodium glutamate

Mash garlic into salt and mix thoroughly with remaining ingredients. Marinate pork strips in this overnight. Lift pork strips out and lay in baking pan. Roast meat in open pan in moderate oven (350°) until browned, watching and turning frequently. Swab occasionally with the marinating sauce saved for this purpose. Turn up heat to 550° for final quick browning before serving. Oddly, the Chinese barbecue *Char Siu* over leaping flames, but suspended so high that the flames never reach the meat.

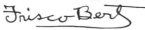

*Investigator, Justice Department
San Anselmo, Calif.*

HAM IN BURGUNDY SAUCE

¼ pound fresh mushrooms
1 tablespoon butter or margarine
1 teaspoon salt
½ teaspoon pepper
½ teaspoon paprika
4 slices uncooked ham
2 tablespoons butter or margarine
1 tablespoon flour
1 cup Burgundy
　Salt and pepper to taste

Wash and quarter the mushrooms. Fry in butter for 5 to 10 minutes, seasoning with the salt, pepper, and paprika. Set aside on a platter and keep warm.

Brown ham slices in butter on both sides, allowing 3 minutes for each side. Remove ham and put on a platter with the mushrooms.

Add the remaining butter to the pan and stir in flour, mixing thoroughly with melted butter until no lumps are left. Add

the wine and stir until the sauce begins to thicken. Add a very small amount of salt (since the ham is quite salty) and some freshly ground pepper. Return ham and mushrooms to the pan and let simmer in the sauce for about 15 minutes. Serve with a green salad. Serves 4.

NOTE: Boiled ham will make an equally satisfactory and often milder dish. If you use it, however, be sure to brown it very briefly—about 1 minute or less per side.

Joachim Remak

*Teacher
Palo Alto, Calif.*

ESTOFADO

3 pounds lean pork, mutton, or venison
¼ cup olive oil
2 cloves garlic, minced
2 large onions, chopped
1 pint red table wine
3 teaspoons chili powder
1 bay leaf
1 teaspoon salt
½ teaspoon liquid smoke
1 teaspoon curry powder
½ teaspoon cumin
½ teaspoon pepper
1 teaspoon dry mustard
1 teaspoon oregano
1 teaspoon monosodium glutamate
2 cups uncooked noodles

Cut meat into 2-inch cubes and put in pan with olive oil and finely chopped garlic and onion. (If you use pork and have to trim off some fat, render it in Dutch oven or skillet and use pork fat in place of olive oil.)

Sauté thoroughly until both meat and vegetables are a rich brown. Pour wine over meat; add all remaining ingredients except noodles; cover and bake for 2 to 3 hours in a very slow oven (250°), or until meat is tender.

Meanwhile, put noodles in salted boiling water and cook until tender. Drain, rinse, and keep warm in a frying pan. Serve Estofado over the noodles, with garlic French bread and a light salad. Serves 6 to 8 with good appetite.

Geo. C. Booth

*Teacher
Long Beach, Calif.*

DEVILED PORK CHOPS

Green olives and pork make a charming couple; we might never have known it if *Chef* Richard Bennett of Phoenix hadn't played matchmaker to bring them together in Deviled Pork Chops.

The rather biting flavor of the olive cuts down the richness and fattiness of the pork and, aided by the green pepper and the pickle juice, makes the pork taste mild by comparison. *Chef* Bennett proposes this as a Dutch oven dish, but you'll need one of larger than standard size to handle eight pork chops as prescribed. Otherwise, use any large, heavy, covered baking pan or kettle suitable for the purpose.

"Green olives, pork—charming couple"

8 pork chops, cut 1 inch thick
1 clove garlic
1 tablespoon prepared mustard with
    horseradish
2 large onions, sliced
1 large green pepper, cut into 8 rings
1 medium sized bottle (8 oz.) pimiento-stuffed
    green olives (including liquor)
¾ cup uncooked rice
¾ cup sweet pickle juice (preferably fig,
    peach, or apricot)
1 can (10¾ oz.) condensed consommé
    Water

Remove any excess fat from chops; rub both sides of chops with cut clove of garlic. Render out some of the fat in a Dutch oven or other cooking kettle. Brown chops lightly on both sides in the drippings. Spread equal amount of horseradish-mustard on each chop. Cover with onion slices, and top each chop with green pepper ring. Chop olives coarsely and divide among chops. Sprinkle rice around chops. Slowly add liquor from olives (about ½ cup), the pickle juice, and the undiluted consommé. Add enough water to barely cover chops. Do not add salt;

the olive liquor and consommé supply all that is needed.

Cover and cook over medium heat for 1 hour. More water may be added if rice becomes dry before cooking is completed. This dish should be almost dry and the rice fluffy when ready to serve.

Richard Bennett
Phoenix

NAPA-SONOMA LAMB SHANKS

As the Livermore region of California is famous for white wines of the Sauterne type, the Central Valley and the south for sweet dessert wines, so the northern counties of Napa, Sonoma, and Santa Clara are renowned for their dry red and white table wines of the Burgundy, Claret, and Rhine types. If you've just a cup of red or white dry wine left in a bottle, here's an excellent recipe:

4 lamb shanks
    Salt, pepper, and flour
¼ cup butter
1 onion, minced
1 clove garlic, minced
1 cup red wine
1 carrot, minced
2 stalks celery, thinly sliced
    Herb bouquet

Select lamb shanks well covered with meat. (Be sure to tell the meat cutter not to crack the bones.) Dust each with salt and freshly ground pepper, and roll in flour. Brown them in butter with the minced onion and garlic; remove them to a casserole. Rinse the pan, in which you have browned the meat, with the wine, and pour all over the lamb shanks. Add the carrot, celery, and herb bouquet, and cook, covered, until the meat is tender, or for about 1½ hours.

If the sauce remaining in the casserole is too thin when the meat is done, thicken it with kneaded butter balls made by blending butter and flour together into marble-like balls.

Philip S. Brown
Rare book dealer
Pasadena, Calif.

BALINESE LAMB

Coconut is the unusual new element added to an old formula here. And if old-fashioned roast lamb is really near to your heart, we advise you to lay on coconut sparingly at first.

```
6  lamb shanks
   Garlic
   Salt and pepper to taste
1  cup sauterne
1½ cups uncooked rice
1  cup chopped onion
1  bell pepper, chopped
1  cup chopped celery
3  tablespoons minced parsley
1  package (4 oz.) shredded coconut
1  teaspoon salt
½  teaspoon mace
½  teaspoon nutmeg
2  cups water
```

Wash and wipe the lamb shanks dry, rub with garlic, and then salt and pepper them. Put in an open roaster as you would a leg of lamb. Cook for one hour at 350°, basting frequently with the sauterne. Remove, add the washed rice, onion, pepper, celery, parsley, coconut, salt, spices, and water. Cover and return to the oven for 30 minutes, or until the rice is quite dry. Serve with a green salad and garlic bread. Serves 6.

George Tripp

Crockett, Calif.

PICKLED LAMB'S TONGUE BASQUO

In his cookery, *Chef* Charles Leicester Palmer has tastes which lean toward the exotic. However, you need have no qualms about his "Pickled Lamb's Tongue Basquo." As long as you don't label it, all your guests are likely to eat it with relish. Since you can always cut back on the garlic, you don't have to take *Chef* Palmer's opening words too seriously:

"It is not a recipe for the timid or the squeamish, but has a robust appeal to the person who likes garlic—and admits it. The ingredients are essentially Basque, with substitutions and variations not only permissible but intriguing. For instance, watercress may be substituted for a portion of the parsley, or a ring of bell pepper added to the chopped ingredients.

"If you prefer fresh lamb's tongues, they should be boiled thoroughly in salted water, cooled, and skinned before slicing."

```
½  bunch of parsley (stems removed)
8 to 12 cloves of garlic
1  jar pickled lamb's tongue (6 tongues)
1  cup Burgundy (or any good red table wine)
¼  cup red wine vinegar
1½ teaspoons salt
1  teaspoon cumin
5  dashes Tabasco
```

Chop together parsley and garlic until very fine. Slice tongue into rounds not quite ¼ inch thick. Place thin layer of parsley and garlic in bottom of jar, cover with layer of tongue slices and repeat until used up, with a final layer of parsley. Mix wine, vinegar, salt, cumin, and Tabasco and pour over to cover. Add more wine if needed to cover. Let stand 24 hours, drain, and serve as appetizers. Will serve about 12 persons.

Charles L. Palmer

Publicity
Fresno, Calif.

SKEWERED LAMB

Marinade and Basting Sauce:
```
½  ounce dry mint leaves
1  teaspoon dry tarragon leaves
½  cup vinegar
¾  cup brown sugar
1  teaspoon dry mustard
½  teaspoon salt
½  cup butter
   Juice of ½ lemon and grated peel
½  cup Sauterne
```

Put all ingredients except Sauterne into a saucepan and bring to a boil. Remove from heat, cover pan, and let steep for about 30 minutes. Strain, and add Sauterne. Cool. Marinate meat in this sauce for 30 minutes.

For *each* serving, use:
```
3  pieces lean lamb, cut in squares
2  small green tomatoes
2  slices onion, cut ½ inch thick
6  squares sliced bacon
```

Place above, alternating items, on skewers. Broil, basting frequently with sauce until done. Serve with rice, French bread, and tossed green salad.

Dick Neily

Mechanical engineer
San Francisco, Calif.

BAKED LAMB NECKS

When a *Chef of the West* scores a bull's eye with a recipe, he should be a little brash in his bragging. So we clap our hands and shout "Olé!" as Ralph W. Felix, of Glendale, California, praises "Baked Lamb Necks":

"I believe it is a dish which can be served to appreciative guests without apology. It will bring some ah's and oh's when they tie on the bibs and get their first taste. If they don't use their fingers and take all that's available, they should be off your guest list for special events."

Not the least of its virtues is the fact that this recipe calls for an inexpensive cut— but there's some surprisingly good meat tucked in around those vertebrae. Lamb can take a very rich sauce. We'd like to give the same treatment to lamb shanks.

We know of one household where lamb necks are always called "punkles." These are mighty good punkles.

> 4 lamb necks

Marinade:

> 2 cans (8 oz. *each*) tomato sauce
> 4 tablespoons wine vinegar
> 4 tablespoons brown sugar
> ½ cup mild red table wine
> ½ clove garlic
> ½ teaspoon rosemary
> Pinch of thyme

Added ingredients:

> 3 tablespoons olive oil
> 1 cup sliced fresh mushrooms
> 1½ tablespoons flour
> 2 tablespoons A-1 sauce
> 1 teaspoon salt
> ¼ teaspoon pepper
> 2 dashes Tabasco

Order lean and meaty lamb necks and have your meat man cut each into 2 or 3 slices about 1¼ inches thick. With a sharp knife, cut off the outer skin, fat, and tissue. Mix marinade ingredients together and marinate lamb necks for 3 hours.

In a heavy skillet, heat olive oil. Add mushrooms and sauté gently for 5 minutes. Remove lamb slices from marinade and scrape off excess marinade. Remove garlic from marinade and sauté 1 minute with mushrooms; discard garlic and set mushrooms aside. Put lamb necks in drippings in skillet, brown nicely on both sides, and arrange in baking pan.

Add flour to ½ cup of marinade; mix thoroughly, to make smooth mixture; pour into drippings and stir well. Add remaining marinade and A-1 sauce, salt, pepper, and Tabasco. Bring to boil and pour over lamb. Place in oven and bake uncovered at 350° (moderate oven) for 1½ hours, or until meat is tender, basting occasionally. If sauce gets too thick, add small amount of water. Sauce should be liquid and about ½ inch deep when cooking is finished.

Serve with Italian-style spaghetti or over steamed rice. Serves 4.

Ralph W. Felix

Civil engineer
Glendale, Calif.

LAMB LAURATTINI

> 5 cloves of garlic
> 1 teaspoon powdered marjoram
> 6 anchovy fillets
> 1 leg of spring lamb (5 pounds)
> Salt and pepper
> Flour
> Butter
> 1 cup undiluted canned consommé

Boil garlic cloves in three changes of water until tender. Mash, add marjoram and anchovy fillets. Mash together and mix well.

Cut slits, about 2 inches deep and 3 inches apart, in fat side of lamb, and stuff with the above mixture. Rub roast with salt and pepper, and dredge with flour. Sear well in butter. Add consommé. Cover closely and bake in a moderate oven (350°) about 2½ hours. Baste frequently.

Serve with wide noodles buttered and mixed with Parmesan cheese. Sprinkle chopped pimientos on top of noodles. Serve pan gravy on side.

JAMES G. ROSS
Special investigator
Santa Barbara, Calif.

LAMB KIDNEY COLBY AND FINE HERBS

Our taste testers rated this dish high. Even some who don't ordinarily care for kidneys liked it, remarking how the taste resembled that of chicken livers. It's a good dish for a supper, a midnight snack, or hors d'œuvres.

Most of the cooking is done in the first 15 minutes. After that it is important to keep the heat very low, lest you toughen the kidneys.

    16 to 20 small, cleaned lamb kidneys
     2 tablespoons olive oil
     4 tablespoons butter or margarine
    ¼ teaspoon *each* dried oregano, rosemary,
        thyme, marjoram, and crushed celery seed
    ¼ teaspoon American saffron (optional)
        Salt and pepper to taste
    ½ cup black muscat or tawny port wine
     8 to 10 slices buttered toast
        Butter
        Parsley

Cut kidneys into small chunks. Place in frying pan with all remaining ingredients except wine, toast, butter, and parsley. Bring to high heat for 15 minutes, stirring and turning constantly. Then turn heat down to very low and let simmer for an hour. Put on a tight cover to trap all the steam and condensed juice. Thus the dish will be self-basting and you can forget about it while it simmers, except to have a tasty sample every now and then, and stir it a little.

Just before serving, add wine. Serve on hot buttered toast, on piping hot plates. Place a small bit of butter on each serving and garnish with parsley. Serves 8 to 10.

Edward P. Colby

Oahu, T. H.

LAMB STEAK CARAMELLI

    1 leg of lamb
        Salt and pepper
        Butter

For each serving, cut slices about ¾-inch thick from the leg of lamb. Dust with salt and pepper, and while doing that, heat some butter in an iron frying pan, using a very hot flame. Now drop the steak (or steaks) into this hot butter and cook very fast on both sides, sealing in all their juices. Enough will escape to help in making the sauce at the end. About 10 minutes will brown the steak on both sides and cook the center sufficiently. Then turn out onto a hot platter while the sauce is being prepared.

Sauce

    1 or 2 tablespoons butter
    1 wineglass dry white wine
    2 or 3 tablespoons sliced mushrooms
        Dash of lemon juice

To the juices in the pan, add the butter and wine. Into this pour the sliced mushrooms and cook until the mushrooms are done—a matter of minutes only. At the end, a squeeze of lemon juice, and then over the steak it goes.

Arthur H. Deute
Executive

VEAL CHOPS CAGNES

Chef Donald Currie sets up his thesis on veal: "Probably more than any other meat, it is adaptable to, and at the same time in need of, flavor variations." He proves it with this recipe.

    1 large onion, finely chopped
    ½ pound fresh mushrooms, sliced
    ¼ cup salad oil
     4 veal chops
     1 clove garlic
        Salt and pepper to taste
        Flour
     1 can tomato soup (11 oz.)
     1 tablespoon dry sherry
        Bouquet garni (sprigs of thyme, parsley,
            mint, tied together)

Sauté onion, mushrooms in oil. Remove from skillet. Rub the chops with garlic; sprinkle with salt, pepper, and flour. Brown in the same oil in the skillet. Cover with onion and mushrooms, pour over can of tomato soup, sprinkle with sherry, and add bouquet garni. Cover skillet and simmer 1 hour over low heat. Remove bouquet garni before serving. Serves 4.

Donald Currie

San Francisco

VEAL ARTURO

    4 pounds veal round steak, cut ¾ inch thick
    1 cup flour
    3 tablespoons seasoning salt
    ½ teaspoon black pepper
    1 cup salad oil
    4 green onions (tops and all), chopped
    1 tablespoon mixed herbs including:
        oregano, thyme, savory, sweet basil
    1 tablespoon chopped parsley
    1 bay leaf
    1 can (6 or 8 oz.) mushrooms
    ½ cup Sauterne, or any white table wine

Cut the veal into strips ¾ inch wide and tie into knots, making hearty chunks. Toss the chunks into a paper bag containing the flour, seasoning salt, and pepper, and shake well. Brown them in the hot oil in a Dutch oven for about 15 minutes, stirring frequently. Add onions, mixed herbs, parsley, and bay leaf. Turn heat very low, cover, and cook for 1 hour, stirring now and then. Add mushrooms 15 minutes before serving, and wine 5 minutes before serving. Serves 6 to 8. Very good with noodles.

ARTHUR STROCK
Attorney
Los Angeles, Calif.

SCALLOPINI OF VEAL WITH PROSCIUTTO AND CHEESE

    2 pounds veal round steak, about ⅜ inch
        thick
    ½ pound prosciutto (Italian ham)
    1 egg
    ½ pound Monterey jack cheese
    3 tablespoons olive oil
    1 lemon
    Salt and pepper

Cut the veal into small pieces and pound until very thin. Place a thin slice of *prosciutto** over each slice of veal and roll the two together. Dip the rolls in flour, then in beaten egg, and again in flour. Fry them quickly in olive oil, and place in a glass ovenware dish. Cover with thin slices of cheese, dot with butter, and sprinkle with salt and pepper. Bake for 10 minutes at 325°. Add the lemon juice, and as soon as it is absorbed, serve the savory scallopini.

*The enlivening *prosciutto* (a specially salt-cured raw ham) is available in most good Italian markets of the West. And you will find that added lemon juice to be a stroke of genius.

A. J. ZIRPOLI
Attorney
San Francisco, Calif.

VEAU À LA ST. COLOMBE

In authentic French cookery, the terms *blanquette* and *fricassée* each specify particular, and usually unalterable, methods of preparation. For the blanquette, or stew, you simmer the meat in a simple white stock, adding garnishes and sauce just before serving. For the fricassee, you sear the meat in butter, flavor it, then moisten it with white stock, season, and cook with the sauce.

By combining the merits of these two distinctive methods of meat cookery, Paul de St. Colombe of Hollywood, California, has created a worthwhile hybrid form. He

"He adds sherry to the meat, then introduces lemon juice and brandy"

goes even further—adds sherry to the meat while it is simmering, then introduces lemon juice and brandy to the sauce. This may seem like heresy to a purist, but undoubtedly accounts for the rich, winy flavor that permeates the dish.

    ¼ pound (1 cube) butter
    1 large onion, minced
    1 clove garlic, mashed
    1 tablespoon chopped parsley
    ¼ teaspoon rosemary
    1 whole clove
    1 tablespoon flour
    ½ cup consommé
    6 tablespoons sherry
    3 pounds veal (with all fat removed), cut
        in small flat pieces
    2 teaspoons salt
    ½ teaspoon pepper
    2 egg yolks
    1 cup half-and-half (milk and cream)
        Juice of ½ lemon
    3 tablespoons brandy
    ¼ teaspoon tarragon
    1 large can (6 or 7 oz.) mushrooms

Melt butter in a large, heavy saucepan, then sauté minced onion until lightly browned. Add garlic, chopped parsley, rosemary, and whole clove. Stir in the flour, and quickly add consommé and sherry. Add the meat, which has been salted and peppered, and simmer for about one hour, or until meat is very tender. If there is too much liquid, uncover pan and cook down liquid so that it barely covers the meat.

Just before you are ready to serve, combine the egg yolks and half-and-half in a small bowl. Add lemon juice, brandy, tarragon, and the can of mushrooms. Mix thoroughly, and stir it into the cooked veal. Simmer for about 4 or 5 minutes, removing it from the heat the instant the sauce thickens. (Timing and a watchful eye are all-important during this final warming process since you run the risk of curdling the sauce if it is overcooked.) Serve on hot buttered noodles or in individual crust cases. Serves 6.

Writer and columnist
Hollywood, Calif.

GOOP

    ½ pound egg noodles
    1½ pounds veal
    2 tablespoons fat
    1 large onion, chopped
    1 pint sour cream (or 1 pint sweet cream
        mixed with 2 tablespoons lemon juice)
    1 cup sliced fresh or canned mushrooms
        Seasonings to taste

Drop noodles in boiling salted water; allow to boil 5 minutes; drain off water.

Cut veal into ½-inch cubes and brown in hot fat; add the onion and mix well. Combine noodles, veal and onion, cream and mushrooms; season to taste; place mixture in a greased casserole. Bake in a moderate oven (350°) for 1¾ hours. Serves 3 to 4.

DON W. LOOMER
Inglewood, Calif.

VEAL SCALLOPINI A LA MILLICK

A request for "elegant but simple" recipes struck a responsive chord with Jack Millick of Berkeley.

If you want to save time, you can buy a packaged, seasoned flour and use it in place of the flour, salt, pepper, celery salt, and paprika indicated here.

    2 pounds veal steak
    2 tablespoons olive oil or butter
    2 tablespoons flour
    1 teaspoon salt
    ½ teaspoon *each*, pepper, celery salt, paprika
    1 can (6 or 7 oz.) mushrooms
    3 cups red table wine
    ½ teaspoon monosodium glutamate

Cut veal into chunks about 2 inches square. Lightly grease an iron pot with the olive oil or butter and quickly heat it until the grease begins to smoke. Toss in the meat and brown it on all sides quickly. Remove the browned meat, shake in a paper bag with flour and seasonings, and set aside.

Keep the heat under the pot and add the mushrooms, liquid and all. Boil off the liquid and continue with the heat until the mushrooms are browned. Add a little more oil or butter if necessary. Put floured veal into the pot with the mushrooms and cover with the wine. Add monosodium glutamate. As soon as the wine begins to boil, reduce heat to simmer and put a lid on the pot. Let simmer for about 10 minutes until veal is tender; but don't—repeat, don't—overcook. This *may* serve 4.

Berkeley

VEAL SCALLOPINI

When the Sierra Club establishes a base camp near the 10,000-foot elevation in one of California's high mountain areas, there are apt to be upwards of a hundred hungry mouths yapping to be fed—and fed well at least three times a day. The *Chef* who renders full satisfaction under these trying conditions has earned an advanced degree in camp cookery.

Such a one is Edward G. "Ned" Thompson of Van Nuys, California, who fills in between these summer engagements as vice principal of San Fernando Junior High School.

He admits, "I have loved to cook since I could first see over the stove into a frying pan." However, he is modest about his achievements. "The best thing we do is to have plenty of good quality foods and then try to give them all the loving care we can. If we then serve them high in the Sierra, to hungry people, it is easy to get a reputation as a good cook."

We still can't ignore the lavish praise from his satisfied customers for what he manages to cook on three portable wood stoves, using nearby snow pits for refrigeration.

"Take a Paul Bunyan mallet, pound it!"

"The most important thing about this 'Veal Scallopini' is to really beat the meat almost to a pulp. You should see me happily pounding meat on a bread board nailed to an old stump. No we don't thin-slice it; we just take a Paul Bunyan mallet or potato masher and pound it!

"We have never even bothered to recopy the family size recipe. When cooking for 200, we only make a few calculations. We start with 80 pounds of veal and work from there."

    1 pound thin veal steak (approximately
        ¼-inch thickness)
    ½ teaspoon salt
      Pepper to taste
      Flour
    1 tablespoon butter
    3 tablespoons olive oil
    1 clove garlic
    ½ small onion
    ⅔ cup bouillon, consommé, or soup stock
    ⅓ cup dry white wine
    ⅔ cup tomato juice
    ½ teaspoon rosemary (or less if you prefer)
    1 tablespoon chopped parsley

Cut veal in small strips; then pound out each piece to half its original thickness. Salt, pepper, and roll very lightly in flour. Heat butter and oil in skillet and brown meat slowly on both sides. Remove meat from skillet. To the fat in skillet, add garlic and onion, minced, and cook slowly until tender, about 5 to 10 minutes. Add stock or consommé and wine, mixed with tomato juice.

Cook 10 minutes, add herbs, then return meat to skillet. Spoon liquid over it, cover, and cook slowly 1 hour. Meat should be turned several times so it will be moist on both sides. If sauce cooks down too much (it should just barely cover the meat), add a little more stock. The sauce should never become really thick. Serves 4.

Edward G Thompson
Van Nuys, California

VEAL BORDELLAISE VITE

    2 cloves garlic, chopped
    2 tablespoons olive oil
    4 veal loin chops
    1 can (10½ oz.) onion soup
    ½ teaspoon salt
    ⅛ teaspoon freshly ground pepper
    ½ cup chopped parsley

Sauté garlic in olive oil until brown. Brown veal chops in the oil (do not remove the garlic). When they are browned

"To my mind veal is a very tasteless meat unless jazzed up"

on both sides, add onion soup, salt, pepper, and chopped parsley. Cut the heat to just above simmer, cover the pan, and wait 30 minutes. Serves 4. The tasty onion and parsley sauce is not only wonderful for the meat but also for rice or noodles on the side.

Howard A Bailey

Newspaperman
North Sacramento, Calif.

VEAL BIRDS A LA PROVENCALE

    4 veal cutlets
    1 teaspoon salt
      Pepper to taste
    1 small can (4½ oz.) chopped ripe olives
    4 tablespoons finely chopped salt pork
    2 cloves garlic, finely chopped
    1 pinch each of oregano, marjoram,
        tarragon, thyme, cayenne pepper
    1 cup dry white wine
    4 tablespoons tomato paste
      Butter or margarine for sautéing
      Juice of ½ lemon
    1 tablespoon minced parsley

Veal birds are best when made from extremely thin slices of veal, about 4 inches long by 2 inches wide. After seasoning them with salt and pepper, cover with a mixture of chopped olives, salt pork, garlic, herbs, and cayenne.

Roll up each cutlet and tie it well (two or three times) with string so it will keep its shape and retain the stuffing while cooking.

Sauté meat rolls in hot butter until brown on all sides. Add the wine and tomato paste. Cover and simmer gently on top of stove or in a slow oven (300°), basting often. After the "birds" have cooked for one hour, remove and keep warm in oven or chafing dish, while you make the following sauce:

Sauce: Boil juice in pan until reduced a little. Add the 2 tablespoons butter and juice of ½ lemon. Mix well, pour over cutlets, and sprinkle with chopped parsley. Serve with any green vegetable. Serves 4 persons.

Robert G. Amesta

Wine importer
San Francisco, Calif.

SAUTÉ OF VEAL CHASSEUR

    2 pounds shoulder of veal
    2 tablespoons oil
    2 tablespoons butter
    2 teaspoons chopped shallots
    ½ pint white wine
      Soup stock
    1 tablespoon tomato paste
      Salt and pepper to taste
    1 clove garlic, minced
    1 pinch thyme
    1 small pinch sage
    ½ bay leaf
    ½ pound sliced mushrooms
    2 tablespoons butter
      Chopped parsley, tarragon, and chervil

Cut the meat into pieces about as large as a golf ball. Fry these in a mixture of the oil and butter until brown, add shallots and wine; let cook for 5 minutes. Put into a casserole and add enough soup stock, in which the tomato paste has been dissolved, to all but cover the meat. Add salt and pepper to taste, and the garlic, thyme, sage, and bay leaf. Cover and cook in a slow oven for about an hour. Fry the mushrooms in the 2 tablespoons of butter and add them to the veal after it has cooked 45 minutes. Remove from oven. Sprinkle with chopped parsley (and tarragon and chervil, if available). Serves 4 persons.

Frank Schoonmaker

Writer
San Francisco, Calif.

ELAH

    2 pounds beef shoulder
    2 pounds pork shoulder
    I lamb heart
    I beef kidney
      Salad oil
    2 cups beef bouillon
    I onion, cut fine
    I clove of garlic, cut fine
    I tablespoon lemon juice
    ½ teaspoon sugar
    6 caraway seeds
    6 anise seeds
    ¼ teaspoon paprika
    ¼ teaspoon chili powder
    I teaspoon soy sauce
    I teaspoon Worcestershire sauce
      Salt and pepper to taste
    I can (4 oz.) mushrooms

Cube the beef and pork, dice the heart and kidney, and sauté these meats in salad oil. Then simmer them very slowly for 2½ hours in the beef bouillon, to which the remaining ingredients have been added.

While the stew is simmering, add water as needed. Just before serving, thicken the gravy slightly with flour, and add a small can of mushrooms.

Harry Hale

Newspaper production manager
Portland, Oregon

MEAT LOAF À LA BANANA SQUASH

    I pound ground round steak, for quality
    ½ pound ground shoulder, for fat and juice
    ¼ pound ground pork sausage, for flavor
    ¼ cup chopped celery, slightly cooked
    2 tablespoons chopped onion, or minced chives
    ½ cup dry cereal flakes
    I egg, beaten
    I banana squash
      Shortening
      Seasonings to taste

Mix the meat together, or have it ground together; add the slightly cooked celery, onion, dry cereal, and egg; form into a long, narrow loaf.

Select a fat banana squash and cut a thin lengthwise slice from the top. Remove the seeds and wipe the inside of the squash with shortening and a bit of seasoning. Put the meat loaf in the squash and bake in a moderate oven (350°) for

1 hour, or until squash is tender. For the first half hour, keep the top of the squash on as a cover. Then remove it and let the meat brown and get slightly crusty on top. The juice from the meat will remain in the "boat" and no basting is required.

G. PROCTOR COOPER III
Plant and animal research
La Mesa, Calif.

BOOLKOKI

    3 pounds lean beef (chuck, sirloin tips, or steak)
    1 cup salad oil
    ¼ cup sugar
    2 tablespoons soy sauce
    4 tablespoons finely chopped green onion
    2 cloves garlic, minced
    ½ teaspoon salt
    ½ teaspoon pepper
    4 tablespoons sesame seed

Cut beef in rather thin slices or strips. Mix remaining ingredients and pour over meat. Be sure that meat is well covered with sauce. Let stand overnight in refrigerator. When ready to broil over hot coals, drain off surplus sauce. Baste with sauce as necessary during broiling. Serves 6.

Howard W. Ellsworth

Orange rancher
Fillmore, Calif.

OLD ENGLISH YORKSHIRE HOT POT

    1 large roundsteak, cubed
    1 bay leaf
    1 tablespoon vinegar
    1 teaspoon Worcestershire sauce
    1 teaspoon minced parsley
    3 drops tabasco sauce
    ¼ teaspoon pepper
    ½ teaspoon salt, or to taste
    3 medium-sized potatoes, or an equal
        weight of small new potatoes
    4 or 5 turnips, diced
    4 large carrots, diced
    1 medium-sized onion, diced

Dredge the cubed round steak in seasoned flour, and sear in a skillet. Remove seared meat, add a little water to the meat juices, and simmer for a moment. Pour this gravy off into a large bean pot or caserole. Add the seasonings to the liquid, and then the meat and vegetables. Pour on enough water to cover, place the pot in a slow oven (300°), and bake 3 hours. Then remove the hot pot from the oven; thicken the gravy with flour, if desired, and set the pot where it will keep warm. Turn the oven up to 500°, and put in a batch of buttermilk biscuits, each with a dab of butter on top. As soon as the biscuits begin to brown, reduce the temperature to 400°. They should be cooked in about 10 minutes. After that, try to fight off the customers!

Claude M (Mike) Forbes

Editor
Salem, Oregon

AUSTRIAN GOULASH

    1 medium-sized onion, diced
    2 tablespoons butter
    1 flank steak, cut in 1-inch cubes
    2 cups water
    2 bouillon cubes
      Salt and pepper to taste
    1 tablespoon flour
    1 teaspoon caraway seeds
    4 slices bacon
    4 medium-sized potatoes, pared and cubed
      Paprika

Brown the onion in the melted butter; add meat and brown lightly. Add water and bouillon cubes dissolved therein. Add salt and pepper. Sprinkle flour over the mixture. Add caraway seeds and simmer for 2½ hours. About 40 minutes before mixture is done, fry bacon and render out all grease. Remove bacon and add with potatoes to meat mixture; simmer ½ hour. Serve on a platter and sprinkle well with paprika.

M. J. LOWELL
Insurance broker
Fresno, Calif.

MEAT LOAF A L'ECONOMIE

    1½ pounds lean beef
    ¼ pound salt pork or bacon ends
     1 clove garlic or ½ medium-sized onion

Place the above ingredients, all ground fine, in a large bowl. Add 4 slices of bread (crumbled), ¾ cup of milk, 1 beaten egg, salt and pepper to taste, ½ teaspoon celery seed or celery salt. Mix thoroughly until the bread disappears. Mixture should be just thick enough to mold. Place in bread pan or loaf-shaped container and bake in 400° oven until well browned, from 45 minutes to 1 hour.

Serve with the following sauce:

Mince 1 onion, 1 green pepper, and 2 diced medium-sized zucchini (or ½ pound of diced summer squash or 2 diced cucumbers). Sauté in shortening or butter. Add the following liquid:

Beat 1 tablespoon mayonnaise into one cup of consommé, beef stock, or chicken stock. Add 1 teaspoon of Worcestershire sauce, 1 tablespoon catsup or chili sauce, Tabasco sauce (depends on you), ½ teaspoon salt, pepper to taste. Bring this mixture to a simmer. Add flour to thicken. (Your choice, also. I like it creamy.) Combine this liquid mixture with the zucchini-onion-green pepper mix.

Serve meat loaf on a platter. Pour the sauce over it, or put in separate bowl and pour over individual slices, or do both. Serves 6.

A. B. Woodworth.
Tacoma.

STUFFED ROAST BEEF

    1 (8- or 9-pound) standing rib roast of beef
    3 oz. pitted Spanish green olives, sliced
    1 oz. capers, drained
    6 slices of bacon, or chunk of salt pork, cut in
      small pieces
      Salt and pepper

Make 3 incisions in the roast, laterally, with a sharp knife. Sauté the olives, capers, and bacon over a low flame until the bacon is cooked. Season. Holding the incisions open with a skewer or knife blade, poke the mixture deep and full into each. Rub remaining fat over the roast.

Place roast in open pan in the oven. Sear at 500° for 20 minutes. Reduce heat to slow oven (300° to 325°) and continue roasting. For medium-done roast, allow 22 minutes to the pound or approximately 3 hours for 8-9 pound roast.

Albert F Boosey
Avocado rancher
Fallbrook, Calif.

SAVORY CORNED BEEF

The last word on corned beef has never been spoken. There is no reason why excellent variations like that of James C. Bock of Piedmont, California, shouldn't continue to appear until the end of time. It is only prudent to remind you that corned beef varies greatly in saltiness, depending on the time that it has been in the brine. Judge it by sight. The paler and "grayer" the corned meat, the longer it has been in the brine. If too salty, it can be freshened by pouring off the first water when it comes to a boil, and re-starting the process with fresh water.

Cover a seven-pound brisket of corned beef with cold water and simmer slowly for about four hours. Remove from water, place in open pan, and cover with the following sauce.

    1½ cups catsup
    1½ tablespoons brown sugar
     1 teaspoon celery seed
    1½ tablespoons dry mustard
     3 tablespoons Worcestershire sauce
    ⅛ teaspoon cayenne pepper or Tabasco

Bake in moderate oven (350°) about 45 minutes or until brown, basting frequently. Serves 8.

James C. Bock
Piedmont, Calif.

CHUCK ROAST ON-THE-COALS

    3 pounds chuck roast, cut 3 inches thick
    1 clove garlic
    ¼ cup olive oil
    ½ jar prepared mustard (approximately)
      Salt

Put the meat in a flat pan or on a platter. Rub it thoroughly with garlic, then smear it with olive oil. Spread plenty of mustard on it, and pat in *all* the salt that will cling to it. Repeat on the other side. Let stand an hour or more.

Let your fire burn down until you have a *deep* bed of glowing coals. Gently place the meat *right on the coals*—no grill. Turn *only once* during cooking, and allow 20 minutes to a side for rare. To serve, slice the meat in strips. Serves 4 generously.

In testing this culinary triumph, we found that the oil and mustard absorb a con-siderable amount of salt, thus forming a coating which adheres to the meat. This salty crust prevents the meat from becoming charred and, in addition, keeps the juices inside. By the time the meat is ready to be lifted from the coals to a carving board or platter, the crust has mostly been dissipated, and what remains is a mere zesty reminder which contributes to the flavor.

Howard Evans
Investments
Manhattan Beach, Calif.

BACHELOR HASH

Here is a corned beef hash so full of vegetables that it is practically a stew. We wouldn't quibble over a name. It is a good, well-flavored, moist hash.

"With a bottle of cold Western beer, this is a dish to suit either logger or banker," says William Bloch, Jr., of Seattle.

It was concocted during the "absence of the household's chief cook on a trip to the Middle West." Hence the name.

"dish to suit either logger or banker"

    12 medium-sized green onions, finely chopped
     3 slices bacon, diced
     1 medium-sized green pepper, finely chopped
     1 small kosher dill pickle, finely chopped
     1 can (12 oz.) corned beef, diced
     1 medium-sized potato, boiled and then diced
     1 tablespoon Worcestershire sauce
     1 cup brown gravy, soup stock, or beef bouillon

Sauté onion with the bacon until onion is light brown. Stir in green pepper and dill pickle. Continue to sauté until green pepper is tender. Add corned beef and potato. Pour in Worcestershire sauce and brown gravy, soup stock, or a cup of boiling water in which you have dissolved two beef bouillon cubes.

Continue cooking until all ingredients are thoroughly heated. All seasoning is in the ingredients; no salt or pepper is needed. Serve with fried or poached eggs. Makes two large servings.

Wm. Bloch Jr

Seattle, Washington

CORNISH PASTIES

In the words of William H. Young of Seattle, "Below is a real he-man dish brought to America by the Cornish miners who came to Butte in the old days— Cornish pasties. And be warned to pronounce it *pass*-ties, not *pace*-ties. That is a very sore point among connoisseurs. In the early days these standbys were carried in lunch baskets and Cornishmen valued them highly because they held their heat over long periods. No Cornish picnic was complete without them.

"My wife always says, 'Why, that's just a form of meat pie!' But I assure you it is not, nor does it have anything like the taste of meat pie. It is a Cornish pastie, and there's nothing like it in the world! Ask any 'Cousin Jack'."

The pastry for each serving:

    ⅓ cup shortening
    1 cup flour
    ⅓ teaspoon salt
    1 to 2 tablespoons cold water

Cut shortening into flour and salt with a pastry blender. Add water and mix in with spoon edge until you have formed moist balls of pastry. Handle very little. Form as many balls as you have servings.

Inside mixture for each serving:

    ½ pound round steak, cut into ½-inch cubes
    ½ large potato, cut into ½-inch cubes
    ½ medium-sized onion, chopped
    1 turnip, cut into ½-inch cubes, desirable
        though not necessary
    ½ teaspoon salt
      Pepper to taste
      Pinch of monosodium glutamate

Mix meat with potato, onion, turnip, and seasonings. Roll out each ball of pastry to the size of a pie tin. Moisten the outer edge of circle. Add generous handfuls of inside mixture, placing it on one half of the circle so that you can form a turnover by doubling over the other half. Then roll back the edge to secure the seal. Now make a hole in the top about the size of a nickel. Bake in a 450° oven for 10 minutes, then in a 350° oven for one hour. Remove when golden brown and add a half-teaspoon of butter in the hole of each crust. Cover with a cloth and allow to stand for a few minutes to steam.

William H. Young

Newspaperman
Seattle, Washington

NORWEGIAN MEAT PUDDING

The "Norwegian Meat Pudding" that *Chef* Frank O. Duro cooks is not the usual meat pie—stew with the crust on top. It both looks and tastes like a tender and well seasoned meat loaf, with a felicitous touch of nutmeg.

    1½ pounds finely ground beef
    3 medium-sized potatoes, cooked and mashed,
        or 3 cups unseasoned mashed potatoes
    2 tablespoons flour
    1 small onion, minced
    1 egg
    3 teaspoons salt
    ½ teaspoon pepper
    ½ teaspoon nutmeg
    1 cup evaporated milk

Combine meat and potatoes. Add flour, minced onion, slightly beaten egg, salt, pepper, and nutmeg. Gradually work in undiluted evaporated milk, adding a tablespoon at a time. Blend thoroughly. Pour in well-greased 1½-quart deep casserole. Bake in a slow oven (300°) for 1½ hours, or until done. Test by inserting a sharp knife; if it comes out clean, pudding is done. Cut into individual portions and separate to make them easy to lift out. Makes 6 to 8 servings.

Frank O Duro

Tooele, Utah

CORNED BEEF HASH ENNOBLED

Chef Captain Edward S. Shaw, U.S.M.C., slices and fries canned corned beef hash and serves it forth with a cheese sauce seasoned with savor salt and minced parsley. This simple trick has earned the captain the right to call himself a *Chef of the West.*

Edward S. Shaw

San Diego, Calif.

*"Can be polished off by five men and a small boy if
they have been tramping the woods all day"*

SEVEN DEVILS DINNER

Chef F. Seymour Faurot has "a meat
dish that should feed eight hungry men
but can be polished off by five men and
a small boy if they have been tramping
in the woods all day." All hail to the
"Seven Devils Dinner."

Cooks of all nations seem to agree that
veal and pork—as in the famous French
Canadian "Veal and Pork Pie"—are good
candidates for a happy marriage.

    2½ pounds short ribs of beef
    8 small pork chops
       A 4 to 5-pound round bone pot roast
       from a veal shoulder
    2 large onions, minced fine
    2 green peppers, minced
    4 large stalks celery, thinly sliced
    2 cloves garlic, minced, or squeezed through
       garlic press
    ½ cup olive oil
    4 large fresh tomatoes or solid pack canned
       tomatoes
       Beef stock or canned bouillon
    4 tablespoons vinegar or 1 cup white table
       wine
    ¼ teaspoon *each* summer savory, sweet basil,
       rosemary, oregano
       Salt and pepper to taste

Trim excess fat from beef and pork.
Brown all meat in a heavy skillet. While
it is browning, put onions, peppers, celery,
garlic, and olive oil in a large oval roaster
and set it over low heat. When vegetables
begin to soften, add peeled ripe tomatoes
with the seeds and pulp squeezed out, or
canned tomatoes well drained.

Now lay the veal pot roast in the center
of the roaster on top of the vegetables,
and put pork chops at one end and short
ribs of beef at the other. Add enough
stock or canned bouillon to half cover the
meat. Cover and let simmer for 2 hours
over very low heat. Add vinegar or wine
and herbs, turn the meats, spoon vegetables and liquid over them, cover, and
cook 30 minutes more at a slow boil.
Don't forget to salt the meat well and
use the pepper with a generous hand.

Serve with plain boiled potatoes, a good
green salad, and toasted rolls or French
bread. Serves 8 or more, the exact amount
varying tremendously with appetite. Remember, it is good eating cold for lunch
the next day. *F. Seymour Faurot*

Cuprum, Idaho

BARBECUED STEW

For the barbecuer, here is an unusual
twist on stew. We entertain a strong
suspicion that the following recipe was
born when W. A. Leak of Cupertino,
California, found himself with some left-

over barbecued beef and determined to utilize it for stew.

Whether you follow the recipe verbatim and use freshly barbecued meat, or whether you purposely barbecue an over-abundant supply in advance, our taste panel recommends the idea as sound.

Since the stewing process does seem to minimize the unusual smoky taste, you might be wise to concentrate on the

"He found himself with some leftover barbecued beef"

smoke flavor at the time of barbecuing— a Chinese oven or barrel barbecue would be ideal for the purpose.

    2 pounds lamb shanks
    2 pounds lean short ribs
    1 cup dry white table wine
    1 large onion, chopped
    1 clove garlic
    6 whole cloves
    1 bay leaf
    ¼ teaspoon sage
      Salt to taste
    6 medium sized carrots, scraped
    6 medium sized potatoes, peeled
    6 stalks celery, cut in 1-inch-long pieces
    2 green peppers, cut into squares
    1 cup coarsely chopped peeled tomatoes,
      fresh or canned
    1½ teaspoon Mexican hot sauce (optional)

Have the butcher cut through the lamb shank and short-rib bones so that you can later cut meat into 2-inch pieces. Place lamb shanks and short ribs over low coals to which you have added aromatic wood chips. Broil meat slowly for at least an hour, turning occasionally. (This is an ideal way to utilize an over-supply of glowing charcoal after broiling

steaks or chops—barbecue the stew meat, then place it in the refrigerator until the next day.)

Bone the smoke-barbecued meat, place in a Dutch oven, simmer for about 3 hours with the wine, onion, garlic, cloves, bay leaf, sage, and salt. Then add carrots, potatoes, celery, and peppers. Add tomatoes and hot sauce and heat for another hour. Allow to cool, remove fat, then reheat and serve.

Four hungry stew-lovers should be content with this amount.

W. A. Leak
Machinist
Cupertino, Calif.

Chef Leak's recipe for stew has a special virtue: It satisfies the taste of both the confirmed stew lover and the outdoor barbecue chef.

VERY SOUND STEW

Now here's a recipe that disguises the flavor of venison almost entirely. As a matter of fact, it's such a good mixture that it scarcely matters what kind of meat you use. If you have no venison, beef will certainly do.

    1 pound venison cut in ½-inch cubes
    ½ cup cooking oil
    12 small onions, whole
    1 medium sized carrot, finely diced
    6 dried prunes, pitted and cut into
      ½-inch cubes
    2 thin slices (1/32 inch thickness) of lemon cut
      into ½-inch segments
      Juice of ½ lemon
    2 teaspoons salt
    ⅛ teaspoon pepper
    ¼ teaspoon monosodium glutamate
    ¼ teaspoon marjoram
    2 cups water
      Flour or cornstarch for thickening (optional)

Brown the meat lightly in the oil; add balance of ingredients except the flour. Simmer over low heat until meat is tender. Thicken if desired. Serves 4.

Flank steak also makes an excellent stew when cooked in this manner.

W. Knowles
Mechanical engineer
Seattle, Washington

"With my graying sideburns shoe-polished, I was riding a red motorcycle"

CABBAGE CORRIDA, OR
THE TERROR OF 101

"I should have preferred to report that, with my graying sideburns shoe-polished, and wearing a black leather jacket with an eagle painted on it, I was riding a red motorcycle which had its early training along this stretch of highway—when the cycle turned in of its own accord to this drive-in. But I'll stick to the truth.

"While exploring the lower reaches of U. S. Highway 101 a few years ago, I ordered a hot dog at a drive-in. Presently a girl approached me carrying something swaddled in a huge coifed napkin which she placed in my arms carefully. Peering in, I was momentarily reassured by the familiar bland countenance of a 'tube steak' resting on a split and toasted bun. But the wiener had been split, too, then blanketed with a thick layer of sauerkraut, topped by a swish of some sort of meaty spaghetti sauce.

"Ah, Youth, I sighed, preparing to chuck the bundle into a trash can and take my hunger to a more sedate poke-out. But I'd paid for it, and I'm pretty tight, so I nibbled a little at the edges to sort of get some of my own back. Of course it was good, and I ate two before I left.

"Back home here I worked out a sauce that seems reasonably like that which drenched the wiener-and-sauerkraut-on-a-bun that I enjoyed so much alongside 101.

"A girl carrying something swaddled in a huge coifed napkin"

116   MEATS

These hefty hot dogs are regular meals, and there's no better beach food."

We'll add our "Amen" to that last. This is picnic food, outdoor eating food, well suited to the young and hearty of appetite. Your approach to it must be relaxed. Caution from one of our testers: "Difficult to eat and keep your dignity, especially when you wear a big mustache."

½ pound ground beef
1 tablespoon olive oil
1 large onion, minced
1 clove garlic, minced
1 can (8 oz.) tomato sauce
2 tablespoons chile powder, or to taste
1 teaspoon salt
1 can (No. 2½) sauerkraut
6 hot dog buns
6 wieners

Brown beef in olive oil till it can be crumbled. Add onion, garlic, tomato sauce, chile powder, and salt; simmer till blended, adding water if necessary to maintain loose paste consistency.

Empty can of sauerkraut into saucepan and cook until it "gives up" completely and lies flaccid and dormant, mellow and brown, but juicy. Split buns and toast them. Cook wieners and split them.

Lay each split and toasted bun in the center of a large napkin. Put a split wiener in the center. Cover with sauerkraut, tucking in the ends neatly. Top with the meat sauce. Serves 6.

Sailor
Seattle, Washington

BEAN-SAUSAGE CASSEROLE

2 medium sized onions, chopped fine
4 tablespoons (½ cube) butter or margarine
1 slice center cut ham, ½ inch thick, diced
1 tablespoon flour
1 can (10½ oz.) consommé
1 cup Pinot Noir or Burgundy wine
2 cans (No. 303) red kidney beans
6 small pork sausages
   Rusk crumbs
   Grated Parmesan cheese

Sauté onions in butter until limp, but do not brown. Add ham, mix with onions, sprinkle flour on top, and mix again. Then, constantly stirring, slowly add consommé mixed with wine. Let this mixture

simmer over low heat for 10 minutes. Add kidney beans. Brown sausages but do not crisp them; add to mixture.

Put all in a baking dish, stirring the sausages and bits of ham throughout the beans. Bake uncovered in a moderate oven (350°) for 1 hour.

Let stand until about 30 minutes before serving. Cover top with rusk crumbs and Parmesan cheese and reheat in a moderate oven (350°).

Public relations consultant
San Francisco, Calif.

BEEF SKIRTS-KEBABS

2 skirt steaks, cut into 4 lengthwise strips
¼ cup salad or olive oil
1 cup dry red wine
1 clove garlic, crushed
1 medium-sized onion, minced or grated
½ teaspoon pepper
2 tablespoons soy sauce
2 tablespoons prepared mustard
   Fresh mushroom caps, quartered; onions,
      green peppers, and tomatoes as desired

Soak the meat in the marinade (all the remaining ingredients except the mushrooms, onions, peppers, tomatoes) for at least 5 hours—the longer the better.

When the charcoal fire is ready, thread the meat on metal skewers in a ribbon style, alternating with mushrooms and other whole ingredients thusly:

The fire should be 6 to 8 inches from the skewers. Cooking time is between 45 minutes and 1 hour. When you serve, give each of your drooling customers a Skirt-Kebab, sliding it deftly off the skewer. This is a wonderful accompaniment to lasagna, a green salad, and garlic French bread. Serves 4.

Newspaperman
North Sacramento, Calif.

BEEF STROGANOFF

Rear Admiral G. van Deurs, U.S.N.(Ret.), of Belvedere, California, has eaten around the world enough to recognize a good Beef Stroganoff. He knows it so well that he can improvise a copy of his own just as good as any original. He knows, too, that there is no need to dress up the rather neutral color of the Stroganoff. Just wait, and watch your guests lick the platter clean. He writes:

"My formula for Beef Stroganoff is a composite of the ideas of several cooks. I claim no authority for it. It was never used at the Czar's court. A Russian even insisted that I should not call it Stroganoff because it had onions in it.

"It was never used at the Czar's court"

"Call it what you will, in the years that I have been serving it, no one has ever declined seconds."

There are four steps to my system. The first is the preparation of the materials. The next two involve cooking. The fourth may be omitted if you are in a hurry.

In order to prepare about eight very hearty servings, you need 4 pounds of lean round steak. I really mean lean. Cut out and discard all bone, fat, and white fibers. You may toss these into a soup pot to good purpose, but get them out of the Stroganoff. Shred the lean meat into slices about ⅛ inch thick. Then cut these into ¼-inch strips.

In spite of any contrary opinions, quarter, peel, and slice 3 big brown onions. Mush-

rooms come next. A couple of medium-sized cans of "stems and pieces" will do nicely. Pour juice off these into a bowl with 3 tablespoons flour and stir to a smooth paste. Complete this sauce by stirring in ¾ cup tomato juice, 1 tablespoon Worcestershire sauce, and 1 quart (4 cups) sour cream.

Heat 2 large skillets. Put ¼ pound butter in one and fry the onions in it. When they are golden and translucent, stir in the mushrooms and seasoned mushroom liquid and allow the mixture to cook for a few more minutes.

At the same time, put a split clove of garlic and a bay leaf in the other pan, along with about 1 tablespoon shortening. When the pan is very hot, put in the shredded meat and stir it so that all pieces sear quickly on all sides. When they are brown, sprinkle with salt, pepper, and plenty of paprika. You must use a rather heavy hand in this, for the seasoning must be strong enough for all the other ingredients, too.

Add mushrooms, onions, and sauce to the meat and simmer all for ½ hour. It will need almost constant stirring. Serve now, or . . .

If there is time, I prefer to set the Stroganoff aside for about 24 hours, or overnight. In this interval, some further blending of flavors occurs that makes the dish superb. Take right out of the refrigerator, reheat in a moderate oven (350°) for about 30 minutes, and serve immediately to 8 hearty or 10 average eaters.

Gran Deurs

Rear Admiral, USN (retired)
Belvedere, Calif.

CONEY ISLANDS DELUXE

This next recipe is a little like the merchant's weekend special, "Two for the price of one!"

Charles W. Laurens of Portland has presumably been working a long time on this invention—hot dog and hamburger combined in the same dish (patent pending). A word of warning so you won't be caught

unprepared: chili-wise, this is very hot
stuff. We liked it.

  2 dozen wieners
  2 dozen wiener buns
  Prepared mustard to taste
  Chopped onion (about ½ cup)

Heat wieners on a griddle over low heat.
Avoid puncturing them when turning.

"Working a long time on this invention"

Cut wiener buns about three-fourths
through and then steam them. Lay a
wiener into a sliced bun; add mustard,
chopped onion, Coney Sauce, and serve.

Coney Sauce:

  1 pound ground beef
  1 medium sized onion, chopped
  2 cloves garlic, minced
  2 cans (8-oz. *each*) Spanish style tomato sauce
  2 tablespoons chili powder
  1 teaspoon Worcestershire
  1 teaspoon monosodium glutamate
  4 small whole red chili peppers, crumbled
  Salt and pepper to taste (but easy on the pepper)

Start ground beef on cold skillet over low
heat, *without cooking fat or oil.* Cook
slowly, breaking up with a fork until very
fine. Then add other ingredients and simmer for 30 minutes. Sauce may be thinned
with water if necessary. This recipe makes
enough sauce for 2 dozen wienies.

Chas. W. Laurens

Truck driver
Portland, Oregon

SPARERIBS AND SAUERKRAUT

  1 can (1 pound 11 oz.) unsalted sauerkraut
  Caraway seeds, allspice, paprika, pepper,
    garlic salt, and 4 cloves
  About 3 pounds spareribs
  2 cups cottage cheese

Place sauerkraut in a glass bowl and separate strands. Add plenty of caraway
seeds, allspice, paprika, pepper, garlic
salt, and the cloves. Mix well and let
stand at room temperature for 1 hour.
Rub baking pan well with a little fat
from ribs; spread half of seasoned kraut
in thin bed over bottom of pan. Layer
on cottage cheese; cover with the rest of
kraut. Brown ribs in flat pan in hot oven
(450°); then place ribs over kraut. Bake
in a moderately hot oven (400°) about
40 minutes, basting frequently with kraut
juice. The last 5 minutes, put some kraut
over ribs so moisture soaks through.
Serve with sprinkling of paprika. No
sauce necessary as it makes its own.
Makes a wonderful simple dinner with a
salad, garlic French bread, and cold beer.
Serves 3 to 4.

William E. Selwyn

Motion picture executive
North Hollywood, Calif.

SPARERIBS CHINESE STYLE

  2 slices bacon, cut in small pieces
  2 pounds spareribs, cut in 1-inch pieces
  1 large onion, sliced
  1 small can (No. 1 flat) sliced pineapple
  2 green peppers, chopped
  ½ cup brown sugar (less if you prefer a dish
    not so sweet)
  ¼ cup vinegar
  2 tablespoons soy
  2 tablespoons cornstarch
  2 tablespoons water

Sauté bacon in large pot or heavy skillet;
remove bacon and save. Brown spareribs
and onion in the bacon drippings, then
pour off excess fat. Add juice from can
of pineapple. Cover tightly and simmer
40 minutes. Add peppers, pineapple slices
cut in bite-size pieces, bacon, brown sugar,
and soy; then add cornstarch mixed with
the water. Simmer slowly for about 20
minutes, or until sauce is thick and well
browned. Stir constantly. Serves 4 to 6 as
an appetizer—2 to 3 as an entrée.

Daniel W. Julian

San Rafael, California

ALMOND PINEAPPLE SPARERIBS

"I have read with much interest the recipes for Chinese dishes contributed occasionally by your American readers," writes Dr. Henry D. Cheu, San Francisco. "However, I have yet to find one sent in by a Chinese reader of your magazine. Here is one, from a Chinese amateur cook, with which I have tickled the palates of many of our friends."

His spareribs have excellent texture, appearance, and sweet-sour taste, in which thirteen well-managed ingredients play an important part.

    2 pounds spareribs
    ½ cup flour
    2 teaspoons salt
    ½ cup salad oil
    1 can (No. 2½) sliced pineapple
    1 tablespoon vinegar
    2 tablespoons brown sugar
    2 tablespoons water
    1 small onion
    1 green pepper
    ½ cup water
    2 tablespoons flour
    2 teaspoons soy sauce
    2 teaspoons catsup
    ½ cup chopped toasted almonds

Cut spareribs into 1-inch sections, roll in flour, and sprinkle with salt. Brown spareribs in hot oil. Pour off excess oil. Drain juice from pineapple and mix with vinegar, brown sugar, and the 2 tablespoons water; add to spareribs. Cut each pineapple slice into 8 pieces, quarter the onion, cut green pepper into inch squares. Add these, cover, and simmer 20 minutes. Make a smooth paste of the ½ cup of water, flour, soy sauce, and catsup. Remove spareribs from pan, stir flour paste into drippings and cook until slightly thickened. Pour over spareribs, and sprinkle with chopped, roasted almonds. This will serve 4.

Henry D Chew M.D.

Physician and surgeon
San Francisco, Calif.

CHINESE RIBS

These Kai spareribs were equally popular with our taste panel; one member claimed they were the best he had eaten. We'd say that these spareribs will equal or top the very best you've ever eaten in a true Polynesian or Cantonese restaurant. We suspect that the trick of drying the honey-marinated meat before cooking may play the most important part in the resulting crispy, crackly surface texture.

    2 sides pork spareribs
    ¼ cup soy
    1 teaspoon pepper
    4 tablespoons honey
    ¼ cup sherry
    2 teaspoons monosodium glutamate

Marinate whole sides of the spareribs in a mixture of the soy, pepper, honey, sherry, and monosodium glutamate for at least 30 minutes. (We've heard of some *Chefs* who let this marinating period last as long as 5 days, leaving the ribs in the coldest section of the refrigerator.) Remove the ribs from the marinade and allow to dry thoroughly.

Hang the ribs from the top of a moderate Chinese oven for 1¼ to 1½ hours. The closer you place the ribs to the actual fire, the more carefully you have to watch for charring. (The timing on this recipe and the preceding one was checked in a true Chinese oven, with the meat located about 40 inches away from the fire.)

Ernest Z. Kai
Honolulu

SPARERIBS PILLY-MINTON

"This is a good recipe," says Robert Bard of Palos Verdes Estates, California. "It carries a strange name inasmuch as the first time I prepared the dish I was called to the telephone and returned to the kitchen to find that my Siamese cat, named Pilly-Minton, had eaten the entire thing." A likely story, *Chef* Bard. But we lick our lips—like your cat allegedly did—after tasting your non-greasy and flavorful spareribs.

Put 1 side of spareribs on edge (rounded side up) in a roasting pan and dust with oregano, thyme, and salt. Bake in a 350° oven for 1 hour. Remove and pour off all fat. Dredge ribs in flour, ginger, and brown sugar, in that order. Put back in pan and pour over the heavy syrup from a can of Bartlett pears. Bake until very brown, about 1½ hours more, turning and bast-

"Pilly-Minton had eaten the entire thing"

ing several times. Serves about 4, depending on the "meatiness" of the ribs.
This is so simple it sounds pedestrian, but try it!

Robert Bard

Interior decorator
Palos Verdes Estates, Calif.

CROWN ROAST OF SPARERIBS

Commander Malcolm C. McGuire of Mill Valley works his legerdemain with spareribs, good with or without special fixin's, as he is the first to admit.

"We do not decry the time-honored way of fixing spareribs. Crisp barbecued spareribs, sizzling in their spicy sauce, didn't become an American tradition by happenstance. But sometimes there is need for variety. Crown Roast of Spareribs is capable of reaching culinary heights. The paper frills are the finishing touch that put this dish in the glamour class."

    2 pounds spareribs
    2 cups cooked rice
    2 cups dry bread crumbs
    1 carrot, finely chopped
    1 large onion, chopped
    ¼ cup raisins
    3 tablespoons shortening
    ½ teaspoon sage
    ¼ teaspoon pepper
    2 teaspoons salt
      Parsley

Remove heavy end from spareribs. Tie the spareribs in a crown shape. Trim top end to expose about 1 inch of bone. Stand upright in an oiled baking dish. Blend all other ingredients together to make the stuffing. Fill cavity of "crown" of ribs with stuffing mixture. Bake for 2 hours in a 325° oven. Arrange on platter, cover rib ends with paper frills, garnish with parsley, and serve. Serves 6.

Cdr Malcolm C McGuire USCG

Cmdr., USCG
Mill Valley, Calif.

SPARERIBS IN SOY SAUCE

Spareribs fit almost any occasion. They satisfy our antediluvian urge to gnaw on a bone.

"Antediluvian urge to gnaw on a bone"

The marinade is the noteworthy contribution of *Chef* J. A. (Al) Perkins to this particular sparerib recipe. As a bacteriologist, he carries the scientist's passion for exact knowledge into his private culinary labors. From his years of residence in the Hawaiian Islands, he has learned the valuable properties of *shoyu* or soy sauce, which he uses as a principal ingredient.

    2 cups soy sauce
    1 cup dry red wine
    3 cloves garlic, crushed
    1 teaspoon powdered ginger
    1 teaspoon monosodium glutamate
    2 tablespoons brown sugar
    1 cup catsup
    4 pounds spareribs
      (the short back ribs are best)
    3 onions, sliced

Combine all the above ingredients, except the meat and onion, into the marinade mixture. Lay spareribs in pan with slices of onion between layers. Pour marinade over and leave overnight. Drain well and barbecue over charcoal. Serves 4.

J. A. Perkins

Honolulu

"Favorite trail food for Indians and whites who roamed the West in the early days"

OREGON JERKY

Although jerky was eventually known throughout the Far West, it has a distinctly southern origin. When the earliest Spanish explorers came to the Americas—from the southwest United States down into South America—they found the Indians eating a kind of meat that had been cut into long strips and then dried quickly in the sun and wind. Their rendering of the local word was charqui (pronounced SHAR-key). The Portuguese explorers in Brazil called it *xarque*. The later rendering in the English tongue came out jerky, or, sometimes, jerked beef.

Made from buffalo meat, venison, or beef, and no matter what it was called, it was a favorite trail food for both Indians and whites who roamed the West in the early days. Sometimes the Indians pounded it to a powder and then mixed it with dried fruits and vegetables to form pemmican. Sometimes they ate it straight, which is the way most favored today. It was the forerunner of all the later dehydrated foods by which long distance hikers now contrive to lighten their packs.

In our experience with jerky, dryness and a certain degree of saltiness are the only essentials. In a rainy winter climate, we have even produced a satisfactory tasting product by hanging strips of venison or beef alongside a hot water tank that was heated by a wood burning cook stove.

"Through testing and experimenting, I have found a short and easy way to make jerky," says Phillip White, of Eugene, Oregon. Either venison or beef can be used to make a product that is equal to that made by the long smoke process. I bone the venison neck and freeze it, then thaw it just enough to cut. But beef neck or any part of the deer or beef can be jerked. I make jerky the year round."

If, by some grievous oversight, you have never experienced jerky, this recipe offers an excellent means of making up that defect in your education.

"My seven-year-old daughter and her friends will clean the oven out by noon"

3 pounds venison or beef
Salt to taste
½ teaspoon liquid smoke (more if desired)
Pepper to taste

Slice the meat very thin, or have your meat man do it on his electric slicer. (In some shops, you can have this done free; in others there may be a charge of as much as $1 for the service.) Be careful to remove all fat—it will become rancid if the jerky is stored for any length of time.

Salt the meat generously, adding just a dab of liquid smoke to one side before salting. Place the strips layer upon layer in a large crock or bowl, and pepper each layer as you complete. Place a plate and a weight (a quart jar filled with water will do) on top of the meat. Let stand overnight or at least 6 hours.

Remove racks from your oven and stretch the strips of meat across these racks, allowing pieces of meat to touch but not overlap. Put the racks back into the oven so that the upper one is at least 4 inches from the top of the oven and the lower one at least 4 inches from the bottom. Set the oven temperature at 150° and let the meat dry for about 11 hours. Most convenient time to do this is overnight; from 9 P.M. to 8 A.M. will dry the meat just right.

Phillip White

Sales engineer
Eugene, Oregon

ROAST SADDLE OF VENISON

Lloyd (Bud) Winter, from San Jose, California, does his hunting and fishing both north and south of the Mexican border. Here's his recipe for saddle of venison. This is one of the choicest parts; avoid overcooking. The Winter treatment involves marinating, roasting, and topping with an unusual and delicious sauce.

    Saddle of venison
    1⅓ cups water
    2⅔ cups dry red table wine
    2 teaspoons mustard seeds
    2 bay leaves
    1 teaspoon thyme
    2 onions, sliced
    ½ teaspoon pepper

Other seasoning:

    2 cloves garlic, cut into slivers
    1 tablespoon salt

Sauce:

    ½ cup sour cream
    1 glass currant jelly
    1 tablespoon brandy

Trim all fat off the venison. Soak meat in marinade for 24 hours, turning occasionally. Insert slivers of garlic in meat, salt it, and place in a 350° oven. Roast uncovered until done (depending on size, usually from 2 to 4 hours), basting frequently with remaining marinade (until all used up) and then with meat drippings.

Remove meat and add sauce ingredients to drippings in roasting pan; cook until the mixture thickens. Spoon sauce over servings of meat, or serve separately. Figure on ½ to ¾-pound venison per person. Serve this with a fairly light, dry red wine.

Bud Winter

Athletic coach
San Jose, Calif.

DEER LIVER

    Deer liver, thinly sliced
    Vinegar
    Flour
    Salt and pepper
    Deer fat
    1 onion, thinly sliced
    1 clove garlic, halved

Let the slices of liver stand in a mixture of equal parts of vinegar and water for 30 minutes. Drain and wipe dry. Dip each piece of liver in flour that has been seasoned with salt and pepper. Heat some deer fat, and in it sauté the onion to a golden brown. Rub the pieces of garlic together over the pan until the juice runs into the sauce. Sauté liver slices in a separate pan. When brown and cooked on both sides (5 or 6 minutes cooking time), add the onion-garlic sauce and serve.

HAROLD RICE
Feature writer
San Francisco, Calif.

"The pre-soaking makes tough venison just tender enough"

ROAST LEG OF VENISON WITH SAUCE PAMALA

If yours is a tough cut of venison from an old buck, here's a formula from a hunter-chef appropriately named Charles Hunt. The pre-soaking, unnecessary for tender venison, makes tough venison just tender enough. The sauce is quite sweet, but many should find it very much to their liking.

    Leg of venison
    2 cups white distilled vinegar
    2 cups ice cream salt
    Water
    Lard or shortening
    Flour
    Salt and pepper to taste

Sauce Pamala:

    1 glass currant jelly
    1 tablespoon raisins
    1 teaspoon grated lemon peel

Soak venison overnight in vinegar, salt, and enough water to cover. Next morning, remove and place in plain water for 2 hours. Remove and wipe it dry. Spear meat with lard, flour it, put in open pan in 350° oven until browned. Then add small amount of water and cover the roasting pan. Cook until done (about 2 to 3 hours), basting frequently. Salt and pepper just before serving. Serve with "Sauce Pamala," made by cooking currant jelly, raisins, and the lemon peel together over low heat until they reach the thickness desired.

Charles Hunt
Van Nuys, Calif.

VENISON, HUNTER'S STYLE

    3 pounds venison
      Salt and pepper
    2 tablespoons butter
    1 onion, chopped
    1 square inch ham, finely minced
    1 clove garlic, finely minced
    2 bay leaves, finely minced
    2 sprigs thyme, finely minced
    1 tablespoon flour
    2 cups warm water
    1 quart consommé
    ½ pound fresh mushrooms, chopped
      Grated rind of 1 lemon

Cut venison into pieces 2 inches square. Salt and pepper well. Put butter in a skillet with the venison and let the meat brown slowly. When it is nearly brown, add onion and let it brown slightly. Then add ham, garlic, bay leaves, and thyme. Stir and simmer for 2 minutes. Add flour and cook a few minutes longer. Add the warm water and let come to a good simmer. Now add the consommé and let all cook slowly for 1 hour. Season again according to taste and add the mushrooms and lemon rind. Let all cook ½ hour longer and serve on very hot plates. Serves 6 to 8.

ROD LA ROCQUE
Actor
Ventura, Calif.

VENISON ROAST WITH SOUR CREAM

"Before roasting either leg, loin, or rack of venison," says *Chef* Posch, "place it in a cheesecloth bag and hang it in a cool drafty place out in the open (a shady lightwell is excellent) for a few days. Just before roasting, clean and trim all of the extra tissue, as a butcher does with a leg of lamb."

"The Posch bacon-with-venison method"

½ pound bacon (in a slab)
  Venison roast (about 2½-pound)
  Pepper
2 cloves garlic
2 cups water
1 pint sour cream
2 teaspoons salt
¼ teaspoon pepper
6 kernels allspice
2 onions, quartered

Cut bacon into strips approximately ¼ inch wide and ¼ inch thick. If you don't have a larding needle, use a hunting knife to punch holes in the roast deep enough to receive the bacon strips after they have been rolled in black pepper. Insert the bacon strips all around the roast at intervals of 1 to 2 inches. Crush the garlic and rub all over the meat. (If you are very fond of garlic, insert small pieces with the bacon strips.) The meat is now ready for the oven.

Heat the meat at 400° for the first 15 minutes (without any water in the pan). Then add the water, half the sour cream, salt, pepper, allspice, and quartered onions. Cut heat down to 350° and cook for about 20 minutes to the pound, same schedule you would use for roast beef medium. Baste frequently with liquid in the pan.

Shortly before meat is done, add balance of cream. Then season gravy to taste and serve immediately. Serves 4 to 6.

Paul N. Posch
Contractor
San Anselmo, Calif.

SADDLE OF VENISON

1 saddle of venison (5 pounds)
1 carrot
1 onion
  Salt
  Butter
½ cup consommé
1 cup currant jelly

Skin venison and remove all sinews from the surface. Take fine larding needles and lard closely. Tie the saddle around with a cord 4 times. Slice carrot and onion into a roasting pan. Place the venison on top of these, sprinkle lightly with salt, and spread with butter. Set in a brisk oven and roast for 40 minutes (or longer if less rare meat is desired), frequently basting the venison with its own gravy. Before taking it from the pan, remove the cord which binds it. Place on a hot platter. Then pour consommé into the pan, set on the stove, and let it come to a boil. Skim the gravy of all fat and strain over the venison.

Serve with a hot Currant Jelly Sauce made as follows: Blend currant jelly with melted butter, and stir until jelly is dissolved. Put it in a saucepan, combine with some of the venison gravy, and let it come to a boil.

ROD LA ROCQUE
Actor
Ventura, Calif.

VENISON ROAST

1 roast of venison
Claret
1 cup olive oil
½ cube melted butter

Unless you have unusually good meat, venison cooked by beef roast methods is dry and uninteresting. However, venison of almost any age becomes a good roast when treated this way:

Cover the meat with claret and let stand overnight. Remove to a pan containing the olive oil and turn several times during the day. Roast, basting frequently with the oil in which the meat was standing and to which the butter has been added.

HAROLD RICE
Feature writer
San Francisco, Calif.

LIVER-STUFFED PEPPERS

4 large green peppers
1 lb. beef or pork liver
1 cup uncooked rice
1 can (8 oz.) tomato sauce
¼ teaspoon mustard
1 tablespoon Worcestershire sauce
¼ teaspoon, each, savor salt, garlic salt,
     onion salt, *fines herbes*
1 can mushroom soup
1 can tomato soup
Bread crumbs
Grated cheese

Cut peppers in half lengthwise, remove seeds, and parboil a few minutes. Scald liver, dip in flour, and fry until browned, then dice.

Cook rice in boiling salted water, drain well, and mix with liver, tomato sauce, and seasonings. Stuff peppers with the mixture.

Heat mushroom and tomato soups together and pour into the bottom of a baking dish. Place peppers on this, sprinkle with bread crumbs and grated cheese, and bake until browned in a moderate oven (350°) for 20 to 30 minutes.

Colin Radford
Bellevue, Wash.

SPICED BEEF TONGUE

1 beef tongue
1 clove garlic
1 teaspoon salt
1 cup tongue stock
1 can (No. 2) (2½ cups) tomatoes
1 large onion, finely chopped
½ cup vinegar
2 tablespoons sugar
1 tablespoon butter
½ teaspoon each cloves, allspice, and
     cinnamon
½ teaspoon salt
½ teaspoon pepper

Place the beef tongue in a kettle with enough boiling water to cover; add garlic and salt. Simmer, covered, about 1½ hours, or until tongue is tender. Remove tongue, and skin it. (Save the liquid.) Place tongue in iron kettle and add the remaining ingredients.

Simmer tongue slowly for 2 hours in this sauce. Serve hot, on a platter, garnished with crisp watercress.

M. A. CONEY
Real estate broker
Piedmont, Calif.

BAKED MOCK TERRAPIN

Let us hear how *Chef* W. W. Williams of Seattle felt moved to explore new culinary heights and discovered a creature you won't even find in Disneyland.

"When I was a kid in Wisconsin, my grandfather had a cottage on a lake and occasionally he would tie into a good sized water turtle. My grandmother cleaned it out and used the shell for a footstool by stuffing it with something or other; the red flannel would protrude from the openings in the shell. But the things she could do with that turtle meat were, according to my mother, out of this world.

"I was too young to remember how it tasted, but I can recall her saying that every turtle has 11 different kinds of meat in it, some tasting like chicken, some like beef, some like pork, and some like liver. Now I don't know whether that was true or not, but I never forgot her saying so.

"Occasionally my grandfather would tie into a good sized water turtle"

"At any rate, I have tried in this recipe to duplicate it (my mother's description of turtle meat—the flavor I have forgotten). I used flank steaks the first time; but, because of the cross grain on the outside, they were inclined to shred somewhat when cut through the edges. The round takes the knife better, but there will be little patching jobs to do where it spreads open—a trouble you don't have with the flank steak. As the main thing is to keep the flavors locked in, any tears in the round steak have to be stitched."

```
1 tablespoon margarine or oil
1 medium sized onion, chopped
1 small green pepper, chopped
2 small cans (2 oz.) mushroom stems and pieces
1 teaspoon sage
1 tablespoon Worcestershire
1 teaspoon celery seed
7 slices dry bread
2 large slices round steak or flank steak
    (about 1½ pounds each)
2 teaspoons salt (approximately)
  Garlic powder to taste
1 pound calf or beef liver
6 lean pork chops
½ teaspoon pepper
1 can (7 oz.) chicken slices or ½ cup leftover
    chicken cut in small pieces
2 cups water
  Flour
```

First prepare the dressing, which can be cooking while you prepare meat: Melt margarine in deep skillet or Dutch oven and add onion, green pepper, 1 can mushrooms, sage, Worcestershire, and celery seed, and cook over medium heat until onions and pepper are soft. Then add the bread, which has been lightly rolled but not powdered, so that it is in coarse particles about pea size. Stir this mixture occasionally while working with the meat; when it appears thoroughly mixed, pull it off to cool.

To make the "terrapin," lay one steak out flat and sprinkle with salt and garlic powder. On top, make a layer of the liver slices, which have been lightly salted; then make a layer of about half the dressing. Next, layer evenly the pork chops, which have been boned, trimmed of excess fat, then salted and peppered lightly. Then layer up the other half of the dressing and place the chicken slices on top evenly. Finally, cover with the other slice of steak and sew up the edges with any light cord in a simple stitch—this makes a neater job, for the later slicing, than nails or skewers.

If necessary, add a tablespoon of oil to the bottom of the previously used pan so that you can brown this terrapin well all around. Then add 2 cups water, cover, and bake at about 350° for 2½ to 3 hours. Remove terrapin from the pan to a platter while you make gravy by adding two or three tablespoons of flour to the drippings and stirring in the other can of mushrooms. Salt and pepper to taste.

Put gravy over terrapin and serve with mashed potatoes, baked squash, tossed salad, and creamed onions—as a suggestion. Serves 10 to 12 generously.

Seattle

SWEETBREADS À LA HANSEN

3 pounds sweetbreads
1 tablespoon salt
2 tablespoons lemon juice or vinegar
¼ pound fresh mushrooms, sliced
3 green onions, sliced
4 tablespoons butter
1 tablespoon Sauterne or Sherry
  Buttered toast

Soak the sweetbreads in cold water for an hour. Remove and cook for 20 minutes in a pot of boiling water containing the salt and lemon juice or vinegar. Drain, and pour cold water over them to whiten and firm the meat. When cold, remove the membrane and tubes from the sweetbreads and cube them. Now sauté the mushrooms and green onions in 2 tablespoons of the butter. In a separate pan sauté the sweetbreads in the remaining butter, seasoning them to taste with salt and pepper; add the wine. Both pans should be done about the same time. Mix the mushrooms and onions with the sweetbreads and quickly clean the mushroom pan for the sauce.

3 tablespoons butter
1 tablespoon cornstarch
1 cup cream or rich milk

Melt the butter; stir in the cornstarch, but do not brown; add the cream and cook slowly for 15 minutes. Empty the sweetbread pan into this sauce. Have individual plates ready with a slice of buttered toast on each and cover the toast with the sweetbreads. Serve with boiled potatoes in their jackets, plus a cup of steaming hot coffee. Serves 6.

FRANK W. HANSEN
Railroad engineer
Richmond, Calif.

CIRVELLI ALLA GORDONI

4 sets calves' brains
1 egg, well beaten
  Cracker meal
1 medium onion, chopped
1 clove of garlic, minced
1 teaspoon chopped parsley
  Pinch of thyme and marjoram
1 teaspoon Worcestershire sauce
1 can mushroom sauce
1 small can sliced mushrooms
  Cooking oil (preferably olive oil)
⅓ cup white wine

First, prepare the brains: Put them to soak in cold water for 1 hour; drain, then cover with fresh water, adding 1 tablespoon lemon juice. Boil slowly for about 30 minutes. Cool, remove membrane, and dry thoroughly. Roll in cracker meal, dip in egg, and again in cracker meal. Fry in oil until brown.

While the brains are cooling, prepare the sauce: Fry onion, garlic, and parsley in oil until a golden brown; add thyme and marjoram, Worcestershire sauce, mushroom sauce, mushrooms, and wine; simmer gently while the brains are browning in the oil. Just before serving, pour the sauce over the brains.

Assistant cashier
Hayward, Calif.

MACARONADA

1 beef pot roast (2 pounds)
  Salad oil or shortening
½ pound hamburger
1½ large onions, chopped
1 can (4 oz.) mushrooms or equivalent in dried mushrooms
1 can (8 oz.) tomato sauce
½ clove garlic, minced
2 stalks celery, chopped
3 strips bacon or salt pork, minced
  Peel of ½ orange, grated
  Peel of ½ lemon, grated
¼ teaspoon each nutmeg, cinnamon, and cloves
  Salt and pepper to taste

Brown roast in a skillet, using oil or shortening. Remove meat, place remainder of ingredients in the skillet, and simmer gently for 20 minutes. The resulting sauce should be fairly thick. If there is too little liquid, add a little water or red wine and cook a few minutes longer. Transfer meat to a well-oiled or greased Dutch oven or covered roasting pan. Pour sauce over it and bake in a slow oven (300°) 3 hours.

This dish is served with long macaroni or spaghetti.

ANTHONY MARINCOVICH
Everett, Washington

sauces
marinades

SPECIAL BARBECUE SAUCE

These days we keep very sensitive antennae out to try to intercept any arrival of a new barbecue sauce more worthy of attention than the usual "everything in and around the kitchen sink" variety. This, by Pierre Coste of San Francisco, is such a one. For a change, there is no Worcestershire sauce, no garlic, no herbs.

"We keep very sensitive antennae out"

It has a fresh taste and is easy to make. In our taste test, it received high marks.

> ½ cup chopped shallots or green onions
> ¼ cup olive oil
> 2 cups sauterne
> 1 cup soy
> 2 cups catsup
> ½ cup prepared English mustard
> ¼ cup sugar
> Salt and pepper to taste
> ¼ cup chopped parsley

Cook chopped shallots in olive oil for 5 minutes. Add sauterne and let reduce about half. Add all remaining ingredients except parsley. *Do not boil at any time.* Remove from fire, correct seasoning to taste, and add parsley. Makes about 1 quart sauce which can be kept in refrigerator until needed.

To use for barbecued meat: Rub meat with sauce and rest 10 minutes before broiling. Then broil meat slowly until tender.

Pierre M. Coste

San Francisco

BARBECUE SAUCE FOR CHICKEN

Many barbecue-minded *Chefs* today are broadening their repertoire, forsaking the exclusive diet of steak and hamburger, and discovering that there is nothing very mysterious about barbecuing chicken. You can do it with a minimum of seasonings. Or you can develop a process for making it more moist, flavorful, and tender, like this barbecue sauce contributed by A. R. Bone, Jr., of Pasadena.

The citrus-soy-honey-butter combination is most effective if you baste just as often as possible. There is no salt in the recipe because it tends to dry out the chicken. Salt to taste after cooking is completed.

> ¼ cup butter
> 1 cup orange juice (as you drink, not
>   concentrated)
> Juice of 1 large lemon (3 tablespoons)
> ¼ cup honey
> ¼ cup chopped parsley (not too fine)
> ¼ cup soy
> 1 tablespoon dry mustard
> 2 medium sized garlic cloves mashed
>   (optional)

Combine all sauce ingredients. Chickens should be of small fryer size, split, with wings and necks removed. Place chicken on grill and cook *very* slowly and baste with the sauce constantly. Cook chicken halves, cavity side down, for 40 to 45 minutes. Turn and cook meat side down for an additional 7 to 10 minutes. Recipe makes enough sauce for 2 chickens of 2 to 2½-pound size—sufficient to serve 4.

A. R. Bone

*Airline executive
Pasadena, Calif.*

LAMB BARBECUE SAUCE

Some meats can take a barbecue sauce or leave it alone, but a meat with a decisive flavor like lamb usually benefits. Especially compatible with lamb are the ingredients grown or used extensively in those eastern Mediterranean countries where lamb is the most served meat.

"This sauce is delicious as a marinating and basting sauce for all cuts of barbecued lamb," says *Chef* Ambrose P. Macdonald of Orinda, California. He recommends that the meat be marinated for at least two hours.

We would raise his ante and say that four hours is about the optimum time for thorough penetration of flavor, especially for the thicker cuts.

    1 cup olive oil
    ½ cup red wine vinegar (flavored with garlic
        or eschalot, if desired)
    1 teaspoon thyme
    1 teaspoon monosodium glutamate
    1 teaspoon mint (fresh or dried)
    1 teaspoon freshly ground pepper
    ½ teaspoon salt
    ½ teaspoon paprika

Mix all ingredients. Marinate lamb for at least 2 hours before barbecuing. Baste frequently with sauce while cooking in a Chinese smoke oven or broiling over charcoal. Makes enough sauce for about 6 chops or a 3 to 5-pound roast.

Ambrose P. Macdonald.
Orinda, Calif.

ALL-PURPOSE BARBECUE SAUCE

"I, too, would like to present for *Chefs of the West* consideration a tenderizing, marinating, and basting sauce recipe," vouchsafes Paul Swensson, of Seattle.

"This seems to be rather good on wild game (slowly barbecued), salmon steaks (or whole salmon), lesser cuts of steak or chuck roast . . . turkey and chicken, too! It can also be used for oven type broiling or roasting."

From our test we'd say it is one of the subtlest sauces we've ever used for barbecuing. It has a choice overtone, and it keeps things delectably moist. We suggest for any meat or fish that needs or deserves any special "saucing." It does not smother a meat (it's all soluble, no solids); it coaxes out the best of its flavor.

    ¼ cup salad oil
    ¼ cup bourbon
    2 tablespoons soy
    1 teaspoon Worcestershire
    1 teaspoon garlic powder (not salt)
        Freshly ground black pepper to taste

Blend all ingredients well. Pour over meat or fish and marinate in refrigerator

(turn when you think of it). . . roasts: 24 to 48 hours . . . steaks: 4 hours . . . salmon or fowl: 2 hours. Also use as a basting sauce during broiling or roasting.

Paul Swensson
Seattle

CREAM MEAT SAUCE

A meat sauce that doubles as a salad dressing comes by way of *Chef* Anderson. He combines cream cheese with horseradish and a few other seasonings to make an exemplary sauce. Then, with a slight adjustment of the recipe, he produces a salad dressing. We suggest that you grind fresh horseradish root to get the fullest flavor.

    1 package (3 oz.) cream cheese
    1 tablespoon prepared hot horseradish
    ¼ teaspoon salt
    1 teaspoon dry mustard and about
        1 tablespoon cider vinegar or
        2 teaspoons prepared mustard

Place cheese in a bowl and work with fork to soften. Blend in horseradish, salt, dry mustard, and cider vinegar, adding just enough of the latter to make the mixture creamy. Or use the prepared mustard. Serve with any meat.

Salad Dressing: To make this into a salad dressing, we add 4 or 5 tablespoons vinegar (garlic vinegar) and 1 tablespoon sugar.

C. McK. Anderson
Civil engineer
Glendale, Calif.

FRENCH MUSTARD

    3 tablespoons dry mustard
    1 tablespoon granulated sugar
    1 whole egg, unbeaten
    1 cup white wine vinegar
    1 tablespoon olive oil

Mix mustard and sugar well. Stir in the egg until the mixture is smooth. Add vinegar slowly, mixing well. Place over low heat and cook for about 4 minutes, or until the mixture thickens, stirring constantly. When cool, add the olive oil and mix thoroughly. Excellent wherever mustard is indicated.

M. A. CONEY
Real estate broker.
Piedmont, Calif.

DUCK SAUCE

If you already own a Chinese oven, chances are you've used it to roast duck.

We leave the stuffing and roasting process up to you. Then Ambrose Macdonald takes over with a sauce that is bold, rich, and tangy—all at once.

    ½ cup red currant jelly or bar le duc
    ¼ cup port wine
    ¼ cup catsup
    ½ teaspoon Worcestershire
    2 tablespoons butter or margarine

Combine jelly, wine, catsup, Worcestershire, and butter in a saucepan. Place over low heat until jelly melts. Serve hot over your very best smoke roasted duck. Makes 1 cup of sauce.

Ambrose P. Macdonald.
Orinda, California

Our tasters liked this sauce so well that they began speculating on other foods that it might go well with—among their suggestions were venison, ham, even a bland white fish such as halibut.

LAMB SHISH KEBAB SAUCE

The glaze and crustiness produced by Robert J. Hall's lamb *shish kebab* sauce may remind you of spareribs cooked in the best brown-and-crisp tradition. We thoroughly agree that, "The honey appears to be the key to a delicious crusty crispness hard to achieve and really seldom experienced by most amateur cooks."

    1 can (6 oz.) tomato paste
    ½ cup olive oil
    1 cup honey
    1 cup dry white table wine
    2 cloves garlic, crushed
    ½ teaspoon *each* crushed rosemary and oregano
    1 teaspoon salt

Mix all ingredients. Thread squares of lamb (cut from shoulder or leg) on skewers, pour over sauce, and let stand a few minutes before cooking. (You can marinate lamb in your favorite wine-and-oil marinade first and use 1 cup of the marinade instead of the dry white wine.) Barbecue about 20 minutes, basting often with sauce during the process. Sauce is ample for about 3½ pounds of meat on 7 large skewers—to serve 7.

A highly complimentary (and complementary) dish with this entrée is a brown rice casserole: 1 cup of rice sautéed with butter and minced green onion, moistened with a can of chicken consommé, then baked (covered) in a slow oven (300°) for about 1 hour.

Insurance
Santa Cruz, Calif.

ALKI SAUCE

Alki Point in Seattle was the site of the first settlement there. *Chef* H. P. Lawrence of that city calls his favorite sauce Alki Sauce, and recommends it for grilled fish or hamburgers. Alki, by the way, is an Indian word meaning "by and by." It seems singularly appropriate for those slow barbecues when you think the food is never going to show up.

    2 tablespoons finely minced onion
    3 tablespoons finely minced green pepper
    1 tablespoon butter
    ½ cup water
    1 medium-sized tomato, diced
    ½ teaspoon salt
    ⅛ teaspoon pepper
    ¼ teaspoon Kitchen Bouquet
      Dash of celery salt

Sauté onion and green pepper in the butter until they are golden brown. Add water, tomatoes, and seasonings. Bring to a boil. Simmer for 10 minutes, stirring frequently. Makes enough sauce for four meat servings.

Mining engineer
Seattle, Washington

TERIYAKI STEAK

One of the best marinades to come out of the West (the Really Far West—Hawaii, Japan) goes by the Japanese name of *Teriyaki*. For its simplest form, you mix just four ingredients—garlic, ginger root (or powdered ginger), sherry, and soy—in any proportions that please your taste. This marinating sauce is most frequently recommended for steak, but it has been known to produce beneficent results on poultry, fish, and other kinds of meat, as well.

"Best marinade to come out of the West"

    1 large clove garlic
    Half of a fresh ginger root chopped fine or
        1 to 2 teaspoons minced dry ginger root
    1 tablespoon sugar
    1 tablespoon cider vinegar
    ½ cup soy
    4 tablespoons dry white table wine
    2 pounds top round steak

Mash garlic and ginger in a bowl. Dissolve sugar in vinegar; combine with garlic and ginger, and add soy and wine. Marinade steaks in this liquid for several hours, turning occasionally. Broil or grill steaks as desired. Serves 4 to 6.

Edwin L. Snyder
Honolulu

MARINADE FOR SPARERIBS

This marinade, originated by *Chef* Wilbur G. Graf, adds substance, which really sticks to the meat, as well as excellent flavor. The most interesting ingredients are the last two. He adds almost any odd bits of jelly or jam but considers orange marmalade best. The banana contributes a good but practically unidentifiable flavor and gives the meat an unusual glaze.

    2½ to 3 pounds small spareribs
    1 cup water
    3 cans (8 oz. *each*) tomato sauce
    4 level tablespoons mayonnaise
    1 cube (¼ lb.) butter, melted
    3 tablespoons brown sugar
    1½ tablespoons vinegar
    3 tablespoons pineapple juice
    1 tablespoon Worcestershire
    ½ teaspoon garlic salt
    ½ teaspoon celery salt
    ½ teaspoon monosodium glutamate
    1 teaspoon salt
    1 tablespoon orange marmalade
    1 crushed ripe banana

Crack spareribs, and cut into small serving pieces. Place in kettle with tight fitting cover, add water, and cook until almost tender—about 30 minutes. Mix the remaining ingredients in the order listed. Drain spareribs, spread with part of marinade, and bake in a 400° oven for 45 minutes, spooning the remainder of marinade over ribs as they cook until glazed and very tender. Serves 10 as appetizer.

Wilbur G. Graf
Tucson, Arizona

DR. MOOSE'S MARINADE

    2 tablespoons soy
    1 cup boysenberry or loganberry jelly
    2 tablespoons lemon juice
    1½ teaspoons powdered ginger
    ½ teaspoon fresh ground pepper

Mix together soy, jelly, lemon juice, ginger, and pepper. Heat gently in a saucepan until jelly is melted. Marinate chicken—the inside as well as the outside—in this mixture for about 1 hour, then hang in a Chinese oven. About 10 minutes before you expect to remove the chicken from the oven, lift it out, brush it liberally with marinade, and return it for the final cooking.

This quantity of marinade should be ample for two chickens.

Sanford M. Moose
Oral surgeon
Atherton, Calif.

This marinade is also ideal for broiled chicken. The lemon cuts the sweetness of the jelly, but leaves just a hint of refreshing fruity flavor on the cooked meat.

GREEN CHILI RELISH

If you like relishes at all, especially those that are good and sharp, you should find good uses for this one. *Chef* Brooks recommends for most any meal but "especially good with barbecued foods and with any of the many usual Mexican dishes."

    48 large green chile peppers
     4 large onions
     8 large cloves garlic
     1 bottle (4 oz.) horseradish
     1 quart cider vinegar
     1 pint cold water
    1½ cups sugar
     2 teaspoons ground cumin seed, or to taste
     1 tablespoon celery seed
     1 tablespoon salt, or to taste

Open peppers and remove seeds and veins. Place in cold water for several hours.

Put peppers, onions, and garlic through coarse blade of a food chopper. Add all remaining ingredients. Simmer in a large kettle till the relish becomes thick. Pour into sterile jars and seal. Makes 2 to 3 pints of relish.

Comet Brooks
Biochemist (retired)
Rolling Hills, Calif.

MARINADE FOR BROILING

     1 tablespoon dry mustard
     1 cup water
     3 cups soy
     3 cloves garlic (about the size of the end
        of your thumb)
     6 tablespoons brown sugar
     4 tablespoons sherry or bourbon

Mix mustard gradually with 1 cup water to form a paste, then add to soy. Thinly slice garlic or compress it in a garlic press; add it—juice, pulp, and all—to soy. Add sugar and the sherry or bourbon. The entire sauce should be kept at room temperature. The meat should be marinated in this sauce at room temperature from 1 to 2 hours, depending on how thoroughly the *Chef* wishes to have this sauce permeate the meat. Makes approximately 1¼ quarts marinade.

J. B. Herman
Honolulu

SALSA

     4 large sweet Spanish onions
     6 large fresh tomatoes
     2 cans peeled green chilis (seeds removed)
        Salt and pepper to taste
     2 tablespoons red wine vinegar
     4 tablespoons olive oil

Cut onions, tomatoes, and chilis into ¼-inch cubes. Salt and pepper as desired, then add oil and vinegar. Allow to marinate for at least 2 hours. This is a sauce used commonly (with variations) throughout Mexico and California. It is good served on steak sandwiches.

Wes Wilson
Barstow, Calif.

AL PESTO (GREEN GRAVY)

     4 large cloves garlic
     1 teaspoon salt
     1 cup chopped fresh basil, or ¼ cup dried basil
     1 cup chopped fresh parsley
     ½ cup grated Parmesan cheese
     ½ cup olive oil (approximately)

Cut up garlic and then mash with salt with a mortar and pestle.

Gradually add chopped basil and parsley to the garlic as you keep mashing and crushing. Then alternate the cheese and olive oil, still mashing all the time, until the sauce is the consistency of a soft paste. Add more salt to suit taste. Serve with fresh tagliarini or other *pasta*, about a teaspoon of the Al Pesto for each serving. This recipe makes about 8 portions. The usual procedure is to put the hot *pasta* in a dish, spread the sauce on top, then cut up the paste, mixing in the Al Pesto as you cut. Additional grated cheese may be sprinkled over the top. Al Pesto can also be used with beans or boiled potatoes, and a spoonful of it in minestrone is a *must*.

Al Pesto may be stored in the refrigerator in a tightly closed jar (to keep the flavor from penetrating other foods) with the surface covered with olive oil to prevent oxidation and loss of flavor. It keeps for a long time.

Leon P. Matthews
Traffic consultant
Oakland, Calif.

vegetables

"We kids fetched the chili in a water pitcher and often had to rush back for more"

YANKEE CHILI

Across our southern borders has crept a dish now so definitely Western by adoption that we almost forget its origin. It's a stout fellow, this one, more favored by grown men than by women or moppets; fit to stand alone, but already a boon companion to the barbecued meats we serve at patio suppers.

Chef H. R. Paradise of Seattle offers a recipe for Chile con Carne con Frijoles and describes it this way:

"Chili con Carne con Frijoles is the full name, but lists the ingredients in reverse order of importance. It should read Frijoles con Carne con Chili. Sounds better that way, and that is the order in which they are cooked.

"In Manitou, Colorado, when I was a boy, the family went on occasional chili binges. We kids fetched the chili in a huge water pitcher and often had to rush back for more. 'Rushing the growler' used to mean running to a saloon for a bucket of beer. Well, we also did that with a chili pitcher.

"I have since tried many times to recapture the well remembered bouquet of that chili. I have sampled specimens in dining palaces and dining cars, opened cans, bribed chefs, and even considered going back to Manitou and walking around with a pitcher. As a last resort, I

have taken to making my own, and have developed an alchemist's faith that the next potpourri I brew shall yield the golden bubble.

"My formula for chili seems to pick up and drop off ingredients as the years pass, much as a street bus picks up and lets off passengers. I seem to be moving farther out toward the end of the bus line; out where *Haute Cuisine* is the name of an Oregon steelhead river, maybe, and we simple people cook a dish called 'Beans, with Meat and Peppers.' "

Chef Paradise brews a mild to medium hot chili. Kidney beans are his preference —"Less starchy, hold up better." He adds no oregano or cumin—"Both are well blended in the commercial chili powders." He puts in no onions—"It is my opinion that a good chili recipe should tell the novice the basic facts and describe one of the easier methods of getting the ingredients cooked and together."

    1 pound dry kidney beans
      Water
    2 pounds ground beef
    6 tablespoons olive oil
    2 tablespoons dry mustard
    6 tablespoons chili powder
    2 cloves garlic, mashed or minced
      Juice of 1 lemon
    2 tablespoons salt

Soak the kidney beans in enough water to cover (I still soak them overnight). Brown the beef in olive oil; crumble it; add the mixture of mustard, chili powder, garlic, and lemon juice; simmer until flavors are blended; let stand overnight.

Next day, slow-boil the beans in the same water in which they were soaked, adding the salt when half done. Then add the meat and chili mixture prepared the day before. Further simmering helps, but the dish is ready to serve when this mixture is hot.

Most important, just before serving time, is the salt ritual. The trick is to salt and stir and taste the brew until the flavors fairly leap from the spoon. All this last-minute stirring helps the chili, too. Serves 4 to 6 generously.

Sailor
Seattle, Washington

CHILI BEANS VENTURA

In the next two recipes, two challengers appear before *Chefs of the West*. Both champion the pink bean, onions, and tomato. They both like their chili hot and Latin.

"Two challengers appear before this meeting of Chefs of the West*"*

"A new semester has begun at San Jose State College, where I am an upper division student," says Lonnie H. Ellis. "As I check assignments, what flashes through my mind? 'Discussion and Debate'—*Sunset* and Chili Beans. 'Speech Correction for the Handicapped Child'—*Sunset* and Chili Beans. 'California Government' —*Sunset* and Chili Beans.

"A native of Ventura County, California, I learned tortilla making from Mexican *halp* when small. Having been active in Boy Scouts and other youth organizations, I am submitting a king-sized recipe for chili beans that I have given my personal interpretation, and that has proved tempting, tantalizing, and filling. This dish freezes wonderfully in case you don't have a Scout troop or men's lodge to help eat it."

The recipe is so king-sized that we cut it in half for fear that the full quantity might swamp our electric roaster. We suggest you try it that way first; then you're on your own.

One of the best things about this chili is the way the ground beef retains its identity. The critical point in its preparation is cooking the beans so they are neither watery nor mushy.

3½ pounds pink beans
    Water
3 cloves garlic
5 medium sized onions
3 large cans (No. 2½ *each*) tomatoes
    (10½ cups)
5 chili peppers
2 cans (10 oz. *each*) Mexican hot sauce
6 tablespoons chili powder
3 tablespoons salt
½ teaspoon cayenne
6 pounds ground beef

Put beans in electric roaster, cover with 1 inch of water, and soak overnight. (It must be "good" water. If you live where tap water is so mineralized you use a hacksaw to cut it off, use bottled water.) Next morning plug in your roaster, set at a low temperature. Do not add any of the condiments until the beans are thoroughly done. However the vegetables may be added at any time after the beans start cooking.

Finely chop the garlic, onions, tomatoes, and chili peppers, and add. When the beans are done, add the hot sauce, chili powder, salt, and cayenne. Continue simmering.

Crumble the meat, but not too finely; it should be in small chunks. Drop small amounts at a time into an iron skillet and cook until done but no more than slightly browned. Add to the chili mixture. If correctly manipulated, the meat will hold its shape when added to the already cooked beans and seasonings.

After all ingredients are combined, they may be simmered indefinitely (at no time set the temperature above a simmer). About 5 hours total cooking time should be sufficient. Serves 20.

Lonnie H. E. Vhi

San Jose, Calif.

CHILI BEANS CHIHUAHUA

Chef George C. Booth, who cooks with a Spanish accent, favors "Chili Beans Chihuahua."

"This recipe did not creep over the border," says he. "It came proudly with flourishes and ruffles.

"This recipe did not creep over the border"

"The chili itself is of the essence. All the U. S. commercial comes from mild varieties grown in Arizona and New Mexico. To the south, hotter and more pungent varieties are grown and used. *Chef* Paradise might find it interesting to buy dried chili; seed it, boil a few minutes, then peel and grind. Likely his chili maker in Colorado used a Mexican type chili.

"I also feel that beans should be Mexican red, pink, or pinto. Kidney beans lack character with their tendency to mush. Soak them overnight and hold the salt until the last half hour of cooking; salt keeps the beans hard."

    1 pound red, pink, or pinto beans
      Water
    ½ pound bacon or salt pork, chopped
    2 large onions, chopped
    1 clove garlic, chopped
    1 teaspoon black pepper
    1 teaspoon salt
    ¾ teaspoon oregano
    ½ teaspoon each sage and cumin
      Pulp of 6 chili peppers (boiled, then scraped)
        or 3 teaspoons chili powder with an added
        ¼ teaspoon cayenne
    2 tablespoons cornmeal
    1 can (8 oz.) tomato sauce

Cover beans with water and soak overnight (if desired). Cook beans for several hours, until completely done. Slowly sauté bacon and add onions and garlic. When onions are golden, add all remaining ingredients and use the tomato sauce can to dip a canful of liquid from the beans; add and cook five minutes. Then add whole mixture to beans and simmer at least 2 hours more to give beans *sabor*. Taste and add more salt if desired. Serves 8 generously.

Geo. C. Booth

Teacher
Long Beach, Calif.

CHILI CON CARNE Y FRIJOLES

    3 cups dried beans—kidney, pinto, or pink navy
    1 large onion
    4 small hot chili peppers (optional)

Wash and pick over beans. Cover with plenty of cold water and bring to a boil. Skim if needed. Add whole onion and if desired, the small hot chili peppers. Cook beans slowly from 2 to 4 hours with plenty of water, stirring occasionally. When tender, wash in colander with running water, removing onion and peppers. Set aside, covered with water.

For the Chili Con Carne:

    1 cup coarse-chopped beef suet
    3 pounds coarse-chopped lean beef
    1 pound coarse-chopped lean pork
    2 cups coarse-chopped peeled onions
    ½ cup coarse-chopped peeled garlic
    ¼ cup paprika
    ½ cup chili powder
    ½ teaspoon Cayenne pepper
    4 teaspoons salt

1 teaspoon ground cloves
3 tablespoons cumin seed
1 tablespoon coriander seed
1 teaspoon chia seed (optional)
1 bay leaf
1 tablespoon whole rosemary
2 tablespoons whole oregano
1 teaspoon sweet basil
3 cups tomato puree
2 quarts stock, or leftover coffee, or bouillon

In a heavy iron, steel, or aluminum pot, put beef suet, beef, and pork; brown well over hot fire. Add onions, garlic, paprika, chili powder, Cayenne pepper, salt, and cloves. Fry this dryish mixture about 15 minutes, stirring and tossing. Place seeds and herbs in a pie pan and toast in the oven; then place in cloth and pound into a coarse powder. Add with purée to mixture. Add one-third of the stock or other liquid and bring all to a boil. Reduce heat and simmer for 12 hours or so, adding stock as needed.

Proper chili is neither thick nor thin, and is supposed to be slightly greasy. When ready to serve, stir in the beans which have been reheated by bringing to a boil. Drain them, then dump into the "con carne."

A spoonful of chopped onions and sweet green and red peppers placed on top of each bowl adds to the flavor and appearance. Mexicans eat tortillas with their chili, and pass a dish of whole oregano to crumble over the top as an added seasoning. Gringos favor crackers in place of tortillas. This recipe is very mild, but can be "hotted up" by using more Cayenne.

Lu. Randall

Vallejo, Calif.

BETTY'S BLACK BAHAMAN BEANS

As you near the tropics, you find a certain preference for some foods so dark that they are almost black. You notice it, for example, in Mexico, where one favorite dish called *mole*, often served with turkey, is very dark. Perhaps it is prized for its contrast with other more colorful foods.

One of our taste testers felt the need for this sort of contrast and recommended serving sliced tomatoes with the Black Bahaman Beans described below.

"No clue to the identity of Betty"

If you use your imagination in that direction, you detect an exotic foreign influence here, from the lands of calypso and tropical fruits, those islands and seacoasts that surround the Caribbean Sea. In submitting the recipe, Alex Hawkes, of Laguna Beach, California, gives no clue to the identity of the Betty who appears in its name.

If the black turtle beans aren't readily available, try any black or one of the darker red beans.

1 pound dried black (turtle) beans
  Water
1 large green pepper, diced
1 small can (4 oz.) pimientos, chopped
2 large onions, chopped
2 large cloves garlic, minced
1 or 2 bay leaves, crushed
1 tablespoon salt
½ teaspoon pepper
¼ teaspoon oregano
2 to 3 tablespoons vinegar
½ cup olive oil

Wash beans thoroughly, then cover with water—about 2 inches above the beans. Cook until just tender. Add pepper, pimientos, onions, garlic, bay leaves, salt, pepper, and oregano. When beans are very tender, add the vinegar. About ½ hour before cooking is finished, add olive oil. (Watch carefully for the last half hour because the beans are likely to scorch.) Serve over hot steamed rice. Serves 6 to 8.

Alex D. Hawkes

Laguna Beach, Calif.

SAN FERNANDO VALLEY BEANS

    1 pound dried kidney beans or red beans
    ½ pound bulk pork sausage
    ½ cup brown sugar
    2 cups sliced apples
    4 onions, sliced
    2 cloves garlic, peeled
    1½ cups tomato juice
    3 teaspoons salt
    ½ teaspoon pepper
    ½ teaspoon chili powder

Wash beans thoroughly and soak overnight in cold water. Next day, bring to a boil, cover, and let simmer for 1 to 2 hours, or until tender. Drain, and put the beans on the back of the stove while you prepare the following mixture:

Combine all the remaining ingredients in a saucepan, being sure to mix the sausage thoroughly with apples, onions, garlic, etc. Bring quickly to a boil, then mix with the drained beans. Allow the whole mixture to simmer for at least 2 hours. Serves 12 to 16.

Don't be apprehensive about being able to boil the mixture which is to be added to the beans; there's enough tomato juice to make it possible. However, if you still think you want more liquid, add tomato juice. But when the dish is served, there should be little or no "soup."

For variation in flavor and a touch of the exotic, pour 2 ounces Jamaica rum into the beans in the last 5 minutes of cooking, and serve the beans with sour cream ladled on the side! Contrast is ever the spice of good eating, and the dark, rich, red beans, piping hot, are made even more succulent by the smooth texture of cold sour cream. A green salad, coffee, and a bit of cheese will complete the menu.

Ellsworth D. Gage

Executive
Covina Knolls, Calif.

CHILI CON QUESO

    2 onions, about 3 inches in diameter
    4 tablespoons salad or olive oil
    1 can (4 oz.) green chili peppers
    1 can (No. 2) solid pack tomatoes
      Cheddar, or any other type of
        quick-melting cheese

Chop onions and fry in oil until clear but not browned. Remove membrane and seeds from chilis and chop. Drain tomatoes, reserving juice. Remove any hard cores from tomatoes, then cut up. Add chilis and tomatoes to onions, and heat

"A fast hand with the Tabasco"

to boiling. Add amount of tomato juice necessary to keep mixture fluid but not juicy. Pour into casserole and top with finger-like pieces of cheese to cover. Place in oven until cheese is melted, then brown under the broiler. Serve with warm French bread or garlic bread. Serves 4.

Jack Damron

Audiologist
Fresno, Calif.

BEAN HOLE BEANS

If there is one place where a dish of beans, fortified with other nutrients, will be a success, it's in camp. R. R. O'Neal, of North Hollywood, California, has been making "Bean Hole Beans" for 25 years.

"I first made this about 1920, when I took a group of young boys on an overnight camping trip. It went over so big with them that afterwards it was a must whenever we went on a fishing or hunting trip.

"It can be made in any pot with a tight fitting lid that can be covered with hot coals. The best thing I found was an old Dutch oven."

1 pound sliced bacon, or 3 thin slices ham cut
   into strips
2 cans (No. 303 *each*) whole kernel corn
2 cans (1 lb. *each*) pork and beans
1 cup catsup
2 teaspoons dry mustard
½ cup brown sugar

Line the bottom of the Dutch oven with a layer of bacon strips or ham slices. Pour over about ½ can corn, ½ can beans, ¼ cup catsup, and sprinkle with a little of the mustard and brown sugar. Put down another layer of bacon or ham, then the other ingredients in quantities given above, and repeat this process until all have been used up—be sure to end with a layer of bacon or ham on top. Cover the Dutch oven.

In camp: Dig a hole right next to your camp fire or cooking fire and put the Dutch oven down in it. Before you retire for the night, put some hot coals on top of the oven and throw on a little wood. Serve the beans for breakfast. (Alternate method: Start the beans in this fashion right after breakfast; serve for dinner.)

At home: Bake 4 hours in a 300° oven. Serves 6 to 8 in camp—possibly 1 or 2 more at home.

Photographer
North Hollywood, Calif.

WEST TEXAS COFFEE-CAN BEANS

2 cups pinto or red kidney beans
1 (No. 2) can of tomatoes
1 clove garlic
1 large onion, cut coarsely
½ pound fat salt pork, cut in inch squares
1 dried red chili, seeds and stem removed
1 teaspoon salt

Soak beans overnight in plenty of cold water. Use a 2-pound coffee can or a large can with a tight-fitting lid in which you have punched a hole with a small nail. Wash soaked beans, place in can, cover with water, and add remaining ingredients. Bring to a boil, press the lid down tightly, and barely simmer for at least 24 hours. Serves 4.

BRIG. GEN. NEAL McKAY
U.S. Army

BEANS 'N BACON

"Whether motoring or packing in on a fishing trip, the rule I go by is 'get the beans boiling'," says *Chef* Ned L. Chaffin of Taft, California. Beans are a main dish standby, of course. However, we are more interested in the way *Chef* Chaffin uses his main-dish beans for breakfast.

1 large onion
5 cloves garlic
½ pound salt pork
5 cups pinto beans
   Boiling water
1 pound bacon (16 slices)

Chop onions, garlic, and salt pork into small pieces and place in the kettle to "cook up" for a while before adding other ingredients. Add beans and cover with boiling water. Cook until beans are tender, from 2 to 3 hours, stirring occasionally, and adding a little more boiling water whenever the mixture seems to be getting too thick.

Now, for breakfast . . . cut the bacon into 1-inch lengths and fry until crisp. Then add 6 cups of the already cooked beans, mashing as many of them as you can. Let simmer for 3 minutes and serve hot. Serves 4 to 6, depending on appetites.

Salesman
Taft, Calif.

VEGETABLE WATERCRESS SUPREME

3 cups sliced celery
3 large carrots, finely diced
1 package frozen lima beans
1 package frozen cut string beans
2 cups boiling water
1 large onion, chopped
3 bouillon cubes
1 large bunch watercress, chopped
2 teaspoons salt
¼ teaspoon pepper

Place celery, carrots, lima beans, and string beans in kettle; cover with water and boil 25 minutes. Add onion, bouillon cubes, watercress, salt, and pepper. Simmer 10 minutes longer. Serves about 8.

San Francisco

OREGANO BEANS

    1 pound red Mexican beans
    ½ pound salt pork, cut up
    2 large onions, sliced

Soak beans in water overnight, then drain
and add salt pork and sliced onions.
Cover with water and simmer for 4½
hours, or until beans are almost cooked.

Sauce

    2 onions, chopped
    3 cloves garlic, minced
    1 carrot, diced
    5 stalks celery, minced
    3 tablespoons olive oil or salad oil
    ½ teaspoon oregano (wild marjoram)
    2 cans consommé
    3 cups tomato juice
      Salt and pepper to taste

Make a sauce for the beans in the following manner: Sauté vegetables in olive oil,
sprinkle with oregano, and allow to simmer for·about 10 minutes. Add remaining
ingredients and simmer for about ½ hour.

Drain liquor from beans, saving this for
soup for the following day. Add sauce
to beans and simmer for another hour.
Serve with French bread and tossed salad
of mixed greens. Recipe will serve from
5 to 8 people, depending upon their appetites.

Henry G. Hart

La Cañada, Calif.

CASSOULET

    2 pounds dried lima beans
    1 bay leaf
    2 large onions
    4 cloves garlic
    2 pounds pork sausage meat
      Salt and pepper
      Pinch of thyme
    ½ teaspoon monosodium glutamate
    1 large bunch parsley
    ½ bottle dry, white wine
    ¼ pound butter (1 cube)
    1 cup dry bread crumbs

Soak beans overnight. Next day simmer in
water to cover, adding bay leaf to the
water. Chop onions and mince garlic.
Cook sausage with onions and garlic until
sausage is brown. Break it up with a fork
while cooking. When the beans are almost
tender and most of the water cooked off,
put them in a casserole, add the sausage
mixture, season with salt, pepper, thyme,
and monosodium glutamate, and mix.
Mince the parsley, save half of it, and mix
the remainder with the beans. Pour on
the white wine and put in the oven at 350°
for an hour. Melt the butter, add the remaining parsley and the bread crumbs;
cover the top of the casserole thickly with
the mixture, and return to the oven to
brown. Serve with green salad and hot
French bread with plenty of butter, but
without garlic for obvious reasons. Cheese
is good with this, too. Serves 12.

Ward Ritchie
Book designer
La Canada, Calif.

GREEN BEANS AUX HERBES

One purpose of this recipe for green beans
is to shape you more like one. Or, as
George J. Watkins explains it, "These
days when the accent and emphasis are
upon diet and weight reduction, there is
a great need for flavorsome food of low
caloric value. My recipe is for delicious
string beans prepared without bacon or
salt pork. Eight ounces of beans prepared
in this manner will not exceed 60 calories.
Nevertheless, they will delight the palate
and taste buds."

"To shape you more like one"

Some traditionalists won't go along with
this, and we can't see the kind of calorie
counting that takes all the pleasure out
of eating. But when a dish is low in calo-

ries and tasty as well, we're all for it. If for nothing else, you can use it on a menu as a foil for richer foods.

This has a surprising taste of apple, although there is not even a trace of apple in the ingredients.

    2 pounds green beans
    1½ cups water
    3 dashes Cayenne pepper
    ½ teaspoon tarragon
    ¼ teaspoon oregano
    ¼ teaspoon sweet basil
    2 teaspoons salt
    3 whole black peppers, ground
    1 medium sized onion, chopped
    ½ clove garlic, crushed
    ½ cup sherry

Wash beans and cut in small pieces. Put in saucepan and add water, herbs, seasonings, onion, and garlic. Cook rapidly until water boils; then turn heat very low and cook 2 hours or more, until beans are very tender and practically all liquor has evaporated. Pour sherry and turn up heat until juice begins to boil. Then turn off heat, cover pan with lid, and let stand until ready to serve. Allow at least 30 minutes for wine to permeate beans. Serves 8.

State employee (retired)
Los Angeles, Calif.

GREEN BEAN CASSEROLE

    1 package frozen string beans, whole or cut
    1 medium-sized onion, sliced thinly
    1 clove garlic, minced
    6 large stalks of celery, finely sliced
    ½ teaspoon salt
    ¼ teaspoon cayenne, or less
    ¼ teaspoon allspice
    ¼ teaspoon freshly ground pepper
    1 teaspoon sugar
    ½ lemon
    ½ cup heavy cream
    1 small package Bluehill Pimento Cheese
      spread

Cook string beans just until tender; drain. Add onion rings, garlic, celery, and the mixed and blended dry seasonings. Squeeze lemon half, add juice and whole rind. Mix all together, then cover and cook over very low heat for 20 minutes. When vegetables (celery and onion) are done, pour entire mixture, except lemon

rind, into casserole dish. Pour in cream and cover with thin slices of the cheese. Bake in a moderate oven (350°) for 30 minutes. Serve casserole piping hot.

Property manager
Stockton, Calif.

ARABIAN STYLE GREEN BEANS

Jack M. Saad was born in Jerusalem, within sight of the Church of the Holy Sepulchre. His family—of Spanish extraction—traces its known lineage back to the Crusades. Arabian cooking, in which lamb is virtually the only meat, was all he knew until he came to this country in the 1920's.

He was astonished by American cooking then and he isn't really accustomed to it yet. Although he now lives in Bellingham, Washington, he still tends to adapt American ingredients to the methods and menus of the Middle East.

    1 tablespoon butter or margarine
    1 cup lean lamb shoulder, diced small
    2 onions, minced
    ½ clove garlic, minced or mashed
    2 packages (10 oz. each) frozen cut
      string beans
    1 large can (No. 2½) solid pack tomatoes
    ⅛ teaspoon cinnamon
      Salt to taste

Melt butter in a skillet and sauté the lamb, onion, and garlic until the meat is crisp and brown. Add string beans and tomatoes, season with cinnamon and salt, cover, and simmer gently until beans are tender. Serves 8.

Restaurant operator
Bellingham, Washington

THELEN STRING BEANS

After cooking string beans in the usual manner, pour browned butter over them. Mix well. Then squeeze lemon juice over the beans and mix lightly. Serve.

Govt. employee (retired)
Portland, Oregon

MEXICAN BEAN SPROUTS

4 strips bacon, cut into small pieces
1 large green pepper, diced
3 stalks celery, sliced
1 medium-sized onion, thinly sliced
½ cup peanuts
1 pound fresh bean sprouts
Dash of chili powder
Salt and pepper to taste

Put bacon in large skillet and cook slowly until crisp. Add the green pepper, celery, and onion; brown slightly, stirring occasionally, for about 10 minutes. To this add the peanuts, bean sprouts, chili powder, salt and pepper. Mix thoroughly. Cover and allow to steam for another 10 minutes. This is ready to serve just before the vegetables have lost all their crispness. It can be served over noodles, a la Chinese, or it is excellent as a vegetable by itself. There's no liquid added to this recipe, and none is needed. Serves 8.

Manuel M Lopez

Fresno, Calif.

GUACAMOLE GUAJARDITO

Mexican food in general is not as hot (like pepper) as some uninformed people believe. Warning: This sauce from Charles L. Palmer is *hot!* But it has a beautiful sea green color and lush texture and could ornament a great number of other foods. Try wooing it gently and learn to love it.

Its base is the avocado, native to the tropical Americas.

4 green chili peppers (long—the type
    that is often pickled)
1 large avocado
6 Chilis Tepinos (small, hot)
1 clove garlic
2 teaspoons salt
1¼ cups sauterne wine
¼ teaspoon cumin, if desired

Split peppers, remove seeds, and roast in oven until skin can be removed (or use the canned peppers). Put peppers and all other ingredients into liquidizer or food mill a little at a time and blend until solids are impalpable. Bottle and store in refrigerator. Makes about 1 pint.

Excellent meat sauce. Can be used to flavor and garnish salads, and is fine for hors d'oeuvres or wherever a pepper sauce can be used.

Charles L. Palmer

Publicity
Fresno, Calif.

CHILIS RELLENOS

6 eggs, separated
1 (4 oz.) can peeled, roasted green chili peppers
½ pound Monterey Jack cheese, cut into strips
    1 by 3 inches

Beat egg whites and yolks separately and combine, folding yolks into whites gently. Slit 4 peppers lengthwise and remove seeds. Stuff with strips of cheese, replace tops, and fasten with toothpicks. Using half the egg mixture, spoon 4 oval patties onto a well-greased, heated, but not too hot, skillet. Cook gently and when set, place a cheese-stuffed pepper on each patty; cover with remaining egg mixture. When patties are lightly browned on bottom, turn carefully with spatula and brown on reverse side. Place on individual oven-proof dishes and cover with ample serving of Spanish Sauce. Place a strip of cheese along top of each serving and place under broiler until cheese melts. Serves 4.

Spanish Sauce

1 large onion, minced
1 clove garlic, minced
2 tablespoons olive oil
½ pound ground beef
½ green bell pepper, chopped fine
2 stalks celery, chopped fine
2 (8 oz.) cans tomato sauce
½ teaspoon oregano
1 dash Tabasco sauce
Salt and pepper to taste

Brown onion and garlic in olive oil. Add meat and brown. Add remaining ingredients and simmer over low heat for about 1½ hours. Add water if sauce becomes too thick. If the sauce is placed in a double boiler, you can cook it much longer without scorching.

O. J. Breitwiener

Electrical engineer
San Diego, Calif.

ONIONS AGRODOLCE

You may have boiled, creamed, or fried onions, but we'll wager you've never

"Palatable even to those who entertain a prejudice against that noble bulb"

braised them in the Italian manner described below. The term *agro e dolce* simply means sweet and sour.

Chef William A. Dyer of Seattle long ago established his seniority in the ranks of *Chefs of the West.* His newest offering may make an onion palatable even to those few who entertain a prejudice against that noble bulb.

      3 tablespoons olive oil
     25 peeled small white onions
     ½ cup port
     ½ cup vinegar
      2 tablespoons brown sugar
     ½ cup raisins
     ½ teaspoon salt
        Dash of cayenne pepper

Heat the olive oil in a large skillet, add the onions, and fry, turning occasionally until they start to brown. Add wine, vinegar, brown sugar, raisins, salt, and cayenne pepper. Cover and simmer slowly for at least an hour, or until the onions are quite soft and the sauce has turned to a thick syrup. This dish requires a watchful eye and an occasional addition of water to prevent scorching. Serves 6 to 8 persons.

Secretary
Seattle, Washington

ONIONS SATELLITE

As one who has done honor to the onion, we introduce *Chef* Frank W. Mackey

who contributes this superlative recipe using the mild, white, tiny pearl onion. He credits an enthusiastic guest for its "out-of-this-world title—Onions Satellite."

      ¼ pound fresh mushrooms, sliced
      2 tablespoons butter
     ½ pound bulk pork sausage
      I pint (2 cups) stock (preferably turkey,
        chicken, or pork; or canned broth may be
        used)
      2 pounds little pearl onions (50 to 60 onions)
      I small carton (8 oz.) sour cream
      4 tablespoons (¼ cup) pistachio nuts (or
        sesame seeds, if preferred)

Sauté fresh mushrooms in butter. Remove from pan but leave browned "flavor bits" in pan. In same pan sauté crumbled pork sausage until very brown. Remove sausage but do not rinse pan. While pan is very hot, pour in meat stock. Stir up all browned flavor bits from the mushrooms and sausage into the stock. Then add peeled onions, cover, and cook slowly until onions are tender and almost all stock has been absorbed and reduced (about 30 minutes).

Add sautéed mushrooms and browned pork sausage and mix in well. Just before serving, mix in the sour cream and top with ground pistachio nuts. Serves 6.

Tabulating analyst
Sherman Oaks, Calif.

ONIONS À LA SHERRY

      Onions
      Butter
      Sherry

Slice onions and fry in butter until nicely browned. Then add sherry (about half as much in volume as the browned onions) and simmer gently until onions are quite tender. Serve with steak.

FRANK JOHNS, JR.
Executive, wholesale supply
Visalia, Calif.

ONION PIE

Onion pie is a just-right accompaniment for your leg of mutton. Serve it in place of potatoes and vegetable. A green salad and some cheese will be a fitting finish.

    4 large white onions, sliced
    3 tablespoons butter
    1 cup of "half and half" (milk and cream)
    2 eggs
    1 tablespoon flour
      Salt and pepper
      9-inch baked pie shell

Cook the sliced onions in butter until soft. Add "half and half," beaten eggs, and flour, well mixed. Season with salt and pepper. Pour into a baked pie shell and bake in a moderate oven (350°) for about an hour or until set. Serves 6.

A bottle of robust Cabernet wine is ideal with this meal. Be rewarded by the sighs of contentment from your well-fed guests.

Philip S. Brown

Pasadena, Calif.

HONDURAS ONIONS

Boil very tiny onions until tender. Mix with cream sauce to which a jigger of sherry (per pint of cream sauce) has been added. Add a lot of blanched, toasted, and slivered almonds.

Colin Radford

Real estate
Bellevue, Washington

PLATO BARRATO

Chef George C. Booth can speak food with a Spanish accent. He can invent a recipe in that language, too.

"Because I am a school teacher, I had to design this dish in self defense. Students drop in singly or in groups and lose all track of time. They are always hungry. To fill them up on sandwiches or hamburgers would take a small fortune. So the inspiration for *Plato Barrato* (cheap dish) came to me one day. I have served it many times. It has always had an enthusiastic reception."

    2 large onions
    1 green pepper
    2 tablespoons olive oil
    1 large can hominy
    1 jar tamales with gravy (about 5 in jar)
    1 can cream of chicken soup

Sauté onions and green pepper slowly in oil in large frying pan. Pour water off hominy. Remove tamale wrappers. Add hominy, tamales *with gravy*, and cream of chicken soup. Don't put any water in the mixture! Heat thoroughly and serve. (May be heated in casserole, too.)

This will feed four boys or six girls.

Geo. C. Booth
Teacher
Long Beach, Calif.

ZUCCHINI CREOLE

It's funny how some okra, a little chili powder, and a dash of Tabasco can send that little old Italian squash, zucchini, kiting off in a brand new direction. Without further ado, we introduce "Zucchini Creole" as authored by William D. Weiler, of Watsonville, California. Well done, William Weiler, of Watsonville.

    1 can (No. 2) okra
    1 can (8 oz.) tomato sauce
    1 teaspoon chili powder
    1 clove garlic, minced
      Salt to taste
      Dash Tabasco
    5 medium sized zucchini, sliced

Combine everything but zucchini and cook for about 10 minutes. Then place sliced zucchini on top, cover and cook slowly, stirring occasionally, until zucchini is done—about 10 minutes. Serves 6.

Wm. D Weiler
Watsonville, Calif.

SQUASH WITH ALMONDS

When you're just about ready to serve up some barbecued bit on the patio, here's a beautiful side dish to bring out from the kitchen. It bakes in the oven, but will stay warm in its casserole for a short time in case you don't start the meal with timetable precision. We've never seen quite this combination before. Among other things, it proves that almost anything tastes good if cooked with loving care and plenty of butter and cream; that's not criticism, it's a compliment to the intelligence of the *Chef*.

    1 pound yellow crookneck squash
    ¼ cup butter
      Salt and pepper to taste
    ¼ teaspoon basil
    ½ cup heavy cream
    ⅛ teaspoon ginger
    ¼ cup brown sugar
    ½ cup finely sliced almonds (or as many as
        the budget will allow)

Split squash. In frying pan melt butter,

"It proves that almost anything tastes good if cooked with loving care and plenty of butter and cream"

add squash, and brown lightly. Sprinkle with salt, pepper, and basil. Put all in casserole, add cream, dust with ginger, sprinkle on brown sugar, and top with sliced almonds. Bake at 350° for about 20 minutes, or until tender and the top is brown. Serves 4 to 6.

Forrest Rose

Garage owner
Sunland, Calif.

ITALIAN STUFFED ZUCCHINI

Chef Nonie Moglia has a magical touch with zucchini, and his recipe is an excellent sample of the Italian approach to this too-seldom-glorified vegetable.

    6 medium-sized zucchini
    1 large onion, chopped
    2 cloves garlic, minced
    1 tablespoon olive or salad oil
    1 tablespoon minced parsley
    ½ cup cooked chopped spinach
    ½ cup grated Parmesan cheese
    ¼ cup fine dry bread crumbs
    ½ teaspoon each salt and pepper
    3 eggs

Wash zucchini, cut blossom and stem end off, and boil whole until tender. Cut in half lengthwise and scoop out centers. Arrange in a shallow baking pan so zucchini shells do not touch.

Sauté onion and garlic in olive or salad oil until tender but not brown. Add parsley, spinach, cheese, bread crumbs, and seasonings and mix well. Stir in beaten eggs. Spoon stuffing into each shell. Bake in a moderate oven (350°) until lightly browned, about 20 minutes. Serves 6

Nonie L. Moglia

Hayward, Calif.

ZUCCHINI CAKES

A few years ago, we might still have had our doubts; but now it seems safe to say that zucchini, the Italian squash, is well established on the Western menu. Some of our *Chefs of the West* have made notable contributions to zucchini cookery.

    3 cups grated or chopped unpeeled zucchini
    3 tablespoons chopped parsley
    1 large clove garlic, mashed or minced
    ½ cup grated Parmesan cheese
    1 egg
    1 cup biscuit mix (approximately)
      Salt
      Pepper
      Cooking oil or shortening

Mix together the zucchini, parsley, garlic, cheese, and egg. Add enough biscuit mix to make a thin batter. Season to taste with salt and pepper. Drop from tablespoon into ½ inch of hot oil or shortening in heavy frying pan. Cook cakes until golden brown. Drain on paper towels. Makes 16 medium sized cakes.

These cakes may be prepared ahead of time and heated in the oven before serving. For variation you can substitute carrots for the zucchini.

Joseph M. Bovren

Pressman
Los Angeles, Calif.

BROCCOLI FRITTATA MELROSE

In Broccoli Frittata, *Chef* Kenneth Melrose, Sr., does something really nice for this cabbage cousin. As one of our testers put it, "He took the strong flavor out of broccoli without destroying its character."

That's important. No cook is successful if he removes good qualities too.

The use of frozen broccoli is a worthwhile short cut, but be sure to let it defrost completely and wait till all the water has drained out. Too much water will prevent the eggs in the frittata from setting properly. If you would like a sharper flavor, sprinkle with grated Parmesan cheese.

"If you would like a sharper flavor, sprinkle with grated Parmesan cheese"

2 packages (10 oz. *each*) frozen chopped
    broccoli
4 tablespoons olive oil
2 cloves garlic, chopped
¼ cup chopped parsley
2 teaspoons salt
    Freshly ground pepper to taste
4 eggs

Allow broccoli to defrost, then drain. Heat oil in a heavy iron skillet, but do not let it get too hot; when broccoli is added, it has a tendency to burn quickly. Add broccoli and garlic. Cook over medium heat for 15 to 20 minutes, stirring frequently.

When cooked tender but not mushy, add parsley and salt and pepper. Beat eggs and add to broccoli. Mix well. Cover skillet, turn heat to low, and cook until eggs are firm. Do not let them dry out. They should be brown on top, like an omelet. Turn out on a hot plate; cut in wedges. Serves 6 generously as a side dish.

For a one-plate meal, add 1 cup diced cooked meat and use 6 eggs. Serves 4 to 6.

Kenneth Melrose, Sr.
Sales manager
Santa Cruz, Calif.

BROCCOLI PELLEGRINI

    Broccoli
2 tablespoons olive oil
2 cloves of garlic,
    cut in 6 pieces each
    Grated Parmigiano
    Juice of half a lemon
    Salt and pepper

Wash and boil broccoli until about half cooked. Drain, cut in small pieces, and finish cooking in a pan containing the olive oil, in which the garlic pieces have been fried and removed. Sprinkle with grated Parmigiano, lemon juice, salt, and pepper, and place in the oven for just a few minutes to melt the cheese.

Angelo M. Pellegrini
Teacher
Seattle, Washington

EGG AND ARTICHOKE CASSEROLE

6 large, cooked artichokes
6 hard-cooked eggs
3 cups cream sauce
    Dash of paprika
1 teaspoon Worcestershire sauce

This is a recipe that will reward you well for the time required. Served with parsley-buttered new potatoes, a tossed vegetable salad, and a well-chilled white wine, it will make a delicious meal.

Put the hearts of the artichokes on the bottom of a well-greased casserole and place a hard-cooked egg in each heart. Scrape the leaves of the artichoke into the cream sauce, to which have been added the paprika and Worcestershire sauce. Pour the sauce over the eggs and bake until hot. Serves 6.

JOHN R. GOLDEN
Attorney
San Francisco, Calif.

GREEN ROSE COCKTAIL ARTICHOKES

Commander Maynard Dixon, USN, has a suggestion for the centerpiece on your hors d'œuvre tray—two large artichokes simmered in a typically standard manner, then drenched with an unusually piquant sauce. Though the ingredients don't seem unusual, the results will be a pleasant surprise.

Commander Dixon suggested adding several dashes of green food coloring to the cooking water. Our taste panel recommended that this coloring be omitted because of its unnatural quality and because the color was concentrated in the porous heart rather than distributed evenly over the artichoke.

    2 large fresh artichokes
      Rind of one lemon (save juice for the sauce)
    ½ cup vinegar
    2 teaspoons salt
    1 teaspoon sugar
    ⅓ cup (6 tablespoons) butter or margarine
    1 thumbnail-size clove of garlic, crushed
    1 teaspoon dried marjoram
    1 tablespoon lemon juice

Cut off tops of artichokes 1 to 1½ inches from top, removing tough outside leaves.

Boil enough water in a 2-quart pan to cover the artichokes. Add lemon rind, vinegar, salt, and sugar. Boil trimmed artichokes until the hearts are tender when tested with a fork (about 40 minutes). While artichokes are cooking, combine butter, garlic, marjoram, and lemon juice in a small pan and place over low heat until the butter is melted.

Remove artichokes from the water and drain, upside-down, for a few minutes; cut off stems so that artichokes will stand evenly, then turn upright, separating the leaves slightly. Spoon the butter dressing over the artichokes and place them in the center of your serving dish. Since this is strictly finger food, your guests will probably have to gather around the tray to savor each separate petal.

Commander Maynard H. Dixon

Cmdr., USN
Honolulu, T. H.

We suspect that once you've tried this method of preparing artichokes, you'll also utilize it for a vegetable course, serving each person a whole artichoke.

ARTICHOKES PELLEGRINI

    6 artichokes
      Boiling water
      Juice of 1 lemon
    ¼ pound prosciutto (Italian ham)
      or ham
      Clove of garlic, finely minced
      Green onion, finely minced
    2 small sprigs marjoram, finely minced
    1 cup stock
      Salt and pepper
    2 tablespoons Parmigiano
    2 tablespoons butter
    1 tablespoon tomato paste
      Juice of half a lemon

Trim artichokes and plunge into boiling salted water (enough to cover) to which has been added the lemon juice. Boil for 3 minutes and drain.

Mince and fry the ham. Add garlic, green onion, and marjoram, finely minced, and fry slowly for another minute. Add half the stock, reserving the rest for later, and simmer for 5 minutes. Season and stir in Parmigiano; remove from fire. Stuff each artichoke with some of this mixture and set them in a baking dish into which you have placed the butter, the other ½ cup of stock, tomato paste, and lemon juice. Bake in a moderate oven until tender, basting frequently with the juice in the bottom of the pan.

ANGELO PELLEGRINI
Teacher
Seattle, Washington

SPICED ARTICHOKES

6 medium sized artichokes
1 stick cinnamon
1 dozen whole cloves
1 tablespoon olive oil
1 tablespoon vinegar
2 tablespoons salt
Water

Combine artichokes and seasonings in a pan and add enough water to cover the artichokes. (A little sugar can be added if more sweetness is desired.) Boil gently for about 45 minutes, or until artichokes are tender. Remove from liquid; drain upside down a few minutes. Serve with mayonnaise or melted butter, one to a person.

C. M. Anderson

Burlingame, Calif.

COLE SLAW Á LA SIERRA

¼ cup prepared mustard
¼ cup mayonnaise
¼ cup sugar
1 tablespoon lemon juice
½ teaspoon salt
1 medium size head of cabbage, finely shredded
2 tablespoons finely chopped toasted almonds

Mix mustard, mayonnaise, sugar, lemon juice, and salt in a mixing bowl and pour over finely shredded cabbage. Add almonds and toss gently until every shred of cabbage is coated with the tangy, saffron colored sauce. Serves 6 to 8.

Edward G. Thompson

Van Nuys, California

STEAMED RED CABBAGE

Large red cabbage
½ cup butter
½ cup vinegar
Salt
Pepper
Red currant jelly

Cut the cabbage into thin strips and put into a pot with the butter, vinegar, salt, and pepper. Cook at low heat (do not add any water). Then when tender, add the

currant jelly, with your own taste dictating the amount to be used.

Chester V Emmons

Reno, Nevada

CARAWAY SAUERKRAUT

1½ pounds sauerkraut
2 apples, sliced
2 onions, sliced
2 tablespoons vinegar
2 tablespoons sugar
½ teaspoon salt
1 teaspoon caraway seeds
1 large raw potato, grated

Our *Chefs* agree that cabbage in some guise is as imperative as the fluffy mashed potatoes and gravy, traditionally served with goose.

Put sauerkraut, apples, onions, vinegar, sugar, and seasonings in a large saucepan. Cover with water and simmer 3 hours. Just before serving, add the potato and cook until thickened.

Bradley Blair

Professor
Eugene, Oregon

SLAW A L'INDIENNE

Slaw originated in northern climates where cabbage used to be one of the few winter salad materials available. Grapes are a distinctly southern addition.

2 quarts finely shredded cabbage
1 quart unpeeled sweet red apple, cut into thin strips
1 cup walnut meats
1 pint Thompson seedless grapes
1 pint sour cream
¼ cup white wine vinegar
2 tablespoons olive oil
Salt and pepper to taste
1 teaspoon curry powder, or to taste
Lettuce

Assemble cabbage, apple, walnuts, and grapes. Combine sour cream and vinegar;

then add all remaining ingredients. Mix this sauce thoroughly with the already assembled, crisp, cold salad materials.

Serve on chilled lettuce arranged on iced plates. Serves 10 to 12.

Alec Yuill-Thornton
Architect
San Francisco, Calif.

GARDEN BOUQUET

You'll find that this Garden Bouquet fits into barbecue menus as neatly as a finger in a glove, and many a time you can enjoy it in generous bowls for a light Sunday lunch when dinner ahead promises more substantial fare.

    1 can (No. 2½) tomatoes
    1 tablespoon butter
      Salt and pepper to taste
    1 tablespoon sugar
    1 cup finely chopped celery
    3 tablespoons parsley (packed)

Heat tomatoes steaming hot, not boiling. Add butter, salt and pepper to taste, and sugar. Last, add the celery and chopped parsley. Serve at once.

WARD C. ALDEN
Doctor
Los Angeles, Calif.

SAUTÉED CARROTS CHATEAU

    1 tablespoon butter or other shortening
    2 cups carrots, diced and cooked until tender
    1½ cups California Tokay or Angelica wine
    2 tablespoons lemon juice
      Salt and pepper to taste

Melt butter in frying pan and sauté carrots slowly until slightly browned. Combine wine and lemon juice and pour over carrots. Simmer slowly until candied, and season to taste.

Publicity
Fresno, Calif.

TOMATOES AND PEPPERS

Chef Ross comments: "Regardless of what else is served at our barbecue parties, I can make them all sit up and take notice with this vegetable dish."

    Green peppers
    Olive oil
    Tomatoes, peeled and chopped
    Salt and pepper to taste

Wash green peppers (2 or 3 per person) and soak in ice water for 1 hour before they are to be cooked; then cut in 1-inch squares, discarding the coarse membrane and seeds. Cook in several tablespoons of hot olive oil until soft and slightly browned. Pour off all excess oil and add as much volume of peeled and chopped tomatoes as there is of peppers. Season with salt and pepper. Cook over very low heat 20 to 30 minutes.

HAROLD ROSS
El Cerrito, Calif.

BARBECUED CORN

Pull back the husks on fresh ears of corn, and clean out the silk and brown kernels. Wash, and tie the husks back in place with a piece of string. Soak the ears in a bucket of cold water for at least a half-hour before roasting. Place the ears on the grill, about 10 or 15 minutes before the fire is low enough to broil steaks or other meat. The water in the corn will dampen the fire. Allow the ears to roast about 10 minutes, turning occasionally. Place about one inch of hot water in a suitable vessel, such as a turkey roaster. Put in the roasted ears, with husks still on, and cover tightly. Place the pan on the shelf above the grate, where it will get the heat of the fire, or put it on the stove over low heat, so that the corn is allowed to steam for 15 or 20 minutes before serving.

Medical service representative
Alameda, Calif.

SPINACH BOHEMIENNE

In case medical scientists eventually discover—as thousands of people already suspect—that spinach has very little nutritive value, there will still be a good reason for serving this dish. It adds some nutrition in the eggs, makes spinach palatable to most spinach haters, and forms a combination hearty enough to serve as a main dish for a lunch or light supper.

Chef Clinton R. Vitous says it is an adaptation of the way his mother, who was of Bohemian ancestry, used to fix spinach.

    1 cellophane-wrapped package (10 oz.)
        fresh spinach
    1 heaping tablespoon bacon fat or butter
    3 eggs
        Salt and pepper to taste

Wash spinach; trim off any stem ends that may be tough; and cover and cook in the water that clings to the leaves, simmering for 2 minutes or until leaves are just wilted. Drain off juice. Return pan to low heat and add bacon fat. When mixture begins to steam, add beaten eggs. Stir in with a fork and keep stirring until the mixture is fluffy. Salt and pepper to taste just before serving. Serves 2 to 3.

Clinton R. Vitous.

Dentist
Seattle, Washington

SPINACH CREPES

It is not enough to say that this recipe glorifies spinach. In the opinion of our taste panel it deserves a special star of merit for a degree of excellence found in only a few *Chefs of the West* contributions each year.

    1 package frozen chopped spinach
    ¾ cup thick cream sauce
    2 tablespoons lemon juice
    1 teaspoon Worcestershire sauce
    ½ teaspoon grated onion
    ¼ teaspoon salt
    ¼ teaspoon nutmeg

Cook spinach and drain very well. Make up cream sauce (¾ cup milk, 1 tablespoon butter, 2 tablespoons flour). Add seasonings to taste. (EDITOR'S NOTE: We used quantities given above in our testing. But we give them merely as a general guide.) Mix in spinach.

Assemble the following ingredients for the crepes:

    1 cup flour
    ¾ teaspoon salt
    2 teaspoons sugar
    3 eggs, well beaten
    1 cup milk

Sift flour, salt, and sugar into bowl. Make hollow in flour, then add eggs and milk alternately, stirring constantly. Strain through fine strainer.

Heat small skillet and brush with butter for each crepe. Batter must be thin and cook quickly. A running-over tablespoon is enough batter for each cake. (Roll batter around the pan to make it spread out thin.) This recipe makes 9 or 10 crepes, 10 inches in diameter; more if skillet is smaller.

When crepe is brown on one side, spread about 2 tablespoons of the spinach mixture across the middle. Roll up, and place with edge tucked underneath in a long baking dish. Continue baking, filling and rolling crepes.

Mix together the topping:

    1 pint sour cream
        Cream to thin slightly
        Grated onion, if desired
        Salt to taste

Spread over filled crepes. Then cover with
    1 cup grated Cheddar cheese

Bake in a slow oven (300°) for 30 minutes. Serve 1 or 2 spinach crepes to each person.

Executive vice president
Honolulu, T. H.

EGGPLANT GRANCHIOLINO

William A. Dyer of Seattle brings considerable ingenuity to the task of improving on eggplant. He suspends it in a solution which he calls "Eggplant Granchiolino" (*granchiolino* is one of the Italian names for shrimp). All the scientists in the field who have reviewed his work are convinced that he has made a sound contribution. As one puts it:

"Even an eggplant lover will like this. And if you don't like eggplant, you won't realize that you are eating it."

Hint to those who would like to repeat *Chef* Dyer's process in their own laboratories: After frying the eggplant, put it on paper toweling to drain off all excess oil before combining it with the shrimp in the casserole.

Cut a large eggplant into slices about ¼-inch thick and soak them in salted water for one hour. Prick each slice full of holes with the tines of a fork. Dip slices in beaten egg to which has been added 1 teaspoon monosodium glutamate, ¼ teaspoon cumin, and 1 teaspoon of the juice from freshly mashed garlic. Then coat slices well with dry bread crumbs rolled to powder fineness.

Fry the coated slices in hot oil or butter until they are a rich golden brown on both sides. Place a layer in the bottom of a well-greased baking dish. Cover the layer of eggplant with a layer of minced shrimp mixed with finely minced green pepper. Add another layer of eggplant, then another layer of shrimp, until the casserole is filled, making the top layer of eggplant. Over the top, pour the remainder of the egg mixture in which you dipped the eggplant slices. Sprinkle the top generously with finely chopped green onion tops. Bake in a 350° oven for approximately half an hour. Serve very hot. Serves 8.

Secretary
Seattle, Washington

BETEN-JEN (EGGPLANT) AL RASHID

Almost all nations, except our own, customarily cook their vegetables with some sort of meat. In this Syrian preparation of eggplant, Dr. Philip J. Rashid uses beef —with onions, tomatoes, and cinnamon.

    1 large eggplant
    Salt
    Salad oil
    ½ cube butter
    1 pound round steak, cut into ¼-inch cubes
    2 medium sized onions, chopped
    1 teaspoon salt
    ½ teaspoon pepper
    ½ teaspoon cinnamon
    1 can (No. 2) solid pack tomatoes

Wash eggplant and trim the top, but do not peel. Cut in half lengthwise, then cut each half into 3 long wedges so that you have a wide strip of peel at the bottom of each one. Salt each wedge and let stand for approximately 30 minutes; then wipe off each wedge with a cloth. Heat oil in a skillet; brown eggplant quickly; remove and place on absorbent paper.

In another skillet place butter, round steak cubes, onions, 1 teaspoon salt, pepper, and cinnamon. Cook slowly until meat and onions are very lightly browned.

Make a lengthwise slit in the top of each eggplant wedge, place peel side down in a baking dish, and fill each slit with about 2 tablespoons of the meat and onion mixture. Pour tomatoes over all, place in moderate oven (350°), and bake 45 minutes. Serves 6 as a side dish for a full dinner or a main dish for luncheon or supper.

Doctor
Fairfield, Cailf.

ASPARAGUS TIDBITS RECHAUFFÉ

If you have any taste for asparagus, March is a good month to eat your fill of that tender green stuff. If you overesti-

"Eat your fill of that tender green stuff"

mate capacity and cook a little too much some evening, don't worry; you'll have an excellent opportunity to serve it again in delicious little bits—"a sort of hot hors d'oeuvre"—as suggested by A. L. Johnston, Sr., of San Francisco.

These are leftovers in fancy dress, a little hard to classify, perhaps. But just fit them into any convenient place before or during a meal as an unexpected dividend.

Not much point in giving exact measurements, because the quantity of asparagus you have left over is bound to vary. Use only the tender part of each stalk.

First set the leftover asparagus stalks out on some paper to drain, as they sometimes become a little watery when left in the refrigerator overnight. When they are well drained, set a frying pan over low heat and cover the bottom with olive oil. Meanwhile cut asparagus in about 2-inch lengths. In a small bowl mix together some catsup and a small bit of mayonnaise, some pepper, and some hot sauce. You'll have to guess at quantities, but the object is to have just enough of this mixture to coat each asparagus piece, with a little left over. Dip each asparagus bit into this mixture and set on some waxed paper.

By this time the oil and the pan are warm. Place the asparagus bits in the pan and let them simmer for about 30 seconds. Then pour the balance of the sauce over the bits and cook them for about 1 minute more. Serve hot to guests armed with toothpicks, spoons, or forks—whichever is proper protocol for the occasion.

A. L. Johnston Jr.

San Francisco

SOUR CREAM ASPARAGUS

Chef E. J. Durrett, a commander in the U. S. Navy, speaks with a world traveler's assurance when he says, "Surely there is no better asparagus in the world than that grown in the West." We can think of no more fitting end for good Western asparagus than to be buried in *Chef* Durrett's magnificent sour cream sauce. His

easy, inexpensive alternate for Hollandaise sauce would also be delicious on new

"To be buried in Chef *Durrett's magnificent sour cream sauce"*

cabbage, cauliflower, or broccoli.

    1½ pounds fresh asparagus
    2 tablespoons butter or margarine
    2 tablespoons minced onion
    1 tablespoon flour
    1 cup sour cream
    2 teaspoons vinegar
    ½ teaspoon sugar
    ¾ teaspoon salt
    Pepper to taste

Remove tough ends from asparagus; stand asparagus in deep kettle, add about 2 inches boiling water, and cook until tender. Meanwhile melt butter in a saucepan over low heat. Add onion and cook until tender, but not brown. Blend in flour and heat until it bubbles. Stir in sour cream, vinegar, sugar, salt, and pepper. Cook, stirring constantly, until sauce is thickened. Serve sauce over cooked asparagus, sprinkling heavily with paprika. Serves 4.

E. J. Durrett

Seattle

ASPARAGUS FRITTATA

From *Chef* Francis H. Wood of Stockton, California, comes a way to fill out a straight omelet with asparagus. Try it on a late Sunday morning when you're in the mood for luxurious living.

4 strips bacon, cut in fine pieces
1 dozen stalks of cooked asparagus, cut in
    ¼-inch pieces
1 pinch *each* of dried oregano, basil, and
    dehydrated parsley
1 tablespoon minced chives
    Salt and pepper to taste
4 eggs
2 tablespoons dry bread crumbs
1 tablespoon butter
¼ cup Parmesan cheese

Cook bacon until crisp. Add asparagus, herbs, salt, and pepper. Mix thoroughly. Drop in eggs and stir. Cook on top of stove about 2 minutes. Remove from stove; cover with bread crumbs (previously mixed with melted butter). Sprinkle with Parmesan cheese and bake in moderate oven (350°) until mixture is firm. Cut in pie-shaped wedges and serve. Serves 4.

Frances H Wood

Stockton, Calif.

PEAS ITALIENNE

There's nothing particularly Italian except, maybe, the garlic—about *Chef* Jon Weber's "Peas Italienne." Nevertheless, after tasting, we accept his testimony that this dish is "mighty good either with fried chicken or rabbit, or as a side dish with roast turkey." It makes chicken livers mighty palatable to those who ordinarily shun them. It also makes peas much more distinguished than usual. In fact, it could qualify as a main dish for a light luncheon or supper.

2 tablespoons butter or margarine
1 medium sized onion
1 clove garlic, mashed
2 or 3 chicken livers or 1 turkey liver, chopped
2 cups fresh cooked peas or 1 can (No. 2) peas
    Salt and pepper to taste
    Dash of Tabasco
¼ teaspoon paprika
1 can (10¾ oz.) mushroom soup or 1 small
    can (3 oz.) mushrooms, chopped

Melt butter slowly. Cut onion into fine slivers, slicing lengthwise with the grain. Add onion and garlic to melted butter. Cover, sauté slowly, add a little liquid from peas (or water) if needed for moisture, and cook only until the mixture is transparent. Add livers (again adding water if necessary), cover, and simmer

5 to 7 minutes. Add peas and simmer 10 minutes (do not boil!). Add salt and pepper, Tabasco, paprika, and mushroom soup or chopped mushrooms. Keep this simmering until you get that fried chicken and those hot biscuits ready to serve. Serves 4 to 6, but ingredients may be doubled easily when you are serving extra company.

Jon Weber
Seattle

Chef Weber prefers the livers coarsely chopped, but we like them better cut in quite small pieces, to make them approximately the same size as the peas. Take your choice.

MIXED VEGETABLE FRITTATA

¼ cup olive oil
1 clove garlic, minced
2 large onions, sliced
1 large green pepper, sliced
4 stalks celery, sliced
2 medium-sized tomatoes, cut into eighths
2 large zucchini, sliced
    Salt and pepper
    Mixed herbs
    Grated Parmesan cheese
6 eggs
½ cup cream or milk

Heat olive oil in a 12-inch skillet. Add garlic and onion. Sauté for a few minutes. Add other vegetables, and seasonings to taste. Cook, covered, for 15 minutes. When vegetables are tender, level the mixture in pan, and set aside to cool slightly. Beat eggs thoroughly with the cream or milk. Make indentations in the vegetable mixture so that the eggs will run through. Pour eggs over vegetables, sprinkle top with grated Parmesan cheese, and cook in a moderate oven (350°) until eggs are just set. The mixture will pull away from the sides of the pan a little when done. Turn out onto a platter and serve like a pie. This is a dish which takes to your own improvisation. You can add practically any left-over vegetables, meats, mushrooms, or anything else that strikes your fancy —or happens to be cluttering up the refrigerator. Serves 6.

San Francisco.

PASTEL DE ELOTE

Our taste-testers took a real fancy to this recipe; we recommend it to the barbecue crowd as a robust accompaniment for almost any kind of meat.

Monte Millard, of Los Angeles, says *"Pastel de Elote* is native to Mexico, the land of my birth, where it is made of fresh corn

"Pastel de Elote is native to Mexico, the land of my birth"

and is most popular. *(Pastel* means pie or pastry; *elote* is a tender ear of maize.) I have adapted it for American palates, using canned, cream style corn so that it may be served the year around.

"This is very popular with my 'gringo' friends as a bread in lieu of the usual garlic bread at barbecues. It may be served also as a starchy vegetable as one would serve Southern corn pudding. You may make it in advance and reheat before serving. Saludos Amigos."

    ½ pound butter or margarine
    1 cup sugar
    4 eggs
    1 can (4 oz.) green chili peppers
    1 can (No. 303) cream style golden bantam
        corn
    ½ cup grated jack cheese
    ½ cup grated Tillamook cheese
    ¼ teaspoon salt
    1 cup flour
    1 cup yellow cornmeal
    4 teaspoons baking powder

Cream butter and add sugar. Add eggs, one at a time, mixing in well. Chop peppers and add. Add corn and mix well. Add

cheeses and pinch of salt. Sift flour and then measure; sift cornmeal and then measure; sift both together with baking powder and add to previous mixture. Pour into greased and floured glass baking dish (8 by 12 by 2 inches). Preheat oven at 350°. Reduce heat to 300° and bake for one hour. Serves 10.

Monte Millard

Los Angeles

GREEN PEPPER-CHEESE CASSEROLE

A vegetable side dish that goes well with any barbecued meat is the Green Pepper-Cheese Casserole devised by *Chef* J. A. (Al) Perkins of Honolulu. Preparation can hardly be any more simple (strangely enough, no liquid is needed to keep the mixture moist). We like it better than the more common rice-stuffed pepper, of which this is a welcome variation. It's an eye-catcher, too, a gay mixture of yellow, green, and white. We recommend an aged Cheddar if you want a definite sharpness to the cheese.

    Butter or margarine
    6 large green peppers
    3 cups cooked rice
    2 cups chopped or grated Cheddar cheese
    Salt and pepper to taste

Grease an 8 to 10-inch baking casserole with butter or margarine. Cut green peppers in half, remove seeds, rinse, and steam until tender. Put a layer of rice in the bottom of the casserole, then a layer of steamed green pepper, then a layer of cheese, and so on. If the rice seems dry, as day-old cooked rice sometimes does, dot the rice layers with butter. Finish off with a layer of cheese. Place in oven, preheated to 350° (moderate), and bake 30 to 40 minutes. Serves 6.

J. A. Perkins

Honolulu

HARVEST GOULASH

If you like fresh corn to taste fresh, don't let this dish cook a moment too long in its final stage. Cook only until kernels of corn are soft and milky, not hardened into congealed pellets of mush.

This "Goulash" (or succotash, if you prefer) is "he-man food," says *Chef* Lyle L. Groundwater of Olympia, Washington, "something that a man can cook and his wife can enjoy. The recipe originated in the Olympia area, in my family, a long time before Washington became a state."

```
4 slices bacon, chopped
2 large onions, chopped
1 large green pepper, chopped
4 to 6 ripe tomatoes, quartered
2 cups water
1 teaspoon salt
½ teaspoon pepper
½ teaspoon paprika
  Corn kernels cut from 6 ears of fresh corn
  (approximately 4 cups kernels)
```

Fry bacon until faintly brown. Then add onions and green peppers and fry until soft but not brown. Add tomatoes and water. Cook 20 minutes. Add corn and seasonings, cover, and cook 15 minutes if corn is young and tender, longer if old and firm. Serves 4.

This dish does not have to be served immediately. It is even better when warmed up the next day. We sometimes cook it over the coals of a fire outside, in a big iron kettle with three legs on the bottom.

Lyle L. Groundwater

Real estate broker
Olympia, Washington

SNOWFLAKE POTATOES

Take any large vessel, such as an iron pot, kettle, galvanized pail, or automatic gas or electric deep-fat fryer. Set up outdoors.

Put in this cooking utensil 2 pounds of refined rosin (of the Naval store variety) for each potato to be cooked and bring up the temperature to between 220° and 250°. Then add medium-sized potatoes.

Maintain the cooking temperature between 220° and 250° until all the potatoes have floated to the top. Remove potatoes slowly from the rosin, draining excess rosin. Place each potato in the center of any clean porous paper (such as paper towels or newspapers) approximately one foot square, rolling paper around potato and twisting both ends.

Allow to cool for several minutes until rosin left on the outside of potato sets hard. Serve the potato wrapped in the paper. Then slit paper, rosin coating, and skin of potato with a sharp knife from end to end, and then gently force the two ends toward the center. Add butter, chives, or any other desired flavoring.

E. F. Champion

Sales manager
Los Angeles, Calif.

POTATOES KAILUA

Chef MacGuigan says, "Here's a potato recipe that I think the barbecue lads will like. I call these Potatoes Kailua because my home is in Kailua and that's where the recipe was born. The potatoes pick up just enough of the spice flavor to make them different."

```
Potatoes
1 cup bacon fat or oil
1 teaspoon whole allspice
10 or 12 whole cloves
```

Use good-sized potatoes, 1 for each person, with a couple of extras tossed in for good measure. Boil them in their jackets for 5 or 6 minutes. Drain. Now, bring out the Dutch oven and put it on the grill. Put in bacon fat or oil and when it gets hot, toss in allspice and cloves. Roll each potato in the hot oil or fat until coated, then stack them in and put the lid on tight. Push the Dutch oven to the back of the grill while you barbecue the steaks or chicken or what-have-you. Takes about 30 minutes to cook through. Meanwhile, the aroma of the spices serves to whet the appetite.

J. ROGER MACGUIGAN
Theater circuit publicity director
Honolulu, T. H.

MASHED SWEET POTATOES IN CIDER

Peel and slice desired number of sweet potatoes. Place in sauce pan, cover with apple cider, add a pinch of salt, and season with cinnamon. Cook until cider is evaporated. Add butter and sugar to taste, mash, and serve.

R H Flournoy

El Cajon, Calif.

BAKED POTATOES A LA KING

Ralph King claims that the following recipe has an Idaho origin. He says he was up in the country around Boise, where farmers raise both potatoes and onions. They were discussing the problems of marketing these commodities separately, and he suggested, "Why not package them together?" In this recipe he wrapped them together for cooking over coals—campfire, barbecue, fireplace —or in a well-regulated oven. Oil from the onions gives the potatoes a cheese-like flavor.

Use medium sized potatoes. Either peel or scrub well. Slice lengthwise into three or four slices. Between these slices put thinner slices of onion. Salt and pepper to taste. Assemble into the basic shape of a potato. Wrap each one in a piece of heavy aluminum foil, or two or three thicknesses of household weight foil. Bake on the coals for about 30 minutes, turning over once during the cooking to distribute heat evenly. (In the oven, cook for 1 hour in a moderately hot oven 375°.)

Ralph King

Real estate
Berkeley, Calif.

POTATOES POTLUCK

Chef George C. Booth says he has "accompanied, ministered to, and cooked for fishermen for 43 years, so I know something of their migrations and feeding habits."

"On the Rogue River as a kid, I gathered crawdads from under rocks in the riffles and boiled their tails while my mates fished for steelhead, cutthroat, or silverside. In Arcata, California, I learned to outthink and chowder the wily razorback clam. In Klamath Falls the secret of dressing the lake trout was revealed to me (bake him on a board; throw the trout away and eat the board). I have observed my friends catch tarpon below the spillways of Gatun Dam, fight yellow jack in Panama Bay, and spear Manta Rays in Gallapagos.

"Now for the diet of the marine maddened. Stew is the general favorite, but that is in such general use that I shall reveal the secret of Potatoes Potluck.

    2 slices bacon, cut in very small pieces
    6 medium sized potatoes
      Salt and pepper to taste
    6 medium sized onions
    ½ wine glass (¼ cup) sherry, or 1 jigger (2
      tablespoons) either brandy or whiskey
      and 1 jigger water
    1 can (12 oz.) corned beef

A Dutch oven, or a frying pan with a lid, is used for this caper; a skillet covered with a pie plate will work. *Don't let the pan get too hot!* Fry the chopped bacon until half done; then add potatoes, salt, and pepper; cover. Introduce peeled, sliced onions 20 minutes later. Stir thoroughly and add wine. Stir now and then to keep from sticking, and for uniformity. When potatoes are almost done, crumble corned beef, add, and cook 10 minutes. Serves 6 to 8.

Geo. C Booth

Teacher
Long Beach, Calif.

POOFERS

My grandmother brought a recipe for "Poofers" with her when she came out from Virginia to join her husband in San Francisco in 1850. At that time "Poofers" were elegantly called *Pommes de terre et oeufs*, but they can be no less delicious with the 20th century delineation of their name.

3 good-sized raw potatoes, peeled and grated
½ medium-sized onion, grated
½ teaspoon salt
I egg, well beaten

Beat all ingredients together thoroughly and drop by tablespoonfuls into hot, deep fat. Remove and drain when browned.

THOMAS GERBERDING
Los Angeles, Calif.

COWBOY POTATOES

Many experimenters add onion or garlic in rather haphazard fashion. There is nothing slapdash about the way *Chef* Les Johnson uses these—and combines the

"And don't ever, ever forget the pepper"

techniques of boiling, simmering, and frying—in his tested, precise formula for "Cowboy Potatoes."

"It is a favorite in Nevada cow camps where I spent a good many years. I have used it many times on hunting trips. I now find it an excellent dish to accompany barbecued steaks served in the patio."

He carefully specifies quantities (and don't ever, ever forget the pepper!). He has refined the cooking technique to blend ingredients thoroughly in the final product with a texture somewhere between hash and stew.

4 slices bacon
I medium-sized onion
6 medium-sized potatoes
½ teaspoon or more of coarsely ground
     black pepper
Salt to taste

Fry bacon until crisp. Remove bacon and slice the onion in the hot drippings. Fry until golden yellow. Remove onions and pour out bacon drippings until only a tablespoon remains. Break bacon into bits and return it with the onions to the pan. Slice in the potatoes and immediately just cover with water. Bring to a boiling point, then lower the fire and allow to simmer until the potatoes begin to cook to pieces and the liquid thickens. Add the salt and pepper before the cooking is finished. More water may be required. Serves 4 hearty or 6 average eaters.

Les Johnson

Arcadia, Calif.

POTATOES EN CASSEROLE

8 small potatoes
3 tablespoons melted butter
  Salt and pepper to taste
I generous pinch of powdered rosemary
4 celery hearts

Pare potatoes to an even size; soak them for an hour in cold water and drain. Place the potatoes in a casserole; pour melted butter over them; sprinkle with salt, pepper, and rosemary. Cover the casserole and bake in a moderately hot oven (375°) for about 45 minutes or until potatoes are tender. Remove cover, garnish with celery hearts, and serve. Don't be disheartened if you have no small potatoes, for the larger potatoes can be sliced and the amount of butter varied to suit your particular requirements. The principle is still the same—potatoes baked in butter—and the result is a happy combination with any dinner.

A. E. DUNCAN
War department special services
Hollywood, Calif.

POTATO-CARROT PANCAKES

We found *Chef* Jake Klebanoff's "Potato-Carrot Pancakes" a welcome variation on the usual potato pancake. For one thing, the carrot counteracts the starchiness of the potato just enough so that you cease to worry about how much of this dish you should eat. We recommend it as a special side dish to accompany a simple main dish. Try it with a barbecue meal.

    2 cups grated raw potato pulp
    ½ cup grated carrot
    1 tablespoon grated onion
    1 egg
    ½ teaspoon salt
      Pepper to taste
    1 tablespoon flour

Drain off excess juice from potato pulp. Add balance of ingredients in proportion and order named. Mix well with fork or whipping spoon. Heat 4 tablespoons shortening or vegetable oil in a skillet. Drop in the batter by tablespoons and fry to a deep golden brown on each side.

Serve the potato-carrot pancakes along with the main meat course, especially delicious with roast or stewed meats of all kinds. Or, for a different and quick afternoon or evening snack, serve with apple-sauce.

Jake H. Klebanoff
Electrical engineer
San Francisco, Calif.

POTATO PUFFS

    3 medium-sized white potatoes
    1 medium-sized sweet potato
    ½ cup shortening or butter
    ½ cup flour
    2 eggs
    1 teaspoon salt
    ½ teaspoon pepper
      Few grains nutmeg

Pare potatoes, cut them in half, then boil in salted water till done. Pass potatoes through a ricer or food mill (or mash and beat thoroughly).

Put ½ cup boiling water and shortening in saucepan and bring to boiling point. Add flour and cook, stirring constantly until mixture leaves sides of pan. Cool this paste, then add beaten eggs one at a time, beating well after each addition. Combine potatoes and paste; add seasonings and nutmeg. Drop by spoonfuls into hot fat (375°) and cook until nicely browned. Drain on paper towel, dust with paprika, and garnish with parsley.

ANTHONY MARINCOVICH
Everett, Washington

BANANA POI

    6 ripe bananas
    2 tablespoons cornstarch
    1 tablespoon brown sugar
    ½ cup coconut milk
      Grated coconut

Banana *Poi* deserves a permanent place in Western cook books; it is more than a novelty. This adaptation of the original *poi* can be served as an interesting substitute for potatoes.

Boil bananas whole with the skins on until soft; about 30 minutes should be sufficient. Peel and mash, mixing in the cornstarch and brown sugar, and cook 5 minutes more. Pour the mixture into a buttered cake tin (it should be about 1 inch thick), and bake slowly for about 1 hour, or until golden brown. Cut into 1-inch squares and serve hot with a sauce made by combining the coconut milk and the grated coconut.

R. A. GREENWADE
Phoenix, Arizona

BARBECUED PINEAPPLE

Cut pineapple lengthwise in 8 sections. Place these spears in a baking pan and drip honey over the fruit. Let stand for ½ hour, and then grill over the open fire.

M. A. CONEY
Real estate broker
Piedmont, Calif.

eggs

cheese

SCRAMBLED EGGS SUPREME

    4 eggs
    2 tablespoons cream per egg (or a
        little less if desired)
    4 green onions, minced
     Salt and pepper to taste
     Dash of Worcestershire sauce
     Butter or margarine
    I package (3 oz.) cream cheese

Put the eggs, cream, onions, and seasonings in a mixing bowl, and beat well with a rotary beater. Melt a little butter or margarine in the top of a double boiler, put in the egg mixture, and cook over boiling water, stirring constantly, until done "easy." Then crumble the cream cheese into the eggs, folding the eggs lightly over it. Serve at once, with or without more minced green onions on the top. Serves 2.

The secret here is not to let the cream cheese melt; it should just be combined "loosely" with the eggs!

JEAN S. SPIGLER
Plant engineer metal industry
San Francisco, Calif.

SWISS SCRAMBLED EGGS

For a lazy breakfast or brunch, *Chef* Kenneth B. Fry prescribes an egg dish made with Swiss cheese.

To counteract the rubbery consistency of melted Swiss cheese, he sprinkles finely sifted bread crumbs on top of the dish just before it goes in the oven.

    3 tablespoons butter
    8 eggs
    ½ cup milk or light cream
    ½ teaspoon salt
     Pepper to taste
     Seasoned salt to taste
    ½ pound package thinly sliced processed
        Swiss cheese
    I tablespoon finely sifted dry bread crumbs

Melt 2 tablespoons of the butter in skillet. Beat eggs with milk or cream, salt, and pepper, and pour into skillet, stirring constantly with fork. Continue to stir until

eggs are set but still soft and not dry. They are to be cooked more in the oven and, therefore, must definitely be left soft! Pour into a buttered 9 by 1½-inch round baking dish. Sprinkle lightly with seasoned salt, top with sliced Swiss cheese, dot with small portions of the remaining tablespoon of butter, and sprinkle with the bread crumbs. Bake in a hot (400°) oven until the top is lightly browned, about 10 minutes. Serves 4 to 6.

Bureau chief, state fair
Sacramento, Calif.

SCRAMBLED EGGS
AND WATER CHESTNUTS

Few *Chefs of the West* escape exposure to the cooking methods and combinations developed by the Chinese. This influence is obvious in the recipe that follows. Sterling J. May is willing to go to considerable trouble to find the water chestnuts for his dish.

    8 slices bacon
    1 large onion
    4 to 6 water chestnuts
    4 eggs
     Tabasco sauce to taste

Stack up the bacon slices and slice them crosswise into little pieces about a quarter of an inch wide. Put them in a heavy frying pan over medium heat. While bacon is frying, peel and very thinly slice the onion and the water chestnuts. After the bacon is browned, drain off nearly all of the drippings. Then break the 4 eggs into the pan. (Don't break the yolks yet.) Over the eggs, spread the onion and water chestnut slices, adding about 1 drop of Tabasco per egg. (Do not salt.)

As the eggs turn white on the bottom, break the yolks and turn the eggs with a pancake turner. As you do so, mix them with the onions and chestnuts. Avoid letting the onions rest on the hot pan very long, as they burn easily. Cook until eggs suit those who eat them. Serves 4.

When you break the yolks only at the very last, your eggs turn out a molten gold and silver. You get all-yellow color when you mix yolks and whites before cooking.

Sterling J May

Postmaster
Sisters, Oregon

Chef May cuts his onion into slices about 1/16 inch thick. "This I do on a small slow cutter." If you have a mechanical or human "small slow cutter" in the house, by all means put it, him, or her, to work. We did the best we could without assistance.

CURRIED SCRAMBLED EGGS, BEURRE NOIR

E. G. Stockton, of La Jolla, California, sends us an unpretentious recipe which owes its distinction to the pungent and positive characteristics of curry. If you like the racy flavor of the East Indian condiment, your eyes will sparkle after your first mouthful of *Chef* Stockton's concoction, but if your palate craves more mild treatment, a slight pinch or even a few grains of curry powder will suffice.

        6 eggs
        1 teaspoon curry powder
    ½ teaspoon salt
        6 tablespoons cream
        4 slices bacon
        1 small onion, minced
    ½ green pepper, grated or minced
    ¼ cup butter

Beat eggs until light. Dissolve curry powder and salt in cream, and add to beaten eggs. Fry bacon until crisp, remove from skillet, drain, and chop fine. Pour surplus grease from skillet, leaving only enough to sauté the onion and pepper. When they are tender and delicately browned, add the chopped bacon and beaten eggs. Scramble over low heat with as little stirring as possible. Brown the butter in a saucepan and pour over eggs as served. Serves 3 or 4.

When accompanied by hot biscuits and strawberry preserves, this makes a breakfast long to be remembered!

E. G. STOCKTON
La Jolla, California

PORTUGUESE SAUSAGE OMELETTE

On Sunday morning—long after the last night's guests have departed, you have slept long and lazy, you get up with a hearty appetite, but no one in the family can decide exactly what he would like to eat—try the "Portuguese Sausage Omelette," as cooked by *Chef* J. N. Phillips of Honolulu.

Any combination of tomatoes, green peppers, and onions is enough to give a dish the added title, "Spanish," or "Portuguese," especially if the recipe also calls for plenty of pepper. In this case the addition of genuine Portuguese sausage makes the claim legitimate.

Incidentally, you will find a baked omelette easier to produce and far less apt to fall than the usual omelette, especially on those occasions when the gang doesn't respond to the first call.

    ½ cup Portuguese sausage, chopped
        2 tablespoons butter
        1 green pepper
    ½ onion, chopped
    ½ cup sliced celery
        A few green onion tops, sliced
        2 tomatoes, chopped
        6 eggs
        6 tablespoons milk
        Salt and pepper to taste

Fry the sausage in the butter, at the same time gradually adding the pepper, onion, celery, onion tops, and, lastly, the tomatoes. Time the length of cooking so that the vegetables will be slightly undercooked. Beat eggs, mix with milk, add sausage and vegetables to milk-egg mixture, season to taste, and place in a round baking pan of 9-inch diameter so that the depth of the mixture will be 1½ to 2 inches.

Bake for about 20 minutes in a moderate oven (350°) or until done (I use the toothpick test to determine this). Cut into serving size portions and serve with hot buttered toast and plenty of coffee. Serves 4.

J n Phillips

Honolulu

"On the anniversary of the discovery of gold, a celebration was held in Hangtown"

HANGTOWN FRY

Placerville, California, has borne its present name for a century. But old-timers will remember that the town in its brawling youth was called Hangtown—for certain blunt and straightforward reasons. And so it is that the only native dish of the whole Mother Lode region is still called the "Hangtown Fry." Today you still find versions of it listed on the menus of many Western restaurants.

One story has it that this dish came of a gold miner's extravagant hunger, in the days when "Wheelbarrow John" Studebaker and a butcher named Philip Armour were well-known Hangtown citizens. To this miner's request for the most expensive food in the house, an obliging restaurant cook whipped up a spur-of-the-moment creation built around oysters and eggs.

Eggs were probably available within a hundred miles. But oysters came from Baltimore in tins of a dozen. They were $11 a can in Hangtown, or just about $1.00 an oyster.

Now *Chef* George W. Hoffman of Los Angeles has his own story of the Hangtown Fry, backed by a magnificent recipe.

"I have seen several versions of what was *called* the California Hangtown Fry," says he, "but I'm sure my formula as set down here is the *original* and is *correct*."

(Whatever its lineage, his offering is triumphantly right for those times when man comes to the table mightily famished, as at a noonday breakfast.)

"It was handed down to me more than 50 years ago, in 1899, to be exact. I was just a kid then and was working in the Montez Cafe in Grass Valley, California.

"The chef in charge, an old man, had taken quite an interest in me and was trying to help me in my culinary efforts. One day when Hangtown Fry was listed on the menu, he explained it to me and claimed he had seen the original served at a memorable banquet.

"On the anniversary of the discovery of gold, a celebration was held in Hangtown. In the evening, Marshall and Sutter were guests of honor at the banquet in Carey (or Cary) House, the best hotel in Hangtown. The chef, whose name has been lost to history, set forth a remarkably fine repast, whose main dish was a beautiful fried oyster creation."

Serve individually on a large (12-inch) platter or large dinner plate. Spread the garnish for the artistic effect; don't crowd. Remember, the Hangtown is a feast for the eyes as well as the stomach.

Garnish the platter all the way around with leaves of dark green curly mustard, the points of the leaves extending high above the edge of platter. Run shredded lettuce down the center of the platter and douse it liberally with special Hangtown Sauce.

For each platter, bread and fry 6 medium-sized oysters to a beautiful golden brown. Fry 4 little pig sausages (or use 4 finger-size patties of country sausage). Make a tightly rolled 1-egg French omelet. Quarter 1 hard-cooked egg.

Lean 3 oysters against each side of the lettuce bed, on each side of the platter. Place 2 sausages, formed in the shape of a V, at each end of the platter. Lay omelet on top of lettuce bed with a slice of lemon at each end of it. Garnish outer edge of platter with sliced tomatoes, quarters of hard-cooked egg, and radish roses twined in between sprigs of parsley.

Now sprinkle over all a pinch of finely chopped parsley. Serve with generous helping of crisp shoestring potatoes.

Sauce

    1 pint mayonnaise
    1 cup catsup
    ½ cup tomato juice
    1 cup chili sauce
    4 tablespoons chopped ripe olives
    4 tablespoons fine chopped sweet pickles
    2 tablespoons lemon juice
    1½ teaspoons grated onion
    1 tablespoon Worcestershire sauce
    1 tablespoon paprika
    1 teaspoon monosodium glutamate

Blend with electric mixer or wire whisk. Makes about 3 pints of sauce, enough for 12 generous servings.

Geo. W. Hoffman

Los Angeles

Chef Hoffman adds: "In late years we have found all manner of shellfish very suitable to Hangtowns — Pismo clams, scallops, small butter-fried shrimp, large French-fried prawns, and, above all, strips of ABALONE."

ONION OMELET

How do you make an omelet? There are as many ways as there are cooks! This is still another way . . . with results that will please and surprise.

    1 tablespoon butter
    6 or 8 green onions, tops and all, chopped
        fine
    ½ cup dry white wine, or sherry
    5 eggs
    ½ cup thick cream
    ½ teaspoon salt
    ¼ teaspoon celery salt
    ¼ teaspoon Beau Monde seasoning
    ½ teaspoon Worcestershire sauce
    Freshly ground black pepper

Melt butter in frying pan, add onions, and cook over medium heat, stirring frequently. After several minutes, add wine. Cover, and simmer until onions start to soften, then remove cover and cook slowly, stirring often until wine is all cooked away. While onions are cooking, break 5 eggs in bowl and beat thoroughly. Add cream and seasonings. Mix with onions and pour into greased baking dish. Place in hot oven (375°) and bake for 20 to 25 minutes or until light golden brown. Reduce oven heat slightly when omelet starts to rise and color.

Louis A Woodward

Office supplies salesman
Oakland, Calif.

HOLZHACKERSCHMARREN

B. N. Prieth, of Carmel Valley, California, earns his *Chef's* emblem in the breakfast department. "On camping and mountain climbing trips in Germany, I came across an easy and solid breakfast recipe called *Schmarren*, or *Holzhackerschmarren* (wood cutter's *schmarren*)." The addition of flour smooths out the texture of scrambled eggs, counteracts any tendency toward wateriness, and makes the dish more hearthy.

    (for each person)
    1 egg
    1 tablespoon milk
    1 tablespoon flour
    Salt and pepper to taste

Simply mix all ingredients and cook in buttered or bacon greased pan as you would ordinarily scramble eggs. If desired, add 1 sausage, cooked and cut up, or 1 slice partly cooked bacon per egg.

B. N. Prieth

Lumbering
Carmel Valley, Calif

HUEVOS RANCHEROS

Win Wylie of Alma, California, used to drink tequila highballs in Mexico City. The next morning he always breakfasted on *Huevos Rancheros*. As it is an egg dish, and probably has been prepared by a rancher at some time, we suppose it is entitled to its name. Dip a tortilla quickly into a pan of hot shallow oil. Then place two fried eggs on top and pour a heated can of chili con carne (without beans) over them and serve.

Win Wylie, Jr
Alma, Calif.

THE COLONEL'S HAM AND EGGS

Chef Fallows is somewhat modest about his winning breakfast idea, claiming that he just stumbled onto it while brewing up ideas in the kitchen. Ham-and-pineapple combinations are familiar, but we think you'll agree that *Chef* Fallows explores a new taste sensation in his version.

    1 slice ham, cut 1 inch thick
    Sliced pineapple
    4 eggs

Place ham on rack over shallow pan and shove under broiler. Broil on one side, turn, then cover with pineapple slices. When done to proper degree, remove to warm place and break eggs gently into juices that have dripped into pan. Return to broiler until set. Season with salt and fresh ground pepper. Serve at once. Serves 4.

Col. R.F. Fallows
Col. U.S. Air Force
Tucson, Arizona

BAUREN FRÜHSTÜCK

Did you ever notice how a man who enters a restaurant uncertain of his appetite or the quality of the fare is prone to order ham and eggs? You'll find that most dishes popular for breakfast carry a kind of universal passport, honored anywhere, and at any time.

For example, here is a dish just as suitable for tapering off an evening as for welcoming a bright new day. J. Jay Anderson says, "Bauren Frühstück" (Farmer's Breakfast) is "a modification of a breakfast that I tasted in Germany and Switzerland years ago."

The extra amount of milk gives a custard consistency to the whole mixture. For our taste, the potatoes should be well-browned until crisp and chewy.

    6 slices bacon, diced
    1 tablespoon butter
    ½ medium-sized green pepper, chopped
    1 tablespoon parsley, finely chopped
    1 small onion slice, chopped
    2 medium potatoes, cooked and chopped
    4 eggs
    1 cup milk
    ¼ teaspoon monosodium glutamate
    ½ teaspoon salt
    Pepper to taste

Fry bacon slowly in frying pan. Pour off some of the rendered fat and replace with the butter. Add pepper, parsley, and onion; cook just until starting to brown. Then add potatoes (or brown them with the previous mixture, if you prefer). Stir frequently to prevent burning.

Stir up eggs and milk in a bowl, and add monosodium glutamate, salt, and pepper. After potatoes are completely heated, and other ingredients thoroughly browned, pour egg mixture into the frying pan. Stir just enough to incorporate evenly, then cook over low heat to simmer until set.

If you cook in a Pyrex frying pan with a removable handle, serve your *Farmer's Breakfast* in this at the table. Garnish with parsley sprays and toast wedges.

Cut in wedges, like a pie, and serve hot with corn bread or whole wheat toast, marmalade or honey, and plenty of coffee. This will serve 4 generously.

J. Jay Anderson
Salesman
Salt Lake City, Utah

OEUFS AU BEURRE NOIR

"Don't be fooled by the sweet simplicity of this recipe," says A. E. Clamp of Sacramento. Every *Chef* should understand the technique of frying an egg to perfection. The general approach—treat very gently —is implied here, and an interesting new flavor has been added.

    6 tablespoons butter
    6 eggs
    ¼ cup torn (not chopped), washed, and dried
        parsley
    1 tablespoon white vinegar
    Salt and pepper to taste

Put 2 tablespoons butter into a saucepan and heat without browning. Break the eggs and slip them carefully into the hot butter. Fry gently until lightly set. Place 4 tablespoons butter in a small saucepan and heat until it is a deep golden tint. Add torn parsley to the butter. Shake parsley around in the pan until it is crisp.

Butter an ovenproof dish, slide in the lightly fried eggs, pour over the butter and parsley, and keep hot in the oven. Heat saucepan again with vinegar in it, bring to a boil, then pour over the eggs and parsley. Serve. Serves 3 with 2 eggs apiece.

Chemical engineer
Sacramento, Calif.

SUNDAY MORNING BREAKFAST CASSEROLE

    6 tablespoons yellow cornmeal
    1½ cups milk
    ½ teaspoon salt
    ¼ cup catsup
    ½ cup shredded bran
    ½ cup grated cheese
    8 pork sausages, cooked brown
    4 eggs

Cook the cornmeal until thick in salted milk. Add the catsup and the bran and spread it in a greased, shallow baking dish. Sprinkle with grated cheese, and arrange browned sausages in square formation on top. Break eggs inside sausage squares and bake the concoction at 375° for 30 minutes, or until eggs are done to your satisfaction. Serves two with big appetites.

Covina Highlands, Calif.

HAM AND EGGS AND MUSHROOMS À LA A.B. STEFFENS

Robert W. Steffens of Redwood City, California, doesn't favor the modest approach. "If this combination doesn't deserve the term ineluctable, then I'm no chef and don't deserve the title."

(NOTE: *Ineluctable:* not to be overcome; irresistible; insurmountable. We concede. It does. He is. He does.)

"My father claims credit for originating it some sixty years back, and since I have never run across it in any other dining room, public or private, I guess he did." Next time we're going to cut up the ham in pie shaped pieces beforehand to make serving easier than we found it.

    Large slice of ham about 3/16 inch thick
    ½ pound fresh mushrooms
    4 tablespoons butter
    8 eggs

Cut ham in sections to fit in bottom of heavy pan and fry lightly on one side. Slice mushrooms and fry in butter until nearly done. Turn ham sections over and cover bottom of pan with same. Then break the eggs over the top, pricking each yolk with a fork so that it runs and flattens out. Distribute mushrooms over the top. Salt and pepper to taste. Cover well and cook over slow flame until eggs are done. Can also be finished off in oven if so desired, but cover, in either case, to keep in the luscious flavors. Cut out like a pie. Serves 4.

Painting contractor
Redwood City, Calif.

EGGS ANGELICA

"In the television studios, or around any of the other facets of show business, the mention of 'egg' is not particularly flattering," says Bob Glassburn of San Francisco. "But after the TV show is over and the results of our efforts are floating around in space, a mention of 'Eggs Angelica' is greeted with much anticipation."

With work hours and meal hours both quite irregular, *Chef* Glassburn, coming home at odd hours, felt "the necessity to brighten up the table with something tempting to the eye and appetite . . . something easy to fix . . . but containing the condiments that only a true 'kitchen chemist' would use."

The resulting egg mixture is sprinkled with greens, reds, and yellows. It is colorful, but we wouldn't call it gaudy because it has such excellent taste. We suggest that you try it on your color wheel.

For *Chef* Glassburn, the full accolade.

```
2 tablespoons minced white onion
2 tablespoons diced green pepper
2 tablespoons butter or margarine
⅓ cup top milk
3 eggs
  Coarsely ground black pepper
  Salt to taste
2 tablespoons diced pimiento
⅓ cup grated sharp Cheddar cheese
  Parsley
```

Sauté onion and green pepper in butter over low heat until clear. They should be crisp but not brown. Add milk to eggs and beat until light and foamy.

Pour foaming eggs into pan with sautéed onions and green pepper; raise heat slightly and stir for about 1 minute or until well combined; generously sprinkle with coarse black pepper, add salt to taste. Add pimiento and cheese to mixture and fold continuously until cooked to desired consistency. Just before serving, garnish liberally with chopped parsley. Serves 2 to 3 persons.

Note: Eggs should remain foamy until almost cooked. Careful dicing of pepper and pimiento into small cubes distributes color more evenly.

Bob Glassburn
San Francisco

CORONADO SUNRISE

Chef Carl Shumate returns to the fold with a dish whose name, "Coronado Sunrise," sounds like the title of a popular song. It is really two separate dishes, and the serving of the two together calls for some fast and good staging in the oven.

The rolls are so simple and succulent that you could serve them alone for breakfast, lunch, or snacks. They are not at all messy—very easy to eat out of hand.

You serve the eggs with their eyes open— after an unusual bit of preliminary maneuvering. The important thing is to remove them from the oven before the yolks get hard, and serve *immediately!*

Don't forget there are some who don't like eggs "sunny side up," like the facetious member of our test panel who commented, "I just don't like sunrises that look like eggs." It might be well to take a preliminary survey so you could make up special orders of "scrambled" for those who prefer them, or a puffy omelet in which you could use the same seasonings.

```
1 small pinch ground coriander
⅛ teaspoon curry powder
¼ teaspoon chili powder
⅛ teaspoon freshly ground pepper
¼ teaspoon baking powder
¼ teaspoon onion salt
4 tablespoons table cream
6 egg whites
½ tablespoon bacon drippings
4 egg yolks
¼ teaspoon paprika
```

Combine coriander, curry powder, chili powder, pepper, baking powder, and onion salt; then blend these well into the cream. Beat egg whites slightly, gradually adding the cream mixture. Grease 4 individual shallow baking dishes with the bacon drippings. Pour egg mixture into each dish and float one egg yolk in the center of each. Sprinkle with the paprika. Bake at 375° about 25 minutes, or until egg yolks have barely set and the rest of the mixture is slightly browned on top.

Rolls:
```
2 slices canned ham, medium thick
4 slices processed American cheese
2 frankfurter rolls, split
1 tablespoon butter
1 tablespoon prepared English mustard
```

Trim all fat from ham. Cut ham and cheese into pieces slightly smaller than the tops of the split rolls. Sauté ham in butter until slightly browned. Sprinkle rolls with some of the ham drippings. Coat lightly with mustard. On each roll lay a slice of cheese, then a slice of ham; brush with rest of ham drippings. Place on a cooky sheet and put in oven at the same time you put in the eggs. Leave there for 15 to 20 minutes, or until cheese is well melted and ham has browned well around the edges. Remove from oven, cover, keep warm until eggs are ready.

"Fast and good staying in the oven—then serve immediately"

Served with large glasses of fresh orange juice poured over ice cubes, these eggs and ham rolls make a breakfast for 4.

Carl Shumate

San Diego

WHIZ WEDGES

    ¼ pound bacon, cut in small pieces
    4 eggs
    10 soda crackers, crushed
    1 heaping tablespoon flour
    ¼ cup water
    Salt and pepper to taste
    Milk
    Chopped green onions, tops and all, or
       chives
    Thinly sliced white bread

Fry bacon in a skillet until quite crisp. While this is going on, break the eggs into a bowl; add the crackers, flour, water, salt, and pepper; mix all together with a spoon; add enough milk to make a thin batter. Pour this mixture over the hot, fried bacon, leaving all grease in the pan; cook very slowly. When almost done, sprinkle with chopped onions, and then arrange slices of bread over top of mixture.

Continue cooking slowly until egg mixture is set. Cut in wedge-shape pieces, pie-fashion, and serve immediately. (Grated cheese may be sprinkled over the bread if desired, and the whole set under the broiler for a minute before serving.) Serves 4 or 5.

CHARLES E. SWANSON
Langley, Washington

EXPENSIVE SUNDAY BRUNCH

Place ¼ pound butter, or margarine, in heavy iron skillet over slow fire. Then add:

    1 pound well-trimmed beef sirloin chopped
       into ¼-inch cubes
    2 chives, chopped
    1 clove garlic, crushed or minced
    1 can (3 oz.) sliced mushrooms, chopped
    Pinch of oregano
    Pinch of monosodium glutamate
    Salt and pepper to taste

Sauté until meat is well done, stirring occasionally. Break in 6 eggs and scramble the whole business. Serve when eggs are firm but not dry. Serves 2 hungry people.

Suggestion: With this dish, serve toasted English muffins or rye bread toast, and strawberry jam.

Francis H Wood

Stockton, Calif.

MEXICAN RABBIT

When an international dish settles in some localities, it undergoes a subtle change. Nothing is more natural than the process by which Welsh rabbit became "Mexican Rabbit" in the hands of Weldon F. Heald of Flying H Ranch, Hereford, Arizona.

"Living only four miles from the Mexican border, we have stepped up the flavoring in most of our food, including one of my old favorites, Welsh rabbit (or rarebit, if you prefer). What I call Mexican Rabbit really has a tangy flavor, not hot but zestful. Cut your cheese, good American, Cheddar, or what have you, into small pieces. Thin shavings are best.

    2 tablespoons butter
    1 tablespoon cornstarch
    1 cup light cream
    1 pound sharp Cheddar cheese, diced
    ½ teaspoon salt
    ¼ teaspoon celery salt
    ½ teaspoon mustard
      Dash of Cayenne
      Drop of Tabasco
    1 tablespoon Worcestershire sauce
    2 full tablespoons Mexican hot sauce
      Buttered toast

Melt butter, blend in cornstarch, add cream and stir until smooth. Cook until slightly thickened, about 2 minutes. Add cheese and stir until melted. Add seasonings and pour over hot buttered toast. Serves four.

Weldon F. Heald

Hereford, Ariz.

EGGS ROMANOFF

"Eggs Romanoff" has a rich Russian sound, suggesting an imperial ball, or a presentation at the court of the czar. Try it for a late Sunday morning breakfast or brunch when you want to eat like a king. Charles F. Stauffacher, Jr., has a simple way of fitting it to the size of the company: "Use a 7-inch pan for 4 eggs, a 9-inch pan for 6 to 8 eggs, a 12-inch pan for 10 to 12 eggs." We present it in the jumbo size.

    18 slices bacon (approximately 1 pound), cut
       in half crosswise
    ¾ pound American or sharp processed
       Cheddar cheese
    12 eggs
       Juice of ½ lemon (1½ tablespoons)
    ½ teaspoon Worcestershire
       Salt, pepper, garlic salt, monosodium
       glutamate, and paprika to taste
    1 tablespoon chopped chives or parsley

Cover the bottom of a 12-inch frying pan with bacon slices, fitting them close together so they will still cover the bottom of the pan after the shrinkage of cooking. (Thin ham slices may be substituted, if desired.) Cook the bacon on one side, pour off fat, and turn over. Cover bacon with thin slices of cheese. Then drop in eggs so yolks are fairly close together; the final product will be ½ to 1 inch thick.

Mix in a cup the lemon juice and Worcestershire. Season eggs with salt, pepper, garlic salt, monosodium glutamate, paprika, and chopped chives or parsley. Sprinkle lemon juice mixture over top of eggs. Cook slowly until whites of eggs are firm. Place under broiler for just a few seconds to cook whites of eggs on top, but do not let yolks become hard. Use a sharp knife to cut eggs into individual servings. Serves 6 to 12 for breakfast or brunch, depending on heartiness of appetites concerned.

Charles F. Stauffacher, Jr.

San Francisco

pastes

rice

cornmeal

NEW ORLEANS JAMBALAYA

L. J. Adams swears this is a New Orleans favorite—the recipe brought West by his mother. "The secret is to follow the directions explicitly. The long, slow cooking is the key to success, and this is typical of all Creole cookery." We vote "for more attention to the lost art of cooking," too, Mr. Adams.

    1 cup uncooked rice
    2 tablespoons bacon drippings
    2 medium-sized dry onions
    1 small can (6 oz.) tomato paste
    2 green peppers, diced
    4 green onions, sliced, tops and all
    ½ pound boiled ham, diced
    1 pound small link sausages, sliced
        into small rounds
    Salt and pepper

Cook the rice in boiling salted water; drain. Put bacon drippings in iron skillet, add the chopped onions, and fry until the edges begin to brown. Then add the tomato paste, and the green peppers, green onions, ham, and sausages. Cook, stirring constantly, for 15 minutes. Add the boiled rice, salt and pepper to taste, and cook on a slow fire for 1 hour, stirring every now and then. Serves 8.

L. J. Adams

Mathematician
Santa Monica, Calif.

SOPA DE ARROZ

This recipe for Mexican Fried Rice or *Sopa de Arroz* comes from the period in Mexico's history when Porfirio Diaz was its president.

    1 cup rice
    2 tablespoons fat or cooking oil
    1 medium-sized onion, chopped
    2 or 3 small tomatoes, mashed
    3 cups soup stock
    Salt to taste

Wash rice in hot water, drain, and dry. Brown it slowly in the fat, stirring constantly. Add the onion, tomatoes, soup stock, and salt. Cook the mixture over a low flame without stirring until rice is soft and dry. If rice is not soft when

liquid has evaporated, add more liquid. Boiling water may be used in place of soup stock, but stock makes a tastier *sopa*. The finished dish may be garnished with slices of hard-cooked eggs and olives. A Mexican *casuela* or pottery casserole is to be preferred rather than a skillet for making this dish. A *casuela* also simplifies the problem of serving, for it may be brought directly to the table.

E. P. SAFFORD
La Jolla, Calif.

PILAFF

    1 cup raw brown rice
    3 tablespoons oil
    Seasoning
    2 cups soup stock or canned soup
        (or slightly more)
    Butter

Your palate will approve of this way with rice whether you serve it with or without Shish Kebab.

In a large skillet, fry rice in the oil. Stir it constantly until it turns a golden brown. Then season it and pour on enough soup stock to cover. Cover the pan and simmer over low heat until all the liquid is absorbed and the rice is almost dry. Then top it with butter and serve.

RALPH G. DENECHAUD
Hollywood, Calif.

RICE WITH SOUR CREAM AND CHEESE

    1½ cups uncooked rice
    ½ pound sharp cheese, grated
    Salt, pepper, and Cayenne to taste
    Pinch of sugar
    1 cup sour cream
    Milk (about 2 or 3 tablespoons)

Boil or steam the rice until tender, then put it in a mixing bowl. Add cheese, and season to taste with the salt, pepper, Cayenne, and sugar. (The pinch of sugar is to bring out the flavor of the other ingredients.) Now thin the sour cream with the milk and pour it over the rice and cheese. Mix all thoroughly, and pour into a buttered baking dish. The rice and cheese mixture should be well moistened, but not "runny." Bake in a moderate oven (350°) for 20 to 25 minutes, or until the cheese is melted.

ROBERT MIDDLEMASS
Actor and writer
North Hollywood, Calif.

ALMOST WILD RICE

J. D. Stephens of Fresno, California, truly loves wild rice. He loves it so well that he has invented a substitute that he can eat between true wild rice occasions. "One bout with this," says he, "and I'm sure you will concur that those Minnesota Indians can continue sending the wild variety to Fort Knox."

The surprising addition of vermicelli is designed to keep the rice grains separate. Be sure, though, that you break it into very small pieces—about the size of the rice grains, if possible.

    ½ cube (4 tablespoons) butter
    1 twist vermicelli (figure "8" bundle)
    1 cup long grained rice
    1 can (10½ oz.) bouillon
    1 small can (2 or 3 oz.) sliced mushrooms
    ½ medium sized onion, grated
    ½ teaspoon salt
    ½ teaspoon freshly ground black pepper
    2 cups water

Melt butter in skillet, break up vermicelli into very small pieces or crush, and brown in butter. Add the rice, bouillon, mushrooms, grated onion, salt, pepper, 1 cup water, and stir. Cover and simmer for 45 minutes, adding the additional water during the cooking process.

Fresno, California

RISOTTO ALLA RATTO

    1 small yellow onion, chopped
    2 tablespoons butter or margarine
    1 cup uncooked rice
    4 cups clear chicken broth
    1 can (4 oz.) button mushrooms
    Salt
    ½ teaspoon saffron
    ½ cup grated Parmesan-type cheese

Sauté onion in butter until transparent but not brown, keeping the heat low. Add rice and stir until each grain is coated with butter. Add 1 cup boiling chicken broth and cook over low heat, stirring frequently, until rice has absorbed liquid. Repeat process with remaining broth, adding, 1 cup at a time as rice absorbs it. (This will take about 20 minutes.) Add mushrooms. Taste the rice and add salt if needed. If the chicken broth has been seasoned, it may contribute enough salt. Then stir in saffron which has been dissolved in 1 tablespoon hot water or broth. Cook 5 minutes longer. Blend in the grated cheese and serve at once. Serves 4.

Stockton, Calif.

"Those Minnesota Indians can continue sending wild rice to Fort Knox"

PORK FRIED RICE

- 2 cups white rice
- 2 large pork chops, or an equal amount of lean pork, cut into small cubes
- 2 tablespoons olive or cooking oil
- ½ cup chopped green pepper
- ½ cup chopped green onions
- 4 tablespoons soy sauce
- 2 cups water

Wash rice thoroughly and drain. Brown meat in oil, using Dutch oven, over medium flame. Add one-half the chopped pepper and green onions. Continue cooking until pepper and onions are soft. Add soy sauce and cook 1 minute. Stir in rice, and mix thoroughly. Add water (this must always equal the amount of rice), bring quickly to boiling, place lid on pan, and reduce flame to simmer. Cook until dry, about half an hour. Avoid peeking. Remove from heat and mix in remaining green pepper and onion. Serves 6.

Ray A. Lindman *Attorney*
Pasadena, Calif.

CHINA RUN CURRY

- 2 onions, minced
- 6 stalks celery, thinly sliced
- 1 green apple, peeled and thinly sliced
- 4 tablespoons butter or margarine
- 4 teaspoons curry powder (or more, to taste)
- 2 cups diced, cooked chicken, beef, or lamb (free from fat)
- ¼ cup seeded raisins
- 1 cup chicken or meat stock
- Salt to taste
- 2 eggs
- ¼ cup cream or milk
- 1 cup raw rice
- ½ pound salted peanuts, chopped
- 2 bananas, sliced
- 1 bunch watercress
- Chutney or preserved ginger

Here is an exotic recipe for curry as it used to be prepared on the old Pacific Mail steamships on their China runs. It was obtained from the port steward during the first World War, and just as it was a famous course on board ship then, so it will become a favorite in your own dining saloon at home once you've tried it.

Sauté onions, celery, and apple in butter until transparent and tender. Blend in curry powder and cook a few minutes longer. Then add the meat, raisins, stock, and salt, and simmer very slowly for 20 minutes, stirring occasionally. When ready to serve, beat up the eggs with the cream and add to the curry.

(NOTE: If fresh coconut is available, the milk of the coconut may replace all or part of the broth. Also, add 2 tablespoons of grated coconut to the mixture before final simmering.)

Prepare the rice in a double boiler, steaming it so that it is cooked dry.

On a large, round platter arrange a border of watercress. Pack the cooked rice into a ring mold and unmold it in the center of the platter. Fill the center of the rice ring with the curry. Top with chopped peanuts (or grated fresh coconut, if available) and surround the rice with sliced bananas. Serve chutney or preserved ginger on the side. Serves 4.

Wildlife conservationist
San Francisco, Calif.

RICE WITH SWISS CHEESE

There's an unexpected "bite"—nippy and chewy—to the rice that Jack Plotkin recommends serving with any kind of meat. It is not intended as a main dish. And it loses its effectiveness if you let it get cold, or even cool, before eating. "The secret is cooking the rice exactly 15 minutes—no more or no less—and serving immediately."

"Exactly 15 minutes, no more, no less"

1 teaspoon salt
1½ cups water
1 cup uncooked rice
2 tablespoons butter or margarine
¼ pound (1 cup) grated Swiss cheese, chilled

Add salt to water and bring to a boil. Stir in rice; cover tightly. Simmer 15 minutes. Stir in butter; when butter is melted, quickly stir in grated cheese. Serve immediately! Serves 4.

Jack Flatkin

Librarian and lecturer
Palo Alto, Calif.

SPANISH RICE WITH BACON

We recommend this highly as food to take fishing. The addition of dried savory (easy to include in your camp kit) is one of the neat touches that lifts it above the commonplace.

"One of the neat touches that lifts it above the commonplace"

6 slices thick bacon
2 onions, chopped
2 cups canned tomatoes (or 2 cans tomato sauce)
2 cups cooked rice
1 teaspoon salt
1 level teaspoon dried savory (no more)

Cut bacon slices in 1-inch-square pieces, put into a heavy skillet, and cook until crisp. Then add onions. When they are soft, add the rest of the ingredients and simmer until heated through. Serves 4.

Now, for the fisherman: Pour onto a double sheet of aluminum foil, or a single sheet of heavy duty foil, and fold up with a "drug store wrap." This version of Spanish Rice is good eaten cold, or it can be heated over a tiny fire—the foil can be set right in the ashes.

George G. Cooper

Welder
Veradale, Washington

TURTA

Chef Boscacci, who sends us this Italian recipe, suggests that it be "turned out on a cake rack covered with waxed paper, allowed to cool, and cut into 2-inch squares." Try it that way if you wish, but we can guarantee equal pleasure if it's eaten hot, spoon bread fashion, and heightened in flavor with a tomato-herb sauce.

4 eggs
3 tablespoons olive oil
2 cups cooked white rice
1 cup grated dry Monterey Jack cheese
Salt and pepper to taste

Beat 3 of the eggs with a rotary beater; add olive oil and stir well; mix in the remaining ingredients.

Cover the bottom of a 6-by-10-inch baking dish, or a regular sized bread pan, with a little oil, and pour in the above mixture. Spread it evenly in the baking dish and cover with the remaining egg, well beaten. Bake in a moderate oven (350°) for 45 minutes, or until firm.

KENNETH BOSCACCI
Redwood City, Calif.

HUNTERS' TOASTED RICE

1 cup uncooked long grain rice
1 tablespoon olive oil
½ cup shelled almonds
1 tablespoon bacon drippings
½ onion, well chopped
1 clove garlic, minced
2 cups chicken broth or consommé

Toast the rice in olive oil in a skillet until the rice is golden brown. Blanch almonds. (Pour boiling water over them; let stand a few minutes, then drain; the skins come off easily.) Chop almonds into small pieces, and place in a skillet over low fire until browned, stirring occasionally. Remove and set aside. Put bacon drippings, onion, and garlic into the skillet and brown lightly. Add broth or consommé, toasted rice, and almonds; bring to a boil; cover and simmer for about 25 minutes, or until rice is tender. Serves 4 to 6.

A. W. Dolley

Los Angeles

SOUTH AFRICAN VELDT COUS-COUS

Cous-cous is semolina or wheat flour that resembles American farina when properly worked up. Originally it took the art of an Oriental people of great patience to prepare this entirely distinctive, but time-consuming, fare. Here are complete directions:

    1 (3½- to 4-pound) stewing chicken or
        2 or 3 pounds of lamb, beef, or veal
    2 red pimientos
    1 clove garlic
    ¾ cup butter, melted
    1 teaspoon red pepper
    1½ quarts water
    1 cup chickpeas soaked in water overnight
        (Garbanzas and chickpeas are identical)
    1 cup fresh shelled peas
    1 cup diced carrots
        Small white turnips
        A few string beans
        Hearts of artichokes
        Green vegetables in season
        (These are extenders or stretchers if and when
            necessary according to number of persons to
            be served)
    2 pounds of Cous-Cous. (It is best to use hominy
        grits as substitute for Cous-Cous. The grain
        being larger, it does not become as soggy as
        finer grains)

Disjoint chicken or cut up meat into small pieces. Mash the pimientos and garlic together very fine in a mortar, adding salt to taste. Add the melted butter and place this mixture in the lower part of a steam vessel. The steam vessel must have a colander or perforated bottom in the upper chamber, and a fitted cover, if possible. Add the chicken or meat to the mixture in the lower part of the vessel and place over a low heat to simmer in the butter until the meat is tender and well permeated with the seasonings. Add

the red pepper to give color and make the dish hot. Add the water and let boil over very low heat for 20 minutes or more. Add the vegetables. If fresh vegetables are not available, small dried lima beans, peas, beans, and the like may be used. Canned vegetables are not recommended. Place the cous-cous or hominy grits in the upper chamber of the cooking vessel. This chamber must be large enough to allow for the swelling and puffing of the granular substance without crowding. The steam from the cooking meat and vegetables must not be allowed to escape but must rise and penetrate into the cous-cous, flavoring and steaming it at the same time. A circular piece of coarse clean cheesecloth, single thickness, the size of the bottom of the upper chamber of the steam vessel, will keep the cous-cous—farina, hominy grits, or semolina—from running through the colander holes while it is still dry. As soon as steamed, it will hold and cook well by absorbing steam from the lower chamber.

Cook until the meat, water, and vegetables make a rich sauce. The cous-cous on top should be done by this time. Sogginess of the cous-cous is the thing to be avoided as much as possible. As one becomes more skilled in its preparation, the cous-cous will emerge grainy rather than soggy, the grains separating as rice does when prepared in the Chinese fashion.

To serve, use a large soup dish for each person. Place in each, 3 or 4 cups of the steamed cous-cous. Pour over the cous-cous the sauce that is in the lower part of the steam vessel. On top of this, arrange the pieces of meat or chicken. Arrange the peas and vegetables all around so that each dish will be colorful and appetizing.

Use plenty of sauce to moisten the cous-cous, and serve more of the hot sauce for those who prefer a highly seasoned dish.

Frisco Bert

M. BERTRAND COUCH
Investigator, Justice Department
San Francisco, Calif.

PIG IN THE CORN

Here's a dish that, with fruit and coffee, will supply a whole breakfast in camp. At home you can serve it as you would spoonbread.

    1½ cups yellow cornmeal
    ½ cup flour
    1 teaspoon salt
    2 teaspoons sugar
    3 teaspoons baking powder
    3 eggs, well beaten
    1¼ cups half-and-half (milk and cream)
    ½ cube (4 tablespoons) butter or margarine, melted
    1 pound lean sausage meat

Sift dry ingredients together; add to eggs, half-and-half, and butter; blend thoroughly.

Crumble sausage meat and fry until well done. Drain off fat.

Grease muffin tins, or individual foil pie tins. Pour in a layer of cornbread, sprinkle with a generous layer of cooked sausage meat, and pour in another layer of corn bread. Bake 15 minutes in a 400° oven. Makes 10 large muffins.

On a camping trip, just take along a box of prepared cornbread mix and use it with your sausage. If no oven is available, mix cornbread and cooked sausage together and cook as hot cakes in a frying pan on top of your camp fire.

Frank Calvert
Printing executive
Seattle, Washington

YORKSHIRE PUDDING

You can't cook this pudding unless you are roasting beef at the same time. Because the British, who originated the dish, often like it rather soggy, many Americans view it with disfavor. However, *Chef* Richard Simmons has a recipe for "Yorkshire Pudding" which should redeem it in many Westerners' eyes. He speaks with some feeling on the subject.

"Some irreverent persons have described this noble food as 'thick gravy with thin gravy on it.' But let them choke on lumpy mashed potatoes while we enjoy the following:"

"Let them choke on lumpy mashed potatoes"

Get plenty of extra suet with a sirloin tip roast. Break it up and render it in the same roasting pan with the meat—a slow oven (300°). About 45 minutes before the beef is due to emerge from the oven, mix together:

    2 cups flour
    ½ teaspoon salt
    1 teaspoon baking powder
    2 cups milk
    3 eggs
    6 tablespoons of fat from the roast

Sift flour, measure, then sift again with salt and baking powder into a bowl. Beat in milk, eggs, and drippings.

Pour this mixture into a greased deep pan large enough to hold it—batter should be no more than 1 inch deep. Bake for the first 15 minutes in the same oven with the roast. Remove the meat, raise the oven temperature to 425° for another 15-minute baking of the pudding. This will give ample time to make gravy with the rest of the pan drippings. The pudding is done when it attains a golden brown surface. Its texture should resemble that of a custard or an omelet, and the added fat will flavor it. Serve it with lots of gravy. This mixture will yield 6 to 10 portions, depending on how much you like Yorkshire Pudding. It is still good the next day.

Richard W Simmons
Chemical consultant
Bellingham, Washington

SUNDAY MORNING MUSH ALTADENA

After supper Saturday night, mix 3½ cups of cold water with 1 cup freshly ground yellow corn meal, 1 tablespoon salt, 8 whole black peppercorns, 1 cup wheat germ flakes, and 2 tablespoons corn oil in a covered metal (round bottom) pan. Put in oven and cook at 275° for 3½ hours. Then just before going to bed (oven still hot) take out the peppercorns (they float on top; count 'em, 8), stir up the mush and taste it to see if you forgot the salt. Put back in oven.

In the morning, turn cold mush out of the pan, slice it thin, and brown it on a slow griddle. Serve hot, with honey.

Edwin P. Arthur

Altadena, Calif.

STORNAWAY BANNOCKS

"Ideal to serve hot with barbecued spareribs or fried chicken," says *Chef* Chet L. Swital, of Beverly Hills, California, introducing "an old and rare recipe for Scotland's far-famed Stornaway Bannocks." For the record the bannock has come into our language as, "A cake of meal baked on a griddle or hot stone." Our taste testers, in true Western style, started trying it for size in all kinds of eating situations—"fun for breakfast . . . wonderful with baked beans . . . just right for finger eating on a damp Sunday afternoon."

    1 cup quick cooking rolled oats
    1 cup cornmeal
    1 cup buttermilk
    1/3 teaspoon soda
    1 tablespoon molasses
    1 tablespoon brown sugar
    2 tablespoons melted butter or margarine
        Grated peel of 1 lemon
    1/4 teaspoon ginger or mace
    1/2 teaspoon salt
        Honey

Mix all ingredients except honey, in the order given above, to a batter of heavy consistency. (If you like, barley flour may be used in place of cornmeal.) Heat a griddle or frying pan, well greased with ¼ cup bacon drippings. When it is smoking hot, scoop in batter to not more than ½-inch thickness. Fry 12 minutes on one side, then 6 minutes on the other side.

Remove to plate; slice in half as you would an English muffin. Butter like a sandwich and spread with honey. Replace top half, divide into sections as desired, and serve hot. Serves 6 to 8 as a hot bread adjunct to dinner.

Chet. L. Swital

Beverly Hills, Calif.

TAMPICO ENCHILADAS

"This recipe was learned in Tampico, on the East Coast of Mexico, about 30 years ago," says C. M. Carson of Ventura, California. "Ingredients have been 'translated' into products obtainable at any Mexican store. Quantities are all variable to taste.

    1 can (No. 2½) tomatoes with purée (solid
        pack tomatoes can be used, but are less
        desirable)
    1 pound ground beef
    4 pounds onions, chopped
    ½ pound chorizo (Mexican sausage)
    1 can (3 oz.) mole poblano, pipian ranchero,
        or adobado
    1 clove garlic, minced
    ½ teaspoon oregano (rubbed between the
        hands to pulverize)
    ½ teaspoon cumin
    ¼ teaspoon pepper
    1 tablespoon Worcestershire
    ¼ teaspoon Tabasco or hot pepper juice of
        some kind
    2 dozen corn tortillas
        Salad oil
    1 pound Cheddar cheese, sliced

Put tomatoes in a large pot. Fry ground beef until done and add to pot. Save fat and fry onions until soft. Add to pot. Skin and fry chorizo. Add to pot with mole poblano. Add garlic and all seasonings. Simmer several hours and stir frequently to free of lumps.

Fry tortillas lightly in salad oil. Put 1 or 2 heaping tablespoons of sauce from pot on each tortilla, then fold two sides over until they overlap at center. Put slice of cheese on each. Put on flat pan in moderate oven (350°) until cheese is melted. Serve with Mexican beans, green salad, and either red or white wine. Serves 6 persons as a main dish, allowing 4 enchiladas to a serving.

Carlton M. Carson.

Geologist
Ventura, Calif.

ENCHILADAS CALIFORNIA

"Being a native Californian, I enjoy eating in Spanish," says Charles L. Ballard of Los Angeles. "These remain my favorite enchiladas. Perhaps it's the olives, perhaps it's frying the tortillas before filling them; but they seem to have a rich succulence that other versions lack."

This is a nice lively dish. The olives have an excellent stabilizing effect much like that of green peppers. They tend to hold other ingredients in balance and keep them from running off on wild tangents of their own.

Don't overdo the final baking of these or they'll be too dry.

"Always working toward perfection"

    1 dozen tortillas
    Salad oil

Sauce:

    1 medium sized can (10 oz.) red chili sauce
    1 small can (8 oz.) tomato sauce

Filling:

    2 or 3 bunches onions, finely sliced (include
        some of the green tops)
    1 small can (4½ oz.) chopped ripe olives
    ½ pound (2 cups) coarsely grated Cheddar
        cheese

Fry tortillas in ¼ inch hot oil, about 2 seconds per side. They should barely start to huff and puff before being turned or removed from pan. Stack on warm plate and begin immediately on the assembling. (The sauce and the filling ingredients should be already mixed—save a little of the cheese for sprinkling on top of each enchilada.)

Dip warm tortilla in warm sauce (pour a little at a time into a plate or a flat pan to make this task easy), spread a generous tablespoon of filling across center, roll, and secure with toothpick. Place all tortillas close together in a greased baking pan or dish, spread thinly with sauce, and sprinkle with the remaining cheese. Keep in refrigerator overnight, or bake immediately, about 10 to 15 minutes at 350°, just enough to heat without drying out the tortillas.

Serve with refried beans, *guacamole* over lettuce, a fresh fruit dessert, and beer or iced tea. Will serve 4.

Charles L Ballard
Los Angeles

ENCHILADAS DE ACAPULCO

    12 chiles anchas (chee'lace ahn'chahs),
        California long chiles
     6 chiles tepines (tay-pee'nace) small and *hot*
     1 clove garlic
     1 teaspoon oregano (oh-ray'gahn-no)
     1 teaspoon salt
    ¼ teaspoon black pepper
     6 coriander seeds
     3 large onions
     2 tablespoons margarine or olive oil
     1 large can tomato puree
    1½ pounds lean veal or chicken
     1 small can ripe olives
    ¼ pound blanched almonds
    ½ pound dry grating cheese
    24 tortillas (tor-tee'yahs)
     1 pint sour cream

Now an *enchilada* could be almost anything wrapped in a *tortilla* and served with an appropriate sauce. *Tortillas* are the national bread of Mexico. They are circular, about eight inches in diameter, flat as a Texas landscape, and as thin as a day-after-Christmas billfold.

To proceed with the actual work, remove the seeds from the *chiles* and scald in water until tender. Save the water. Run the *chiles* through your finest grinder and then press through a sieve to remove all skin particles possible. Into this, mash the clove of garlic and the spices. (If desired, a small, *very small*, pinch of cumin may be added.)

Now finely chop 3 tablespoons of the onion and sauté in the margarine or olive oil. Add the chile mixture, the water from the *chiles*, and the purée. Simmer slowly for several minutes until the flavors are well mixed. Cool and put in refrigerator.

In the meanwhile the meat should have been simmering gently until tender. When ready, chop into *small* pieces, and into this chop the pitted olives and the blanched almonds and return to broth in which the meat was cooked. Cool and place in the refrigerator. Grate the cheese and place in a jar; the extra drying time will help it. Leave the so-far-untouched onions in a handy place, wash the dishes, and go to bed.

Now we come to *the* day, with the game won, or lost, and everybody with a good appetite. Have a friend mix the cocktails while you go ahead with your work. Put about ⅓ of the sauce back into a deep, broad, heavy pan and heat thoroughly. Place the bowls with the meat, the grated cheese, the rest of the onion, finely chopped, and the stack of *tortillas* in a handy position. Put on a large chef's apron.

One at a time, drop the *tortillas* into the slowly simmering sauce and leave until thoroughly soaked and heated. Take out gently and lay on a large plate and then, into each *tortilla*, roll a reasonable amount of the prepared meat and a teaspoon of the finely chopped onion. Carefully stack the *enchiladas*, folded side down, on a large platter. Sprinkle each layer with a little more onion and a generous portion of grated cheese. Over the entire platter full of *enchiladas*, sprinkle more onion and cheese and another third of the sauce, well heated. Serve from the platter with a wide spoon that will not permit the rolls to break apart. The rest of the sauce (thoroughly heated) together with a generous bowl of finely chopped onions, a bowl of grated cheese, and a bowl of sour cream, should be placed upon the table for handy reference. That, with Mexican beans and a tomato and lettuce salad, or *guacamole* (whah-kah-mol'-lay). and beer, Burgundy, or black coffee, makes quite a meal. Serves 8 to 12. On second thought, better order 36 *tortillas*.

Morgan Hill, Calif.

RAVIOLI À LA VICTOR HERBERT

2 tablespoons olive oil
1 small clove garlic, slivered
1 pound veal round, finely chopped
1 pound loin of pork, finely chopped
1 pound spinach
½ teaspoon cinnamon
Salt and pepper
2 eggs
1 cup grated Parmesan cheese

Heat the oil in a skillet; add the garlic, veal, and pork, and cook quickly until the meat is nicely browned. Boil the spinach until tender; drain. Now, run the cooked veal, pork, and spinach through a fine grinder into a mixing bowl. Add the seasonings, eggs, and cheese. Mix thoroughly and spread between dough made in this manner:

Ravioli Pasta

2 cups flour, sifted
3 eggs
¼ cup water
1 teaspoon salt

Mound the flour on a board, make a pit in the center of the mound, and drop in the eggs, salt, and water. Beat quickly with a knife until the dough is well mixed. Knead the dough for several minutes, then roll it out into two thin sheets. Cover one sheet with the ravioli mixture and top with the second sheet. Roll with a special ravioli rolling pin and cut with a scallop-edged wheel or knife which seals the ravioli as it cuts. (If you haven't this special equipment, place small mounds of the filling about an inch apart on one sheet of the dough, cover with the second sheet, and press the two sheets together at the edges and between the mounds of filling. Cut into squares so that there is a mound of filling in each square; press edges together again with a floured fork.) Dust with flour, and set aside while preparing the sauce:

Ravioli Sauce

1 small onion, chopped
3 stalks celery, chopped
½ clove garlic, chopped
½ cup butter or margarine
2 tablespoons olive oil
½ pound ground beef
½ pound ground pork
½ cup chopped dried mushrooms, soaked in water for 30 minutes and drained
Salt and pepper
1 (No. 2½) can (about 3½ cups) solid pack tomatoes

Sauté the celery, onion, and garlic in the combined butter and olive oil until golden. Add the beef, pork, mushrooms, and seasonings, and cook 10 minutes more. Add the tomatoes and cook 45 minutes longer. Turn the heat low and let the sauce simmer slowly while the ravioli are being cooked.

Boil the ravioli in salted water for 15 minutes and serve with a generous helping of the sauce.

Each step in the recipe blends the complementary flavors in a logical sequence which you will find quite simple. The sauce can be enriched with chicken livers; and you may use basil, rosemary, or a bay leaf in it if you like.

A. J. ZIRPOLI
Attorney
San Francisco, Calif.

SOY NOODLES

Chef Francis L. Pelandini, now of Bremerton, Washington, reminds us how soy has gone island hopping across the Pacific.

"While living in Honolulu," says he, "I developed a taste for soy sauce, and since returning to the mainland, I've continued to experiment with it." The result reported here is a dish that could be the main feature for a fairly light supper, or a side dish at a more extensive meal.

> 2 large pork steaks (about 1 pound)
> 1 tablespoon salad oil
> 1 medium sized onion, diced
> ¼ cup soy
> 2 cups chicken broth
> 1 package (1 lb.) thin noodles (about ¼ inch wide)
> Water
> Salt and pepper to taste
> 3 green onions, chopped

Trim steaks of all bone and excess fat, and cut into narrow strips ½ inch long. In a Dutch oven, fry meat in salad oil until medium brown. Add diced onion and continue to cook until onion is tender; then add soy and chicken broth. Allow mixture to simmer.

Drop noodles into boiling salted water; cook for 2 to 3 minutes, until limp; turn into strainer and drain well. Add to meat-soy-chicken broth mixture. Cover and place in 325° oven for 12 to 15 minutes, or until noodles are done. Stir once during

"Reminds us how soy has gone island hopping across the Pacific"

cooking. Add salt or more soy and pepper to taste. Top with chopped green onions and serve hot. Serves 8.

Francis L. Belandini
Government employee
Bremerton, Washington

PIZZA BASTARDO

Chef Al Perkins of Honolulu calls these hot pizza pies "Pizza Bastardo," if you'll pardon the plain spoken name. We bet they'd have won favor in the Tuscan castles of the Medici, who had a reputation for living it up.

They're not real pizza, of course, but they meet a very special need. As *Chef* Perkins puts it, hot hors d'œuvres are always popular with guests; the problem is to find one simple enough to be popular with the cook, too.

This is it:

        2 cups prepared biscuit mix
        Milk (according to package directions)

Sauce:
        1 can (8 oz.) tomato sauce
        1 can (6 oz.) tomato paste
        1 teaspoon garlic purée
        1 teaspoon oregano
        2 tablespoons anchovy paste
        ½ teaspoon rosemary
        Pepper to taste

Topping:
        Sharp cheese, grated

For the shells mix the prepared biscuit mix with milk according to package directions. Then roll the dough to a thickness of about ¼ inch. Cut into circles with a scalloped cooky cutter and put in greased muffin pans—small size, with muffin cups no more than 1¼ inches across. Bake in a hot oven (400°) for 5 minutes.

Then remove from oven and, with a fork, prick each "pie" shell so it won't rise. You can also use your thumb to push down the dough. The purpose is to keep the dough from rising any more during the baking process. Return to the 400° oven for another 10 minutes, or until the shells are browned. Then remove from the muffin cups and allow to cool.

Meanwhile, mix all sauce ingredients and let them simmer for 15 minutes. Fill each

shell half full of sauce and then top with the grated sharp cheese. Put the "pies" in a hot (400°) oven until the cheese is melted. Remove from the oven and let them cool a minute or two so the cheese-tomato mixture will "jell" and won't be drippy. Serve. Makes approximately 24 pizza pies.

Any leftover sauce will keep in the freezer or in the freezing compartment of the refrigerator.

Honolulu

PASTI LEONI

        1 clove garlic, chopped
        1 tablespoon oil
        1 cup chopped, cooked or canned spinach
            (should be well drained)
        ¼ cup minced parsley
        ¼ teaspoon thyme
        ¼ teaspoon rosemary
        ¼ teaspoon marjoram
        ¼ teaspoon basil
        4 eggs, yolks and whites beaten separately
        1 cup old-fashioned (farmer's-style) cottage
            cheese
        1 cup grated Parmesan or dry Monterey Jack
            cheese
        1 cup bread or cracker crumbs
        1 cup flour

Sauté garlic in oil until nicely browned. Add the spinach and herbs, and cook over low heat for 10 minutes. Beat the egg yolks in a large mixing bowl; stir in, first, the cottage cheese; second, the grated cheese; third, the bread or cracker crumbs, and then the spinach mixture; last, fold in the stiffly beaten egg whites.

Sprinkle the flour over a bread board, shape the spinach mixture into pellets about the size of a golf ball, and roll each pellet in the flour until it has absorbed a heavy coating of flour. When all the pellets are coated, cook them in boiling water to which a tablespoon of salt has been added. (The water must be *boiling* when you begin to cook the *pasti*.) When the *pasti* are done, after about 10 minutes of boiling, they will come to the top of the water. Drain, and serve at once, covered with the following Mushroom-Tomato Sauce, and sprinkled with grated cheese.

Mushroom-Tomato Sauce

½ pound ground lean beef
1 large onion
1 large clove garlic
1 stalk celery
    Several sprigs parsley
1 tablespoon mixed dried herbs
4 whole cloves or ¼ teaspoon allspice
½ bay leaf
1 teaspoon salt
¼ teaspoon black pepper
¼ cup oil
2 cans tomato paste, mixed with an equal
    amount of water
1 package dried mushrooms

Put the meat, onion, garlic, celery, and parsley through a grinder together, or mince the vegetables separately and mix them with the meat; add the herbs, cloves or allspice, bay leaf, salt, and pepper. Sauté the mixture quickly in the oil until nicely browned; then simmer and stir over low heat until well cooked. Add the diluted tomato sauce; cook slowly for at least 1 hour, adding water if the sauce becomes too thick.

Meanwhile, soak the dried mushrooms in warm water. After the sauce has cooked for an hour, add the mushrooms. Cook another 15 minutes and serve.

Chard may be used in place of spinach. Also, ground, leftover cooked beef, ground sausage, or chicken or turkey giblets may be substituted for the raw beef in making the sauce.

L. P. Matthews

Traffic manager
Oakland, Calif.

GNOCCHI ALLA ROMANO

There are many variations of *Gnocchi,* but "*alla Romano*" is the most popular. Unless you go to an Italian grocery, you may have trouble in finding semolina. Farina, the breakfast-food variety, is to be found in any grocery.

3 cups milk
    Salt
1½ cups semolina or farina
    Butter
1 cup grated Parmesan cheese
    Pepper to taste
    Nutmeg to taste
2 eggs

Season the milk with salt to taste, and bring to a simmering boil. Add the semolina or farina, sprinkling it in slowly to avoid lumping. Stir mixture with a wooden spoon, and when it is thick, add 2 tablespoons butter, ½ cup of the cheese, and pepper and nutmeg to taste. Stir until well blended, then remove from the heat and add the beaten eggs. Mix well and pour into a flat, shallow pan to about ½-inch thickness. Cool, then cut into rounds with a very small biscuit cutter. Flour your hands and roll the rounds into balls the size of a walnut. Put balls in a baking pan with melted butter and the remaining ½ cup of cheese. Bake in a slow oven (325°) about 30 minutes.

These same gnocchi balls may be poached instead of baked. Drop them into simmering milk and cook them until done. Use the milk to make a cream sauce, adding the remaining ½ cup cheese.

Gnocchi may also be served with a tomato sauce. Poach the balls in salted water for 10 minutes, then remove them, add the following sauce, and sprinkle with the remaining ½ cup cheese.

Tomato Sauce for Gnocchi

2 tablespoons butter
¼ cup minced lean ham
2 shallots or small green onions, chopped
1 pound tomatoes, peeled and sliced
1 bay leaf
1 sprig thyme
10 peppercorns
    Salt and pepper to taste
1 tablespoon vinegar
1 tablespoon flour

Melt butter in a saucepan; add ham and shallots or onions; cook gently until tender but not browned. Add tomatoes, bay leaf, thyme, peppercorns, salt, pepper, and vinegar. Sprinkle with the flour, stir all together, and boil for 20 minutes, or until mixture is well reduced. Pass the sauce through a tammy-cloth* or fine sieve, heat again, season, and serve.

*Simply a square of flour or sugar sacking which is laid over a bowl. The sauce is poured on its center. Pick up ends and twist the resulting bag until all sauce is expelled.

George A. Selleck

Dentist
San Francisco, Calif.

SIMPLE SPAGHETTI SAUCE

2 tablespoons butter
2 tablespoons olive oil
1 small onion, chopped
1 can tomato paste
1¼ cups water
Salt and pepper to taste
1 sprig sweet basil or ½ teaspoon dried basil

Put butter and oil in small frying pan. Heat, add onion, and cook until a golden brown, crushing onions with a wooden spoon to extract the flavor. Put tomato paste and water in a saucepan and mix until smooth. Strain contents of frying pan into tomato paste mixture, discarding onion. Season with salt, pepper, and basil, and simmer for 15 minutes.

This is a good sauce to use for spaghetti when it is to accompany a meat dish.

JAMES C. FLAGG
Bookkeeper
Claremont, Calif.

SPAGHETTINI, TUNA SAUCE WITH CAPERS

6 cloves garlic
4 tablespoons chopped parsley
4 tablespoons olive oil
1 can (7 oz.) flaked tuna
1 can (No. 2½) solid pack tomatoes
1 can tomato paste
3 cups boiling water
1 bay leaf
Salt and freshly ground pepper to taste
1 heaping tablespoon drained capers
1 pound spaghettini

Sauté 4 cloves garlic, diced, and 3 tablespoons parsley in 3 tablespoons olive oil until the garlic is a light golden brown. Add the tuna and sauté a few minutes longer. Add tomatoes and tomato paste and boiling water, bay leaf, salt, and pepper. Simmer slowly for about 2 hours, or until the sauce becomes quite thick. Just before serving over the spaghettini, stir in the capers.

To cook the spaghettini, add 2 whole cloves garlic and the remaining parsley and olive oil to a gallon of boiling, salted water. Slowly slide the spaghettini into the boiling water and cook until it has an "*a dente*" consistency. Test by pinching between the fingers. Drain, but do not wash. Remove garlic cloves, transfer spaghettini to a hot platter, and cover with the sauce. Serves 4.

It is important that no cheese be served on the spaghettini.

Comet Brooks
Biochemist
Rolling Hills, Calif.

PALLETTE

½ cup dried mushrooms
1 small onion and 1 small leek, finely chopped
5 tablespoons olive oil
½ cup nut meats, finely chopped or crushed
4 ripe tomatoes, seeded and peeled or 1 can tomato paste plus water to make 1 cup liquid
Salt and pepper
2½ cups coarse cornmeal (polenta)
4 quarts boiling salted water
¼ cup butter

First, prepare a sauce similar to spaghetti sauce:

Cover mushrooms with boiling water and set aside. Brown onion and leek in olive oil; add nut meats and tomatoes or diluted tomato paste; cook about 5 minutes. Chop mushrooms and add to the mixture, along with ½ cup of the mushroom liquor; season to taste with salt and pepper; simmer for ½ hour.

Prepare meanwhile a cornmeal paste, or a *polenta*. Sift cornmeal slowly through the fingers into boiling water. Cook about ½ hour, stirring constantly. If mixture gets too thick, thin it with a little boiling water. Before removing from the heat, add butter and stir well. Take up cornmeal in large spoonfuls and arrange on a large platter or on individual dishes. (Cornmeal should be thick enough not to run together when arranged on the platter.) Depress the center of each ball and place in it a thin slice of fresh Monterey cheese (optional). Cover each ball liberally with the above sauce and sprinkle with Parmesan cheese before serving.

This dish is a meal in itself, so accompaniments should consist simply of a green salad and a glass of red wine.

ALBERT BELLI
Fire insurance
Colma, Calif.

pancakes

sandwiches

NUTMEG WAFFLES

Nutmeg and wheat germ seem to cancel out each other's extremes in Francis E. C. Hilliard's Nutmeg Waffles. With whole wheat flour, they produce excellent flavor and texture best described as nutty. *Chef* Hilliard invented it because "all-white flour products do not agree with me." To its already full-bodied health, he sometimes likes to add two additional eggs—"no difference in flavor but some in food value."

  1 cup finely pulverized 100% whole
    wheat flour
  1 cup wheat germ
  4 tablespoons white flour
  2 tablespoons brown sugar
  1 teaspoon salt
  3 teaspoons nutmeg
  3 teaspoons baking powder
  4 tablespoons cooking oil or melted
    shortening
  2 cups milk
  2 eggs, separated

Mix all dry ingredients together, add liquids gradually, then egg yolks (lightly beaten). Stir until smooth. Fold in well-beaten egg whites. Bake well done—about 6 or 7 minutes. Makes 6 large waffles.

Francis E. C. Hilliard

Oakland

RYE WAFFLES

One bite of these waffles will make you shake your head and blink your eyes in surprise. The reaction should be altogether pleasant. The slight bitterness of rye flour is an ideal foil for syrupy sweetness. The caraway seeds are a bonus. Since maple syrup introduces another distinct flavor, you may prefer to serve these with honey.

The inventor, Saul W. Chaikin, likes his humor very dry. "My original intention in devising this recipe was to invent a gastronomical pun by incorporating both rye flour and rye whiskey, but I lost my nerve. Only rye flour is used. I have a hunch that the introduction of the whiskey would result in a recipe title change to 'Wry Waffles' (thus completing a triple pun)."

  1 cup all-purpose flour
  ¾ cup rye flour
  1½ teaspoons baking powder
  ½ teaspoon salt
  1 teaspoon cinnamon
  3 eggs, separated
  2 cups milk
  1½ teaspoons caraway seeds
  5 tablespoons melted butter

Sift flour, measure, then sift again with rye flour, baking powder, salt, and cinnamon. Beat egg yolks, add milk, then combine with dry ingredients, caraway seeds, and melted butter. Fold in stiffly beaten egg whites. Makes 6 large waffles.

Saul W. Chaikin

Research chemist
Palo Alto, Calif.

ORANGE WAFFLES AND BAKED EGGS

  4 eggs
  2 cups orange juice
  2 tablespoons lemon juice
  2 teaspoons grated orange peel
  2 cups sifted all-purpose flour
  4 tablespoons cornmeal
  1 teaspoon soda
  1 teaspoon baking powder
  1 teaspoon salt
  2 tablespoons melted butter

Beat eggs well. Add juices and grated peel. Sift together flour, cornmeal, soda, baking powder, and salt. Add to mixture. Beat until smooth, then add melted shortening. Bake in heated waffle iron and top with Baked Eggs. Makes about 6 waffles. For the eggs:

Fry, not too crisp, one slice of bacon for each egg. Grease small custard cups with bacon drippings and circle a slice of bacon inside each cup. Drop egg into cup and season with 3 drops of Worcestershire sauce and 1 drop Tabasco sauce (if added tang is desired). Do not add salt and pepper until after baking. Bake eggs in a moderate oven (350°) 15 to 20 minutes, or until eggs are set.

Roy E. Matison

Personnel manager
Burlingame, Calif.

BREAD AND BACON WAFFLES

Chances are that every *Chef* who reads this next entry will want to try it. If for no other reason, he will want to find out whether anything so simple deserves consideration by this august body.

"No yen for washing kettles"

Ben S. Hessel recommends it for those times "when your wife has gone to one of those affairs with 'the girls' and you have no yen for washing kettles." We concur. First heat your waffle iron. Line up slices of bread. (No sandwich or thin-sliced bread for this one, please.) Arrange on each slice one strip of bacon cut in two. Pop into the waffle iron (with control set at medium) and toast until beautifully brown. For the average slice of bread, this will take about 3 minutes. (If you lift the lid before the bacon is sealed to the bread, the bacon will curl and spoil the effect.)

Ben S. Hessel

Building contractor
Santa Rosa, Calif.

The bacon flavors the bread but doesn't make it seem greasy.

MR. RINGER'S PANCAKES

Every *Chef* can and should be a prima donna when it comes to hot cakes. Many *Chefs* of our acquaintance have hit upon a certain individual combination they like to cook and eat most of the time; they and many others still like to tinker with variations.

Robert Lee Ringer, of Portland, serves up some that are faintly reminiscent of "flannel cakes" we remember from boyhood. His cakes are substantial and fairly rough textured, at the other end of the scale from the light, soft cakes in which white flour predominates. He has added cornmeal, soda, and vinegar to what might otherwise pass as a recipe for bread crumb pancakes. Try them on your own griddle and see how you like them.

Put 1 cup dry bread crumbs in a bowl. In a cup put about 2 tablespoons more than ½ cup flour. Add 3 tablespoons dried non-fat milk, 1 teaspoon salt, and 1 teaspoon soda; then fill the cup with cornmeal and add to bread crumbs. Add 1½ cups water, 1 egg, ¼ cup melted shortening, and 1 teaspoon vinegar. Mix all ingredients thoroughly and add more water if you desire a thinner batter. Bake on a hot griddle. Makes about 24 pancakes 4 inches in diameter.

Robert L Ringer

Retired
Portland, Oregon

SCOTCH OATCAKES

Harry C. James submits his Scotch Oatcakes with the suggestion: "We like them with wine." They are less sweet than a cooky, more sweet than bread. The coarse flours add a crunchy texture and nut-like flavor, dividends enjoyed by our forefathers who milled their own grains.

        1 teaspoon soda
        1 cup sour milk
        2 cups stone-ground oatmeal (or 1 cup rolled
              oats and 1 cup steel-cut oats)
        3 cups oat flour
    1½ cups sugar
        1 cup melted shortening
        1 teaspoon salt

Mix soda in sour milk. Add oatmeal, oat flour, sugar, melted shortening, and salt. Roll thin, cut as desired, and bake slowly (300°) on cooky sheet until light brown. Makes 6 to 7 dozen cookies.

Harry

Headmaster, boys' school
Banning, Calif.

"Serve the first batch to your mother-in-law"

SOURDOUGH BUCKWHEAT CAKES

Some men who keep strictly out of the kitchen are master cooks over a camp stove. The inner prompting may be just an unusually hearty appetite. Or it may be a deeper urge—understood by most male campers and by all of the early Western pioneers—to prove that a man can work out some of the good things of life with nothing but his bare hands and the minimum elements of subsistence.

If you have a taste for sour French bread, chances are good that you'll like sourdough breads of the kind immortalized by the prospectors who stampeded the Klondike back near the turn of the century. To the miner and mountaineer, sourdough bread is the staff of life with built-in vitamin pills. Some meat and some canned tomatoes are all he really needs to balance out his diet.

By saving some of your last batch of sourdough as a "starter" for your next batch, you have the culinary equivalent of perpetual motion. Most sourdough experts use the starter with a variety of flours and other ingredients to produce pancakes, biscuits, dumplings, and plain bread.

All you need is a point of departure, contributed here by William Buster McGee, M.D., of San Diego. He volunteers this typically masculine advice:

"Serve the first batch to your mother-in-law, as all *Chefs of the West* know that a sourdough culture improves with age, but be sure and save two cups for your starter. Don't add any more yeast or yogurt to future batches."

2 cups buckwheat flour
1 cup prepared biscuit mix
1 heaping teaspoon salt
2 eggs
1 cake yeast or 1 package dry yeast
   (dissolved in a little warm water)
4 tablespoons brown sugar
4 tablespoons salad oil
½ pint yogurt
1 quart buttermilk
1 heaping teaspoon soda

Mix all ingredients. (You can sift the dry ingredients if you happen to be in a kitchen equipped with the refinements of civilization; otherwise, just mix.) Let the mixture set overnight. Next morning, add the soda and fry on a well greased griddle. Should serve approximately 3 to 6 hungry campers. (Save some starter!)

Buster McGee
San Diego

HAM'S FRENCHERS

"My breakfast special is a time and space saver that gets us out for the early morning fishing run so well fortified that a sandwich, candy bars, and fruit will keep us going until the end of the day. I learned it back in '17, from two little ladies in Brest, France, who scurried for their skillets whenever they spotted our navy blues crossing the bridge from the landing docks into the old town, where they ran a very small cafe."

He prefers to make up his own pancake batter, but a prepared mix should work practically as well. His original contribution is the technique for amalgamating egg and pancake (and if you don't like eggs in the syrup, even at a camp breakfast, better skip this recipe).

      1 egg
      1 teaspoon salt
      ¾ teaspoon soda
      3 tablespoons powdered buttermilk
      1 cup flour
      1 cup water
      1 tablespoon bacon drippings
      6 eggs
        Salt and pepper

Beat egg; add the salt, soda, powdered buttermilk, and flour; mix in the water and warm bacon drippings. (By the way, keep the bacon warm and crisp by wrapping in paper toweling and slipping it *under* the camp stove until ready for use.)

Now we're set. Put two large spoonfuls of batter—or enough to make about a 6-inch cake—in the center of the heated griddle. One cake at a time! As the batter begins to set, use your spoon to make a crater, or hollow, in the center of the cake, being careful not to break through the bottom crust that is forming.

Break an egg into this cup, using your spoon to keep any white from running over the edges. Salt and pepper to taste; let the whole thing cook until the batter and white of egg begin to set. Then, using a large pancake turner, make sure that the cake is completely loosened from the griddle, get set squarely under it, and flip! With dexterity and practice, you can make the yolk of the egg land, unbroken, under the center of the cake. (For those who like their eggs hard cooked, I break the yolk before flipping, then cook a little longer.)

Bake this side and serve hot, with plenty of butter, syrup, and bacon. Makes about 6 man-size cakes. One should just about fill the 8-inch plate that fits into your camp set, and just about fill the fisherman, too, or at least keep him busy while you prepare another "Frencher."

Robt. F. Hamilton

Retired
Portland, Oregon

GAER AEBLESKIVER

The Danish *Aebleskiver* (pancake ball) has the taste and consistency of a pancake but the shape of a muffin or popover. By tradition, they are cooked in a special cooking iron which has seven holes or compartments. However, a cast iron muffin pan will serve the purpose.

One popular flavoring is applesauce Put a scant teaspoon or so on top of each cake when it is about half baked, then turn with a fork and continue baking.

      1 cake compressed yeast or 1 package
        dry yeast
      ¼ cup lukewarm water
      1 tablespoon sugar
      ½ teaspoon salt
      2 cups rich milk
      2 cups flour
      4 eggs

Soften yeast in water with sugar and salt. Heat milk to lukewarm, then add to flour. Add yeast. Add eggs, one at a time, beating well after each addition. Cardamom, nutmeg, or lemon may be used for flavoring. Let dough rise for 2 hours.

Heat the cooking irons or heavy muffin pans on top of the stove until a drop of cold water will dance on the surface. Grease the holes well. Then put about ½ tablespoon of the batter in each hole. Currants, seedless raisins, applesauce, cooked prunes, cooked cranberries, peanut butter, or jelly may be added while the pancake balls are cooking. Turn with a fork when the underside is cooked. If the iron is good and hot, aebleskivers will be ready to serve in about five minutes. Makes about three dozen.

Edwin B. Kraft

Optician
Burlingame, Calif.

FINNISH PANCAKE

Be prepared for anything from *Chef W. K. Latvala*, "an old fisherman-hunter from Finnish Lapland and other strange parts" (including the Waldorf-Astoria and Stockholm's Grand Royal). He speaks knowingly of barbecued lampreys and codfish tongues, and a recent experiment called "The Latvala Bear Meat."

On this occasion, he presents a reminiscence from his childhood called "Finnish Pancake" (says he, "any man can make it"). It rises like the full moon, sets rapidly on cooling, has the consistency and fresh taste of a very light soufflé, but should satisfy hunger just as well as the most substantial of flapjacks.

    3 eggs
    1 pint (2 cups) milk
    ¼ cup honey or sugar
    ¾ cup flour
    ½ teaspoon salt
    4 tablespoons butter

Beat eggs with milk. Stir in honey or sugar, flour, and salt. Melt butter in a frying pan until butter is so hot that a drop of water sizzles in it. Add egg mixture and bake in a hot oven (450°) for 25 to 30 minutes.

Variation: Beat egg yolks with milk, add other ingredients, beat egg whites separately until stiff and add to the pancake mix just before pouring into the hot pan.

Both the frying pan and the oven should be HOT. When you pour the mixture into the pan, don't aim for the center. Pour the batter in a circle around the center so that it will spread the melted butter to the edges and also push some butter up to the top as batter gradually fills in the center. Serve with jam, jelly, maple syrup, or strawberries and cream. Serves 6 to 8.

Retired
Ojai, Calif.

YEAST WHEAT CAKES

Chefs of the West do some of their finest work on Sundays. Their favorites by far are Sunday breakfast and Sunday night supper.

In his Honolulu kitchen, *Chef H. W. B.* (Hod) White is working up a batch of old-fashioned hot cakes. Principal ingredients are whole wheat flour ("high enough in protein so you don't have to put in any soda to counteract sour milk"), yeast, and dried milk ("adds a smoothness and richness you can't get any other way"). This hot cake maneuver takes a little time, but our taste testers definitely approved the product. After reading the recipe, don't neglect the postscript. *Chef White*, under the influence of hot cakes, no doubt, bubbles and expands with enthusiasm on the merits of his batter.

    3 cakes yeast or 3 packages dry yeast
    2 cups warm water, sweet or sour milk, or
        buttermilk
    4 tablespoons dark molasses
    3 eggs, separated
    1 teaspoon salt
    ⅓ to ½ cup melted shortening
    1¾ cups whole wheat flour
    ⅓ cup non-fat dry milk

Crumble or sprinkle yeast into water, milk, or buttermilk. As soon as yeast is softened, add molasses, egg yolks, salt, and shortening. Sift flour and dry milk together. (If you prefer, you can substitute some wheat germ or soya flour for some of the flour.) Sift again and stir well into the liquid.

Let stand for about an hour; or, if you are in a hurry, run some warm water into the sink and set the bowl containing this mixture in the water. In 20 minutes you are ready to go. Just before frying the cakes on the griddle, fold in the stiffly beaten egg whites. Serves 4 to 5—depending immensely upon appetite—but in any case makes 50 to 60 small pancakes.

Then hurry and make up another batch, because if you have asked more than three for breakfast, you won't have any left over. If there is any of the batter left over, put in the refrigerator in an open container. But be sure to beat it down a couple of times, or it will run all over the place until it gets cold. Then, next morning, it is ready to go again. You can add a little more flour, another egg yolk and egg white to fluff it up, but you'll find that it is probably all right as is. After you have made these hot cakes a few times, you'll find that you just naturally make more than you can use in order to put some away in the refrigerator.

"Let's see what the early shift has cooking"

You can use this same recipe for waffles if you like, making it a little thicker. If you do that, try adding some apple sauce to the dough.

Executive vice president
Honolulu, T. H.

TWO-TONE PANCAKES

This idea for making pancakes dates back just 50 years. It is simple and it is effective. The man who brings it to our attention now is Ernest I. C. Erlandson of Alameda, California. Let's listen to his story:

"This recipe has long since disappeared from San Francisco, but it was very familiar in all the small restaurants in the days before the great earthquake and fire of 1906, when you could get a stack of the pancakes for about 15 cents, including coffee. They were as popular as the hamburgers of today.

    1 pitcher thin wheat cake batter
    1 pitcher thin buckwheat pancake batter

With the griddle hot and ready, first pour out some cakes of white batter and let them get set a little. Then pour some buckwheat batter on top of each white cake and leave until each cake is set enough to turn over. (Care must be taken

that the white batter is thin enough to spread, so that when the buckwheat is applied, the pancake will not be too thick.) When cakes are cooked on the other side, serve with syrup and slabs of ham or pork sausages.

Leather worker
Alameda, Calif.

SPICED NUT MUFFINS

    2 cups prepared biscuit mix
    ½ cup sugar
    ½ teaspoon cinnamon
    ¼ teaspoon nutmeg
    1 egg, beaten
    ⅔ cup milk
    3 tablespoons shortening, melted
    ⅔ cup nut meats

Mix dry ingredients. Add egg and milk, then shortening. When well mixed, add nut meats. (This may seem like a lot of nuts, but I like muffins that way.) Fill muffin pan about ⅔ full. Bake in a moderately hot oven (400°) 20 minutes or until done. Yield, about a dozen muffins.

Sunol, Calif.

SHEEPHERDER'S POTATO FLAPJACK

From Idaho, Blaine Stubblefield proposes the "Sheepherder's Potato Flapjack." It adds a superlative twist of showmanship to that camping favorite, fried potatoes.

Peel spuds, slice thin and small—this is easiest with one of those hard-to-find washboard slicers. Salt and pepper to taste, and don't be too poky or the batch will oxidize.

Fat or cooking oil should be starting a slow smoke in skillet or heavy frying pan. Dump in the sliced potatoes, pat down to cover bottom of pan, and round up the edges away from pan sides. Fry easy until brown (lift edge with turner and peep under). You find your potatoes stuck together—a flapjack.

So—hold pan over newspaper or the ground, toss, and catch, brown side up. It makes a show if you score; if not, it's a laugh. With practice you never miss.

Cover, and fry the other side brown. Cut in pieces and serve. This makes good eating indoors or out.

Blaine Stubblefield

Hells Canyon navigator
Weiser, Idaho

CORN FRITTERS IN A BEER BATTER

2 cups flour
1 pinch salt
½ teaspoon sugar
¼ teaspoon baking powder
½ cup beer
¾ cup tepid water
1 generous tablespoon olive oil
2 egg whites
1 generous cup fresh or canned
    Golden Bantam corn
    A dash of pepper

Sift together flour, salt, sugar, and baking powder. Gradually add beer, water, and olive oil. Stir only until mixture is smooth, then let batter rest for an hour. When ready to use fold in 2 egg whites, beaten stiffly. Add corn (a 12-ounce can does nicely, drained), and pepper. Drop by spoonfuls into ½ inch hot fat in a shallow frying pan. Fry until a golden

brown on both sides, cooking only a few at a time. Let them drain on absorbent paper before serving. This recipe makes about 12 to 15 fritters.

Long Beach, Calif.

GOLDEN DELIGHTS

Those crisp delights are fine for a barbecue meal, but they also may be served at breakfast with plenty of butter, plus honey, syrup, or warmed apple butter, according to your taste.

2 cups boiling water
½ teaspoon salt
½ cup cornmeal, preferably yellow
1 tablespoon butter or margarine
1 cup diced Swiss or American cheese
¼ teaspoon paprika
1 egg, well beaten
    Cracker crumbs
    Frying fat

Add salt to the boiling water, sift in the cornmeal, and cook for 30 minutes. Add butter, diced cheese, and paprika, and stir until cheese is melted. Remove from fire and spread in a well-oiled pan to cool. When cold, cut into strips; dip each strip in well-beaten egg and then in cracker crumbs; fry in hot fat until crisp and brown. Serves 4.

M. C. Cook
Chico, Calif.

CINNAMON TOAST DE LUXE

Let's speak now of a dish about which there are few quibbles or quarrels. Every recipe for cinnamon toast is good; some are better than others.

"Traveling with the Navy a few years back," says Dr. Richard H. Hall of Garden Grove, California, "we stopped one Sunday morning in a lovely hotel in the Deep South. In an atmosphere of snowy white tablecloths, we were served a basket of the most delicious cinnamon toast we had ever encountered. We brought the recipe to the West with us and have eaten this toast many Sunday mornings in the past 10 years. It is always a favorite with children, guests, the whole family."

One suggestion: To pick up less sugar, put toast on a paper towel to dry for a minute after frying in butter and before you put it in the paper bag. The pieces are just a little sticky to eat, but, unless your guests are quite finicky, this cinnamon toast should be very popular at a Sunday morning brunch

> 1-pound loaf of fresh, enriched, white bread
> ½ pound (2 cubes) butter or margarine
> 1 cup powdered sugar
> 1 tablespoon cinnamon

Cut slices of bread diagonally. Fry the half slices slowly, 2 or 3 at a time, adding butter gradually (at the rate of about 1 tablespoon per half slice), until each piece is golden brown on each side—no darker. Take slices from frying pan and drop in a clean brown paper bag containing a mixture of sugar and cinnamon. Shake gently and serve warm in a basket. There will be calls for more. Makes 24 to 32 pieces.

Richard H Hall, M.D.

Orthopedic surgeon
Garden Grove, Calif.

We also recommend this variation, using the same ingredients: Combine sugar and cinnamon and add a little water to make a paste. Dip bread in this paste and fry in butter until brown. The sugar and butter caramelize in this process to give the toast a very toothsome crisp crust.

SAUSAGE PANCAKES

"This breakfast dish pleases the boat riders hereabouts," says *Chef* F. W. Knowles, of Seattle, "particularly when I am along to man the galley." It's a man's dish, a kind of variation of the farm breakfast custom of serving fried eggs right on top of the pancakes.

> 1 pound pork sausage, seasoned to taste with
>   sage and freshly ground pepper
> 1 cup prepared pancake mix
> 1½ cups buttermilk
> 1 egg
> 1 tablespoon salad oil or melted butter

"Pleases the boat riders hereabouts"

Take portions of sausage and roll into balls about 1 inch in diameter; then pat into thin, very flat cakes. Mix other ingredients to form a batter.

Brown sausage cakes on both sides lightly in a skillet, drop them in the batter, and then remove them to brown on a dry griddle, turning to brown both sides. Serve with honey, syrup, or a tart jelly. Makes about 25 cakes about 2 inches in diameter.

F. W. Knowles

Mechanical engineer
Seattle, Washington

RYE BREAD WITH ESCHALOTS

Edward C. Stalder's rye bread with eschalots (perhaps better known as shallots) is a worthy alternate for the usual garlic French bread. "Years ago we had rye bread fixed with chives. I then tried it with eschalots and we like it much better and so do our guests. It is difficult to buy eschalots in the markets, but they are easy to raise in a small garden plot."

If you can't find shallots in either market or garden, we have suggested two other onion cousins that can substitute on this occasion.

Heed *Chef* Stalder's closing remark: "Be

sure to have seconds for all, as some will return for thirds."

2 bunches eschalots, or I bunch green onions and I bunch chives
I loaf rye bread (about 20 thin slices)
I cube butter or margarine

Chop eschalots fine. Spread rye bread generously with butter that has been well creamed first. Then sprinkle each slice with the chopped eschalots and pile bread back in loaf form. Wrap first in wax paper, then in aluminum foil, and steam in oven at 275° for about 1½ hours—a little longer or shorter time will not matter. Serve very hot. I usually serve this bread with casserole dishes, also with barbecued chicken and other meats. Serves 8 to 10.

Retired
Ben Lomond, Calif.

CALIFORNIA TOAST

The kind of French toast that is usually served doesn't please *Chef* Whiting at all— "It suggests stale bread and leathery egg whites, both cold and soggy. However, that needn't be and shouldn't be. It can be a dream. Here's my way":

6 egg yolks
½ cup evaporated milk or fresh cream
Pinch of salt
Grated peel and juice of ½ orange
¼ teaspoon nutmeg
12 slices fresh bread

Beat egg yolks with fork or rotary beater, gradually adding the evaporated milk or cream. Add salt, orange peel and juice, and nutmeg.

"The important thing is to use fresh bread—why waste good eggs to use up stale bread? *Do* trim off the crusts. Dip bread slices in batter and cook in a heavy skillet greased with butter. As in cooking any egg dish, the skillet should be barely hot enough to do the job. Please don't brown these beauties—leave them golden and lovely. Serves 6.

"We serve the toast with a simple syrup: 1 cup white sugar and enough water to dampen it (2 or 3 tablespoons). Heat to dissolve, then add 1 tablespoon honey. When cool, add ½ teaspoon vanilla."

Richmond, Calif.

BANANA BREAD

"This banana bread," says *Chef* J. K. Connell, "is a specialty of our house and may be used in place of bread or rolls, or, if you prefer, as a dessert."

He gives you a choice of whole wheat or white flour. There's no doubt in our minds which is preferred. The whole wheat gives a texture that transforms banana bread into manna. Guard it well, lest it disappear before you can serve it.

1 cup sugar
¼ pound (1 cube) butter or margarine
2 eggs
3 very ripe bananas
2 tablespoons water
1 teaspoon vanilla
2 cups whole wheat flour
¼ teaspoon salt
1 teaspoon baking soda

Mix sugar, butter; add eggs and mix well. Mash bananas in separate bowl, add the water and vanilla. Sift flour, salt, and baking soda together. Now alternately add the flour mixture and the banana mixture to the sugar, butter, and eggs. Pour into greased loaf pan. Bake in moderate oven (350°) for 1 hour. Turn out and cool on cake rack before slicing.

North Hollywood, Calif.

INDIAN BREAD

Chef Moise Penning's version of Indian Bread "has sort of a pioneer air about it," according to one of our taste testers. As a matter of fact, it is very easy to imagine our great-great-grandmothers mixing it up in the back end of a covered wagon.

The method makes sense only on a camping trip, but the slightly salty and crusty

"Our great-great-grandmother mixing it up in the back end of a covered wagon"

result may tempt some of you to try it at home.

- 6 tablespoons shortening
- Flour (approximately 1½ cups)
- 1 teaspoon salt
- 2 teaspoons baking powder
- 2 tablespoons cornmeal
- Water (approximately ⅓ cup)

Drop the shortening in one lump directly in your flour sack. On top, add salt, baking powder, and cornmeal. With your hands, work these ingredients into the shortening, picking up whatever amount of flour sticks to it. Now, gently and sparingly add water and mix until you have a ball of soft dough. Pat down gently in a well greased, warm skillet and bake over a slow fire. When the bottom side is brown, turn over to brown the other side. Serves 4 to 6.

Lumberman
San Lorenzo, Calif.

CORN ROLLS

French bread is (nearly) always with us at barbecues, and although it's mighty good stuff, a change is welcome. *Chef* Victor H. Reynolds of the VE Ranch in Harbor, Oregon, has to fight off the customers when he puts together a batch of his corn rolls.

- 2 cups flour
- ¾ teaspoon salt
- 4 teaspoons baking powder
- 4 tablespoons shortening
- 1 egg, beaten
- ⅔ to 1 cup milk
- 1 can (12 ounce) whole kernel corn
- Melted butter
- Paprika

Mix the dry ingredients and work in shortening. Add beaten egg and milk; mix to a soft dough. Place on a floured board, roll to ½-inch thickness, spread with drained corn, and brush over with melted butter. Roll as for jelly roll and cut with a sharp knife into ½ to 1-inch slices. Place the slices, cut side down, on a cookie sheet, and dust with paprika. Bake in a 425° oven for about 15 minutes. Serve with country gravy, or simply as a bread with lots of butter. Makes 6 to 8 rolls.

Deputy sheriff (retired)
Harbor, Oregon

BUENA TIERRA RANCHO
SOUR CREAM COFFEE CAKE

When *Chef* Sachse discovered a surplus of sour cream on hand, he explored the nearest cook books and found a couple of recipes for coffee cake that sounded good, but might be better with his sour cream. Using a familiar recipe as his guide, he added the sour cream, tried a few ideas of his own, and invented an original cake. It not only makes morning coffee an event but improves with age.

```
2 cups sugar
1 cup shortening (use half butter or margarine)
5 eggs
4 cups sifted all-purpose flour
3 teaspoons baking powder
½ teaspoon soda
½ teaspoon salt
1 cup thick sour cream or 1 cup commercial
    sour cream plus ¼ cup milk
1 teaspoon vanilla
  Grated peel of 1 lemon
⅔ cup each nut meats, raisins, currants
```

Cream together sugar and shortening until light. Beat in eggs, one at a time. Sift together flour, baking powder, soda, and salt. Add flour mixture alternately with sour cream, beating until smooth after each addition. Add vanilla and remaining ingredients. Turn into a well-greased tube pan, such as is used for angel food cake, and bake in a moderate oven (350°) about 45 minutes. Remove from pan, spread top with butter or margarine, and sprinkle with confectioners' sugar.

(NOTE: If you don't have a tube pan, two cake pans will do.)

Frank R. Sacher

Avocado and lemon grower
Fallbrook, Calif.

CHAPMAN SANDWICH

No finer compliment could be given a chef than the attachment of his name to his creation by admiring friends. Witness the history of this sandwich. *Chef* Schulte writes:

"The fact that the ingredients are placed between two slices of toast places this dish in the sandwich category, but it could never be considered a snack. Years ago Mr. Franklin E. Chapman introduced it into our kitchen. Over the years, frequent use has given the recipe the status of a family treasure. Oddly, although everyone enjoys the sandwich, when, at family gatherings, a Chapman sandwich is called for, preparation is a man's job."

```
4 to 6 slices bacon
4 eggs
4 large slices sharp Cheddar cheese
4 slices Bermuda onion
  Salt and pepper to taste
```

Cut bacon into small pieces and fry until crisp in a large frying pan. Pour off excess fat, leaving just enough to cover bottom of pan. Scatter bacon out evenly in pan; break eggs over bacon so that they are arranged individually. With a fork, break the yolks slightly. Place a slice of cheese on top of each egg; cover with slice of onion. Salt and pepper to taste. Cover the whole business and let it cook over a very low fire until the cheese has melted and the onions are somewhat transparent but still crunchy. Cut into 4 sections and place each serving between 2 slices of toast. Serve with a garden or romaine salad; then go back to the kitchen and start making seconds for the crowd.

B. H. Schulte

Business analyst
Berkeley, Calif.

CAPIROTADA CALIFORNIANA

Chef Ted Hutchison of Barstow, California, submits a recipe that has us puzzled. We don't know whether it is a main dish or a dessert, but we pass it on to the Western world with our blessing. It has to be eaten to be believed—a strange medley of flavors, but surprisingly good.

"Sour dough bread herein is a 'must,' as it is part of the flavor scheme.

```
  Shortening
8 slices, ½-inch thick, sour dough French bread
1 large onion, cut fine
¼ cup sugar
1 tablespoon coriander seed, crushed
1½ cups water
⅔ cup raisins
½ pound cheese (Cheddar or jack) cut in
    ¼-inch slices
```

Use enough shortening to cover frying pan to depth of ¼ inch. Fry bread golden brown; then drain. Pour off most of shortening. Fry onion until clear. Add sugar, coriander, and water and boil a few minutes to make an onion syrup.

In a 1-quart casserole, add alternate layers fried bread, raisins, and cheese. Spoon onion syrup over top slowly so bread will soak it up. Bake in slow oven (300°) until cheese is melted and syrup is absorbed. Serves 6 to 8.

Ted Hutchison

Nurseryman
Barstow, Calif.

ORANGE SCONES

This Scotch cousin to a biscuit may be familiar enough, but the orange lifts it well above the commonplace.

    2 cups flour
    2 teaspoons baking powder
    ¼ teaspoon salt
    2 tablespoons sugar
    ⅓ cup butter or shortening
    2 egg yolks or 1 whole egg
    2 tablespoons grated orange peel
    2 tablespoons orange juice
    ⅓ cup milk
    8 cubes sugar
    ¼ cup orange juice
       Melted butter

Sift flour, measure, then sift again with baking powder, salt, and sugar into bowl; blend in butter or shortening. Add egg yolks lightly beaten with grated orange peel and orange juice. Add milk to make a soft dough. Divide in two equal parts and pat out each part on floured board to fit into two 8-inch greased pans. Cut dough into 8 wedges with a floured knife. In each wedge insert half a cube of sugar, which has been dipped into orange juice.

Brush wedges with melted butter, and bake in hot oven (400°-425°) for approximately 15 minutes. Makes 16 scones.

We often serve these scones for Sunday supper with a fruit salad.

Edw. C. Balder

Retired
Ben Lomond, Calif.

BARBEMUSH

While it may be that meat makes the barbecue, a few extra surprises help sat-

isfy the appetites that always grow with the aromas that float through the air while the chef is at work. Byron Barshinger sends us one of those surprises of genuine originality.

    1 pound salt pork, diced
    3 or 4 large onions, minced
    1 clove garlic, minced
    1 quart water
    1 tablespoon chili powder
    ½ teaspoon oregano
    ½ teaspoon cumin seed
    2½ cups yellow cornmeal
    ¼ cup sliced green olives

The day before the barbecue, fry the salt pork slowly until crisp, and sauté onions and garlic in the fat until golden; set aside.

Put water in the top of a double boiler and bring to a boil; add seasonings and gradually stir in the cornmeal; cover and cook over boiling water for about 45 minutes. When done, add salt pork, onions, and olives. Turn out into a well-greased square pan that will give ample slices. Let stand until the next day.

An hour before barbecuing meat, grill well-oiled ½-inch slices of the cold mush over a fairly hot fire. The slices will lose moisture and shrink, and when thoroughly done, will let go of the grill so they can be turned easily. Cook till crisp, and if slightly scorched, so much the better. Tier them up on the side of the grill while cooking the meat.

Byron W. Barshinger

Gilroy, Calif.

EGYPTIAN ONE-EYED SANDWICH

Take a slice of bread and make a hole in the center. Brown bread in butter (one side only) in frying pan. Add extra butter as required. Turn over and drop an egg in center of bread and fry to suit.

Please do not confuse this with a fried egg and a piece of toast. I do not know why this tastes so much better, but that it does. Never fry just one at a time; you will eat two or three at a sitting.

Doris a Brooks

Pharmacist
Oakland, Calif.

HIGH SIERRA SANDWICHES

Chef Weldon Heald doesn't even claim to be a fisherman, but he has a secret that many fishermen might use.

"Mountains and mountain climbing happen to be my special outdoor enthusiasm. When I climbed my first mountain at the age of eight, my mother put me up some egg sandwiches. When I climbed my 500th mountain last month, I ate egg sandwiches. On the summit of every mountain in between, I ate the same kind of egg sandwich. It has become a sort of rite, like signing the register. These sandwiches are neither too dry nor soggy, and they keep fresh longer than most."

We heartily endorse the formula.

> 3 hard cooked eggs
> 2 thin slices onion
> Salt, pepper, paprika, and cayenne to taste
> 2 tablespoons mayonnaise
> Milk or cream
> Mexican hot sauce
> 4 slices bread
> Garlic butter

Slice hard cooked eggs in 3 or 4 directions so pieces are small (do not chop or mash). Add onion slices, cut into small pieces with shears. Add salt, pepper, and paprika. Add dash of cayenne (if you like things highly seasoned, add 2 or 3 dashes). Mix mayonnaise with enough milk or cream to give it consistency of a thick sauce. Add several drops Mexican hot sauce (here, too, you must use judgment as to personal taste). Combine half the mayonnaise mixture with egg, saving remainder to use later.

Spread all 4 slices of bread (the fresher the better) with garlic butter. On 2 of these slices, spread the remaining mayonnaise mixture. Spread the other 2 slices with the egg mixture. Gently press the mayonnaise-spread slices onto the egg-spread slices. With a sharp knife, cut each in half (do not try to be fancy and cut off crusts or quarter sandwiches—they aren't that type). Wrap each sandwich in wax paper. It will remain fresh for at least 24 hours.

Weldon F. Heald

Writer
Tucson, Arizona

ONION SANDWICH

This looks just like an ordinary onion sandwich, according to one of our taste testers, "but no burn!" The trick is to use a mild onion to begin with, and then subject it to a further mildening.

Let's examine "onion san."

The secret of this sandwich is to cut both the bread and the onion as thin as possible. The bread should be cut not more than 1/8 inch thick and it can be trimmed or left untrimmed, as you desire. The onion should be a mild variety, of sufficient size to cover the slice of bread.

The onion should be sliced razor-thin and placed carefully into a bowl of crushed ice to which 1 cup of skim milk has been added. Let the onion remain in this mixture for at least 1 hour before serving.

"Let's examine 'onion san' "

The dressing—enough for 4 to 6 sandwiches, at least—is a mixture of the following:

> 1/2 cup mayonnaise
> 2 grated or finely-chopped sweet pickles
> 2 tablespoons prepared mustard
> 1/2 teaspoon Worcestershire

Spread one side of the bread with a thin coat of butter, and place on top of the butter the slice of onion. Spread the other piece of bread with the special dressing and lay it on top of onion.

Sales manager
Los Angeles, Calif.

desserts

RIS A L'AMANDE

This Danish dessert is very vivid in color —as if the dark red juice of the loganberry had dripped on snow. It is rich. Serve at a dessert party, or at the end of a light meal. It can be made the day before and kept in the refrigerator. If you'd like to make it several days ahead of time, it should keep equally well in the freezer.

Chef Holger J. Jesperson says that in Denmark it is a favorite Christmas dessert. However, it makes excellent eating any time of the year.

"Makes excellent eating any time of year"

    2 cups milk
    ¼ cup uncooked rice
    1 tablespoon (1 envelope) unflavored gelatin
    ½ cup water
    ¼ cup slivered blanched almonds
    ¼ cup sherry
    1 teaspoon vanilla
    5 tablespoons sugar
    2 cups (1 pint) whipping cream

Bring milk to a boil. Add rice and cook until done. Be careful not to burn it. Add the gelatin which has been previously soaked in the ½ cup cold water. Stir until gelatin is dissolved. Add slivered almonds, sherry, vanilla, and sugar. Cool until almost set. Fold in the whipped cream, pour into bowl, and place in refrigerator.

Sauce

    1 can (12 oz.) sweetened loganberry juice
    1 large stick cinnamon
    1 tablespoon cornstarch
    1 teaspoon vanilla

Bring loganberry juice to a boil with cinnamon stick for 1 or 2 minutes. Remove cinnamon stick. Thicken with cornstarch to thin sauce consistency. Remove from stove and add vanilla. Cool.

To serve, turn out rice mold, cut into wedges and pour sauce over the dessert.

Other fruit juices can be used, but we think loganberry is the best—and certainly colorful. This serves 6 to 8. If you like plenty of sauce, double the recipe.

As they say in Denmark after good eating, *Vel bekomme* (we hope it agrees with you)!

Holger J. Jesperson

Mechanical engineer
Menlo Park, Calif.

SICILIAN NUT PUDDING

    ¾ cup nuts (preferably walnuts)
    ¾ cup sugar
    ¾ cup grated chocolate (cocoa will do)
    4 eggs, yolks and whites separated
      Dash of salt
    1 teaspoon vanilla
    1 ounce candied lemon peel, chopped
      Vanilla wafer or graham cracker crumbs

Chop nuts very fine in a wooden bowl; add the sugar and pound mixture to a paste; transfer to a mixing bowl. Add the chocolate, egg yolks, salt, and vanilla; mix thoroughly. Fold in the stiffly beaten egg whites. Last, add the chopped lemon peel. Grease a pie pan and sprinkle the bottom with crushed vanilla wafers or graham crackers. Pour in pudding mixture and bake in a moderate oven (350°) for 30 minutes. Serves 4 to 6. Don't worry if the nuts and sugar do not make a true paste, or if the batter seems stiff before the egg whites are added—the finished dessert will allay your fears. The only way to improve upon this Mediterranean classic is to top it with Rum Cream. Simply whip some cream, sweeten it, and add a dash of rum.

Dick O'dren

Los Angeles, Calif.

REAL YORKSHIRE PARKIN

"We've all heard of Yorkshire Pudding," says H. T. Gibson of Los Angeles, "but how many know Yorkshire Parkin, which also comes from the 'County of Broad Acres,' England?"

You get a clue from the dictionary:

Parkin (Scot. & Prov. Eng.). *Gingerbread made of oatmeal.*

The texture is somewhat heavy, but if you're partial to fruit cake or plum pudding, you should like this.

"Used in one family for generations"

The contributor adds, "Yorkshire Parkin should be kept a week or two before it is eaten. This recipe has been used in one family for generations."

    6 tablespoons butter
    ½ cup lard (or shortening, if preferred)
    1 cup sugar
    2 cups flour
    5 cups rolled oats
    1 teaspoon powdered ginger
    1⅓ cups molasses
    1 teaspoon soda
    ½ cup milk

Rub butter and lard into sugar, flour, rolled oats, and ginger. Add slightly warmed molasses. Dissolve soda in milk. Add to other ingredients and mix all together. Place in a greased pudding tin and bake in a slow oven (300°) for about 1 hour. Makes enough to fill a 9 by 13-inch baking dish.

H. T. Gibson

Los Angeles

BAVAROISE AU RHUM

    3 egg yolks
    6 tablespoons sugar
    1 tablespoon plain gelatin
    ¾ cup cold water
    3 tablespoons Jamaica rum
    1 cup cream, whipped
    1 pinch salt
    1 package frozen raspberries
    1 tablespoon cornstarch or potato flour
    Sugar to taste

The following smooth-textured sweet will convert anyone who tastes it to a passion for "the good old days" of molded puddings, or cold "shapes."

Beat egg yolks with sugar until lemon-colored. Soften gelatin in the cold water; dissolve over hot water. Add dissolved gelatin and rum to the egg mixture; chill. When mixture begins to thicken, fold in whipped cream and add salt. Pour into mold; chill until firm.

Unmold and serve with a fruit sauce, preferably one made with a package of frozen raspberries. To prepare it, thaw the berries and rub them through a strainer; thicken the resulting juice with about 1 tablespoon potato flour or cornstarch, simmering mixture to desired thickness; sweeten to taste. Chill and serve with the pudding.

Edgar M. West

Retired
Los Angeles, Calif.

FRUIT FROSTING

Take a medium-sized mixing bowl and put in the white of one egg, a cup of granulated sugar, and a cup of fresh fruit. "I prefer a cup of good, tart apple. However, strawberries or blackberries are also excellent choices." Beat this mixture until it is stiff. It covers a two-layer cake with frosting half an inch thick.

Marsden A. Sherman
Professor
Chico, Calif.

BREAD PUDDING, AU RHUM

    ¾ cup seedless raisins, soaked in Jamaica rum
    4 tablespoons sugar
    I teaspoon water
      Sliced, well-buttered day-old bread
    2 eggs
    I pinch salt
    2 cups milk, scalded
    ½ teaspoon vanilla

Soak raisins overnight, using just enough rum to barely cover. Caramel the inside of the top part of a round-bottomed double boiler in this way: Carefully boil over direct heat 2 tablespoons of the sugar with the water until it turns a rich brown. Remove pan from heat and coat sides of pan by swishing the caramelized sugar evenly around and to the top on all sides. Put in a layer of bread, butter-side up, sprinkle with raisins; repeat until pan is full, putting the last layer of bread butter-side down. Beat eggs with remaining 2 tablespoons of sugar and salt. Add slowly the scalded milk. Mix well, add vanilla, and pour over bread. Cover and place over gently boiling water. Cook for 1 hour. Remove from heat and turn out upside down on platter. Serve chilled with:

Rum Custard Sauce

    2 eggs, slightly beaten
    ½ cup sugar
    I pinch salt
    2 cups milk
    2 tablespoons Jamaica rum (drained from
      raisins)

Combine eggs, sugar, and salt in top part of a double boiler. Stir in milk and place over boiling water. Cook, stirring constantly, until mixture thickens, or coats the spoon. Remove, cool, add rum gradually. Chill before serving.

Actor and author
Van Nuys, Calif.

SOUR CREAM DIP FOR STRAWBERRIES

To top off a rich and heavy outdoor meal, few desserts compare with fresh fruit. Cliff Segerblom of Boulder City, Nevada, joins our ranks for suggesting that strawberries should be dunked in a sweet-sour dip. Results: surprising and superlative.

It will be a losing battle to pass this concoction around—the passer won't ever have an opportunity to sit down or sample a berry. Instead, place the berries and sour cream dip on a table and let everyone hover around them.

    ½ pint (I cup) cultured sour cream
    I teaspoon grated lemon peel
    I teaspoon lemon juice
    ½ cup powdered sugar

Beat sour cream, lemon peel, lemon juice, and powdered sugar with an egg beater until light. Place in a bowl and surround with whole strawberries whose stems and antimacassar-like caps are still intact.

Boulder City, Nevada

PICCOLE PASTE

    2 egg yolks
    3 tablespoons butter or margarine, melted
    3 tablespoons sugar
      Salt
    I teaspoon vanilla
    4 tablespoons port wine
    2¼ cups sifted flour
      Mincemeat or marmalade or preserves

Beat together egg yolks, butter, sugar, and salt. Add vanilla and wine. Add to flour and make a stiff dough as for pie crust. Wrap in wax paper and set aside for at least an hour before using. Roll out on floured board to the thickness of ordinary pie crust. Cut in circles about the size of the top of a water glass. Wet edges of the circles with water, using finger. Put in a generous teaspoon of mincemeat, fold over, and press wet edges together with fork. Prick on top to make vent. Fry in heated deep fat (375°) until golden brown. Drain and sprinkle with powdered sugar. Serve hot or cold.

Bows of Nastres: Make bows by cutting the pastry in ribbons ¾ inch wide and about 10 inches in length. Tie in loose knots and fry.

Life insurance
Palo Alto, Calif.

RASPBERRY TORTE

½ pound butter
1 cup sugar
2 egg yolks, well beaten
½ pound shelled almonds, ground
Grated rind of 1 lemon
2 cups flour
1 tablespoon cinnamon
½ teaspoon powdered cloves
Raspberry jam

Cream butter and sugar until light; add beaten egg yolks, ground almonds, and grated lemon rind. Mix and sift flour, cinnamon, and cloves; add gradually to first mixture. Roll out about three-fourths of the dough to ½-inch thickness on a lightly floured board. Fit into a square or rectangular baking pan and spread with raspberry jam. (The amount of jam needed is a matter of taste; you can use just a thin coating or spread it up to ¼ inch thick.) Roll remaining dough to ¼-inch thickness; cut into shapes with a small cooky cutter. Lift "cookies" with a spatula and arrange in rows on top of the jam. Bake in a moderate oven (350°) for about 40 minutes.

When torte is cold, place it in a covered cake or bread container to age for 2 days. To serve, cut in small squares.

The pastry may be hard to handle. If it should break, just patch it by pressing it back together. The finished torte holds together beautifully but, once served, will disappear in a fraction of the time it took to make it!

Burton C. Walker
Supervisor
San Diego, Calif.

NUT TORTE

F. W. Jaques, an engineer at a cheese factory in Tillamook, Oregon, submits a favorite recipe for a "Torte," a kind of spice cake widely baked in German-speaking countries. It resembles many well known German "Torten," which invariably include many eggs, ground nuts, and, often, white bread crumbs in the ingredients. *Chef* Jaques says he believes his recipe came originally from Austria, where many

"How to be frivolous with 10 eggs"

of the world-famous Torten, such as "Sachertorte," originated. When ground nuts are not included, butter is usually added for shortening.

One scoffer suggests that this recipe be titled "How to be frivolous with 10 eggs." But why not, on occasion, if the results are worth it? They are. We would even recommend topping each portion with whipped cream.

10 eggs
1 cup sugar
Grated peel of 1 lemon
½ teaspoon cloves
1 teaspoon cinnamon
¾ cup dry bread crumbs
1½ cups finely ground almonds, filberts, or walnut meats

Separate 4 eggs. Beat 6 eggs and the 4 egg yolks until thick. Add sugar, lemon peel, cloves, cinnamon, bread crumbs, and nut meats, and mix well. Fold in the 4 remaining egg whites which have been beaten stiff. Spoon mixture into a greased 10 by 15-inch pan. Bake in a moderate oven (350°) for 45 minutes. Serves 12 to 15.

F. W. Jaques
Tillamook, Oregon

PERSIMMON MOUSSE

3 fully ripe persimmons
¼ cup sugar
½ pint whipping cream

Peel the persimmons carefully and press the pulp through a strainer. Add the sugar to the pulp and stir until dissolved. Whip the cream until stiff and add the persimmon pulp. Freeze quickly. Serves 3 to 4.

FELIX SAUNDERS
Oceanographer
La Jolla, Calif.

APRICOT JAM STRUDEL

Here's a dessert that rates some kind of special award of merit, to judge by the enthusiasm of our panel of testers. It is undeniably rich, with a fine combination of crisp and chewy textures, and filling that is moist and permeated with the flavor of apricot.

    ½ pound (2 cubes) butter
    2 cups flour
    ½ teaspoon salt
    1 cup thick cultured sour cream
    1 jar (10 oz.) or 1¼ cups apricot jam
    1 cup shredded coconut
    ⅔ cup walnut or almond meats, chopped
      Powdered sugar

Mix butter, flour, and salt as you would for a pie crust, cutting butter into dry ingredients, then mix in the sour cream. Put in refrigerator overnight.

Next morning, remove and let stand until it is room temperature. Cut dough in half and roll each piece into a rectangle measuring approximately 10 by 15 inches. Spread with jam, and sprinkle with coconut and nuts. Roll like a jelly roll; place on greased baking sheet. Bake in a 350° oven for 1 hour.

Remove from oven and allow to cool for 5 to 10 minutes. Cut in pieces, sprinkle with powdered sugar, and serve. Makes 18 generous pieces.

A. Abrahamson
Los Angeles

CRUMB TOP APPLE PIE

Chef C. I. McReynolds offers this dish— a delicious and hearty finish for a meal. It is a refreshing change from the run-of-the-mill apple pie.

    8 large apples
    ⅔ cup granulated sugar
      Cinnamon or nutmeg
      A little lemon juice and salt
    1 cup flour
    ½ cup brown sugar
    ½ cup butter or margarine

Slice apples into a rather deep pie pan, having them well heaped. There is no bottom crust. Sprinkle over the granulated sugar, cinnamon, lemon juice, and salt.

For the upper crust, mix the flour, brown sugar, and butter until it is just crumbly. Be careful not to work it too long or it will become creamy. Sprinkle the mixture over the apples and press into shape. Bake in a 350° oven until the crust is brown and the apples are tender (about an hour). The butter and sugar will melt down through the apples and make it solid enough to cut.

C. I. McReynolds
Tucson, Arizona

HUDSON'S BAY COMPANY PUDDING

"If you are going to be hunting in the wilderness with a friend or two on Thanksgiving and want to have something really special for that occasion, why not try a Hudson's Bay Company pudding?" Why not, indeed? This man's question intrigues us.

Bradford Angier, of Cambria, California, writer, outdoorsman, and connoisseur of cooking, vouchsafes further explanation: "These aromatic delicacies, that by tradition vary in accordance with what ingredients may be at hand, have crowned many a holiday repast since the *Governor and Company of Adventurers of England trading into Hudson's Bay* was founded 2nd May 1670. Whenever some outdoorsmen enjoy one of these gastronomical splendors in the wilderness, often enough they think of Voltaire acidly describing the North two centuries ago as, 'A patch of snow inhabited by barbarians, bear, and beaver.' M. Voltaire should have seen the roof of the continent when it's in a festive mood."

Reduced to more mundane terms, this is a bag pudding, remarkably light for the rich cargo of ingredients it bears. Outdoorsmen readying for a trip can mix the components at home and seal them in a plastic container. Indoorsmen should be encouraged to do the whole job at home and bring forth this nobly rounded dessert on some appropriate plum pudding occasion.

"Hunting in the wilderness with a friend or two on Thanksgiving"

4 cups sifted flour
4 teaspoons baking powder
½ teaspoon cinnamon
½ teaspoon nutmeg
1 cup brown sugar
½ cup white sugar
¼ cup finely chopped glacéed fruit mix
2 cups seedless raisins
1 cup currants
4 tablespoons whole egg powder
6 tablespoons whole milk
¼ teaspoon powdered lemon juice
2 cups finely minced suet
2 cups water

Mix together all ingredients except suet and water and—for a wilderness trip—seal in a plastic container. When the memorable day arrives, mix in the suet; it may be either lamb or beef suet brought along for the occasion, or it may be the suet of some game animal procured on the spot. Then add water and mix well to form a cake batter.

For the next step, you need a heavy cotton bag, one that you have carried along especially for this purpose, or one you can borrow from the food pack. Wring it out in hot water and dust the inside with white flour. Tip the cake batter into the bag and knot the top tightly, making sure that ample room remains for the expansion.

Place the bag of batter without delay in a large pot containing sufficient boiling water to cover it. Keep the water boiling cheerily for 3 hours. When the pudding starts to become hard, carefully turn the bag bottom-side-up so that the fruit will not all settle into one end. Move the bag now and then as the boiling continues, so that it will not be burned by the sides of the receptacle.

At the end of the cooking time, immerse the bag and its contents very briefly in cold water and then gently work the fabric loose so as not to mar the traditional dish of the world's oldest trading corporation.

Serve it hot, with some appropriate sauce steaming from it. Melted butter and sugar, flavored with some camp spice such as cinnamon or something tart such as powdered citrus juice, will enhance it. So will the thick hot juice from boiled dried apricots or peaches. Serves 8 to 10.

Bradford Angier

Cambria, Calif.

A MAN'S PIE

E. F. Champion, a veteran *Chef*, doesn't aim to make cooking easier, but he has the right notion on a pie that goes straight to the hearts of men.

"I am attaching hereto a recipe for an unusual pie. You will again note that I have gone into quite a bit of detail, but I felt quite sure that few men understood the instructions of the pie."

On first glance, it appears to be an apple pie. But it has mince pie and raisin pie appeal as well. It is very nearly all pies to all pie-eaters. Serve it hot, or cold with whipped cream or ice cream on top. That crusty business on top is good.

Bottom crust:

    4 level tablespoons shortening
    1¼ cups flour
    ½ teaspoon salt
    Ice water

Chop shortening thoroughly into sifted flour and salt. Add 3 to 4 tablespoons ice water, scattering it so as to cause no excessively wet dough.

Take dough into hands and form a cylinder or round mound about 2 inches high. Place on floured board and roll to fit a 10-inch pie pan. After dough is placed in pan, prick dough with fork at about 1-inch intervals, and coat with light film of butter. Place in 450° oven for about 10 minutes until it starts to brown, then remove.

Filling:

    3 medium-sized cooking apples
    2 tablespoons flour
    ⅔ cup of chopped, seeded muscat raisins
    1 cup crushed pineapple and juice
    1 teaspoon allspice, if desired
      Juice of 1 lemon (approximately
        3 tablespoons)
    1 cup water
      Pinch of salt
    ⅔ cup sugar

Dice apples into ¼ to ½-inch cubes. Mix flour with apples. Add other ingredients in the order listed above. Place in pan and let come to a boil. Place filling in pie shell. Sprinkle sugar over the filling.

Top crust:

Crush 1 small package (3 oz.) sugar wafers. Mix in 3 tablespoons melted butter. Sprinkle evenly over top of pie. Bake 40 minutes in moderate oven (350°) or until set and slightly puffy. Serves 8.

E. F. Champion
Sales manager
Los Angeles, Calif.

BABA AU RHUM

This firm golden sponge cake holds its shape without becoming soggy—the test of a good Baba! (A tip to first-time bakers: be sure the scalded milk is cool before blending with fresh yeast.)

Dissolve and blend

    1 cake fresh yeast in
    ½ cup lukewarm milk, scalded, then cooled

Add and beat until smooth:

    1 tablespoon sugar
    ½ cup flour

Cover and let rise in a warm place until doubled in bulk, about one hour.
Cream until light, and combine with the yeast mixture:

    ½ cup butter
    ½ cup sugar

Add, and thoroughly blend:

    3 eggs, well beaten
    ½ teaspoon salt
    1 tablespoon lemon rind, grated
    1½ cups sifted flour

Beat for 5 minutes with an electric mixer at medium speed, or 15 minutes by hand. Pour into a well-greased 2-quart casserole, and let rise for 1 hour. Bake in a moderate oven (350°) for about 45 minutes, or until slightly brown. Remove from oven, prick the top with a sharp fork to allow steam to escape. Turn out of pan on to serving plate. Pour Baba Sauce over the top and sides and allow to stand until it is all absorbed. Cover with Apricot Glaze.

BABA SAUCE

Boil for 5 minutes and cool:

    1 cup brown sugar
    1 cup granulated sugar
    2 cups water

Remove from fire and add:

    4 tablespoons Jamaica rum

APRICOT GLAZE

Soak overnight:

    ¼ pound dried apricots
      Water to cover

Press through a sieve. Add equal amount of sugar and boil for 5 minutes, stirring constantly.

J. D. Dimshee
Doctor
Phoenix, Arizona

E AI, KAMAAINA

Chef Louis Beck, back from Hawaii, proposes a concoction that might raise a *kamaaina's* eyebrows. The title gives no

angel food cake

papaya

Sauterne

nuts

sour cream

E ai, kamaaina

"The five ingredients may appear to be strange bedfellows"

warning of what's to come: *"E ai, kama-aina"* means, simply, "Eat, old-timer."

The five ingredients may appear to be strange bedfellows, but this dish was approved by the majority of our taste testers. One did suggest, however, that before serving it to guests, you should be sure of their tastes in food. To wit: they should approve foods sweet, sour, crisp, and soft—and not be too startled by the combination.

        1 large angel food cake
        Sauterne (about 1½ cups)
        1 pint sour cream
        1 cup ground macadamia nuts
        1 large papaya, sliced

(If the papaya or macadamia nuts **are unavailable, you might substitute apricot** halves, peach slices, or cherries, and chopped toasted almonds. *Chef* Beck insists, however, that "They will make the finished product an imitation.")

Pull the cake into 12 to 14 separate servings and arrange on a large plate or platter. Carefully spoon the sauterne over until each piece is well soaked—the nearer saturation, the better.

Place in the refrigerator for half an hour, remove, and transfer each serving to an individual plate, allowing any surplus wine to drip off. Cover each piece with

sour cream, sprinkle with the ground nuts, then dot generously with the fruit. Serve immediately. Depending on size of servings, this will serve from 12 to 14.

Writer
Los Angeles, Calif.

CHRISTMAS HONEY CAKE

        1 cup strained honey
        ¾ cup sugar (1 cup if sweeter cake is
            desired)
        3 eggs
        ½ cup cold, strong coffee
        3 cups sifted all-purpose flour
        3 teaspoons baking powder
        ½ teaspoon baking soda
        ½ teaspoon cinnamon
        ½ teaspoon nutmeg
        1 cup nutmeats, cut rather coarsely

Beat honey until it turns almost white; add sugar and continue beating; add eggs and coffee; continue beating until the whole thing is foamy. Then add all the dry ingredients which has been sifted together. These should be added a very little at a time, beating between each addition. Then go on beating. If an electric beater is used, it is best to do the final beating by hand so you are sure the batter at the edges of the bowl has been mixed in. The beating is the most important part of this cake. Last, add the nuts, then turn the batter into a pan which has been lined with buttered paper, or into an angel food tin which has been thoroughly greased. Bake in a moderately slow oven (325°) for 1 hour and 20 minutes, and *don't look at it* until it has been in the oven 1 hour and 10 minutes. Test with a straw, and take the cake out as soon as straw comes out clean. When cake cools, ice with your favorite frosting.

F. A. McKEAN
Telephone exchange
Hollywood, Calif.

FRANCO-CALIFORNIA SURPRISE RING

⅓ cup butter
1⅓ cups brown sugar
½ teaspoon almond extract (optional)
2 eggs
1¾ cups flour
3 teaspoons baking powder
½ teaspoon cinnamon
½ teaspoon grated nutmeg
½ cup milk
½ pound dates, cut in small pieces
1 teaspoon shaved, candied lemon peel
1 teaspoon shaved, candied orange peel

Cream butter and brown sugar; beat in almond extract; add well-beaten eggs. Sift flour twice before measuring, then sift with baking powder and spices; add gradually to first mixture alternately with milk. Dredge dates and fruit peel in a little flour and add last. Beat well for 3 minutes.

Turn into an angel cake pan which has been greased, lined with waxed paper, and greased again. Bake in a moderate oven (350°) for about 40 minutes.

Serve hot at table, with a hard sauce of confectioners' sugar and butter, flavored with rum or brandy.

Dr. FREDERICK WILSON
Lecturer
Seattle, Washington

VACATION FRUITCAKE

Many people may wonder why this recipe is called Vacation Fruitcake, and the answer is that fruitcake is a delight on any vacation. It will pack in a trunk, suitcase, duffel bag, or even a knapsack, and travel equally well from the seashore to the Sierra. Don't ask me how to keep it, as I have never been able to keep any portion of one over two weeks, and it isn't the pack rats that make it disappear.

2 cups dates
1 cup walnuts
½ pound candied cherries
½ pound citron
½ pound orange peel
½ pound butter
1 cup sugar
4 eggs
2 cups flour
1 teaspoon baking powder
½ cup grape juice

Seed dates and cut into eighths. Shell nuts and break into pieces. Quarter cherries. Cut citron and orange peel into ¼-inch cubes. (I prefer large pieces of citron and orange peel to the smaller pieces in ready-cut packs.) Put all fruit into kettle and mix well.

Cream butter. Add sugar, then cream again. Add eggs and mix into butter and sugar. Sift flour and baking powder several times; then add half of flour to butter-sugar mixture and the other half to fruit mixture. Mix butter, flour, sugar, and eggs well.

Heat grape juice; add this to butter, sugar, and flour, and mix well. Add to fruit mixture and mix again. Turn into angel food cake pan and bake in slow oven (250°) about 3 hours.

NICHOLAS D'ARCY, JR.
Mechanical engineer
Huntington Park, Calif.

DUTCH APPLE PIE

First: Cook ½ cup quick cooking oats in 1½ cups water with ¾ teaspoon salt. When cooked, rub oatmeal through a sieve to remove the chaff.

Second: Make a standard pie pastry. Put it in a 9-inch pie plate, as the crust should be thick. Build up the edge of the pastry around the pan about half an inch or more to keep juice from boiling over.

Third: Pare 6 large cooking apples. Core and cut into eighths, then cut these cross-wise. Put in salt water until ready to use.

Fourth: Mix ¾ cup sugar (more or less, depending on apple tartness), 4 table-spoons flour, ½ cup sieved cooked oat-meal, and 1 tablespoon cream.

Fifth: Mix ½ cup sugar and 1 teaspoon cinnamon.

Sixth: Pour all the oatmeal mixture into pastry. Then arrange apples, thin edge up, around outer edge of pastry. Continue arranging rows until bottom layer is covered with apple wedges. Then sprinkle some of the sugar and cinnamon mixture over this layer and dot with butter.

Now start a second layer about ¾ inch from the edge of the pan and repeat the rest of the procedure. Then a third layer about 1½ inches from the edge of the pan. This builds up the center. When the pie is baked and cooled, the center levels off.

Seventh: Bake in 450° oven for 10 minutes. Then reduce heat to 350° for about 1¼ hours, or until done.

Office manager (retired)
Alhambra, Calif.

FESTIVE CHOCOLATE CAKE

    1 cup shortening
    2 cups sugar
    3 eggs, separated
    3 ounces bitter chocolate
    1 cup milk
    ½ cake compressed yeast, or ½ package fast,
        granular yeast
    ¼ cup lukewarm water
    2¾ cups flour
    ½ teaspoon salt
    1 teaspoon soda
    3 tablespoons hot water
    1½ teaspoons vanilla

Cream shortening and continue creaming while adding sugar and egg yolks; beat well. Add the bitter chocolate, melted with the milk. Dissolve the yeast in the lukewarm water; add this to first mixture and beat well. Beat in the flour and salt, which have been sifted together. When mixed, fold in the whites of the eggs, which have been beaten stiff but not dry. Allow this mixture to stand overnight or until ready to bake conveniently. It will *not* rise like a sponge. It is not necessary to place the batter in the refrigerator. When ready to bake, add the soda, which has been dissolved and mixed thoroughly in the hot water, and add the vanilla. Bake in 2, 3, or 4 layers, as desired, in greased and floured pans, in a moderate oven (350°) from 30 to 45 minutes, depending upon thickness of layers.

For a festive occasion the 4-layer baking is preferred. Between the second and third layers, spread ginger marmalade, and between the other layers, and over the outside, a butter-cream icing.

Chief of exhibits, state fair
North Sacramento, Calif.

GOOD NEIGHBOR CAKE

    ½ cup butter or margarine
    1½ cups sugar
        Grated peel of 1 orange
    4 small eggs, separated
    2 cups sifted cake flour
    4 teaspoons baking powder
    ¼ teaspoon salt
    1 cup milk

Cream butter and sugar until light. Add orange peel. Beat in egg yolks one at a time. Sift flour, baking powder, and salt together. Add alternately to batter with milk, beating until smooth. Beat 2 of the egg whites until they are stiff, but not dry; fold lightly into cake batter. Pour into 2 well-greased and floured layer cake pans. Bake in a moderate oven (350°) 25 to 30 minutes. Remove from pans and cool on rack.

Apple Frosting: Peel and grate 1 green apple. Beat remaining 2 egg whites until stiff, then beat in gradually 1 cup sugar and grated apple. Use as filling and frosting for cake.

Writer
Lemon Grove, Calif.

WHITE FRUIT CAKE

1 pound *each* candied cherries, seeded
    raisins, seedless raisins and candied
    pineapple in red, green, and white fingers
½ pound citron
¼ pound orange peel
¼ pound lemon peel
2 cups brandy or rum
1 pound butter
1¼ pounds sugar
1 dozen eggs
1¼ pounds flour
1 teaspoon baking powder
1 teaspoon *each* cinnamon, cloves, nutmeg,
    and mace
1 pound *each* blanched almonds, hazelnuts,
    and pecan halves
½ pound Brazil nuts

(1) Prepare fruit the day before baking cakes. Cut cherries and seeded raisins in half. Cut pineapple, citron, orange peel, and lemon peel in long, thin strips, not too wide. Place prepared fruit in bowl and add brandy or rum, turning fruit occasionally so that most of the liquor will be absorbed.

(2) Cream butter until soft; add sugar gradually, beating until mixture is light and fluffy. Add eggs one at a time, beating well after each egg is added.

(3) Mix flour, baking powder, and spices, and sift together 3 times.

(4) Split the blanched almonds and hazelnuts, and quarter the Brazil nuts. Add nut meats to the fruit mixture.

(5) Dust some of the flour mixture over the fruit and nuts and mix well. Repeat dusting process until all flour is used.

(6) Add butter-sugar-egg mixture and mix thoroughly.

(7) Line loaf tins with heavy brown paper that has been well oiled or greased. Fill the pans two-thirds full.

(8) Preheat oven to 300°. Bake cakes 2 to 3 hours, depending on size of loaves. Reduce heat to 250° the last hour. To test for doneness, thrust a wire cake tester or a wooden toothpick into the center of the cake. If it is done, no batter will adhere to the tester or pick. Set cakes aside to cool, preferably overnight.

(9) Saturate white cloths in rum or brandy, then wring them out so they are moist but not dripping. Wrap cakes first in cloth, next in paper, and finally in waxed paper. Seal with gummed tape. Store until ready for use, at which time the tops may be decorated with almonds, cherries, etc.

F. A. McKean
Telephone exchange
Hollywood, Calif.

MYSTERIOUS CHOCOLATE CAKE

½ cup shortening
2 cups brown sugar, lightly packed
2 eggs
2 tablespoons cocoa
5 teaspoons vinegar
2 cups cake flour
1 teaspoon soda
½ teaspoon baking powder
½ teaspoon salt
1 cup lukewarm water

Cream shortening, add brown sugar and whole eggs, and beat well until smooth and very creamy. Add cocoa and vinegar, and beat until smooth. Sift flour, measure, then sift again with soda, baking powder, and salt and add alternately with water. Bake in two 9-in. layer pans for about 30 minutes in a moderately hot oven (375°). Frost with caramel or coffee icing, and sprinkle chocolate chips on top. Serve, and just ask any man what he thinks of this cake.

Jack K Green
Building contractor
Santa Barbara, Calif.

HOLIDAY FRUIT BOWL

Chef Wallace S. Wharton favors this dish "for brunch, late snacking, or other nibbling." It is somewhere between a fruit salad and a dessert, could be served as either, or alone.

The general effect is soothing, but you will notice small percentages of rum (optional), vanilla, and maraschino cherries, all mildly stimulating to the taste buds. There are obvious variations to the list of ingredients, says *Chef* Wharton. Other fruits may be added to the base or substituted for those listed—"except the oranges for which there is no substitute." For appearance only—no difference to taste—we recommend that you drain the pineapple thoroughly and don't add the juice to this mixture.

"Drain the pineapple thoroughly"

- 1 large apple, peeled and cored
- 1 large banana, peeled
- 1 large orange, peeled, membrane removed, and sectioned
- 1 tall can (No. 2II) pineapple chunks (1½ cups)
- ½ cup maraschino cherries, halved
- ½ cup sliced dates
- ½ cup walnut meats, coarsely chopped

Sauce:
- 1 egg
- 4 tablespoons sugar
- 1 cup table cream
- ½ teaspoon vanilla
- 2 ounces (4 tablespoons) rum (optional)
- ⅛ teaspoon fresh ground nutmeg (or to taste)

Cut apple, banana, orange segments, and pineapple into small cubes. Place all fruits and nutmeats in a bowl and mix.

Beat one egg until it is a light froth; then beat in sugar thoroughly. Add cream, vanilla, rum, and nutmeg, beating mildly to mix well. Pour this sauce over fruit, cover the bowl, and let stand in refrigerator at least 3 hours before serving. Serves 10 to 12 as side dish or snack.

Wallace S. Wharton

*Farmer and Civil Defense Director
Turner, Oregon*

MORHABA DATE CAKE

From the Coachella Valley of California, Russ Nicoll sends a date cake moist and crunchy, so simple to make that it's practically an idiot's delight, and just the right luscious companion for a cup of coffee.

*"Just the right luscious companion
for a cup of coffee"*

- 2 eggs
- 1 cup sugar
- ½ teaspoon vanilla
- ⅓ cup flour
- 1 teaspoon baking powder
- 1 cup walnut meats, chopped
- 1 cup chopped dates

Beat eggs, then stir in sugar, vanilla, flour, and baking powder, mixing thoroughly. Add chopped nut meats and dates. Turn into a greased 8-inch-square pan.

Bake for 30 minutes in a slow oven (300°). When the cake drops flat, it is done. Cut into squares or bars and serve.

Russ Nicoll

Thermal, Calif.

COCONUT HONEY AND SUGARED CHIPS

Milk from 1 fresh coconut
4 to 5 cups grated fresh coconut meat
    (approximately)
1 cup honey
1 cup sugar
2 cups water

Drain the milk from the coconut and save. Grate the meat on a medium coarse grater, and measure the shreds. If they are more or less than 4-5 cups, adjust amounts of other ingredients accordingly. Put honey, sugar, coconut milk, and water in a kettle of about 4-quart size. Add the grated coconut and stir until the sugar melts; then bring the mixture to a boil. Let it stand until it cools. Bring to a boil again and strain through a mesh strainer. Remove coconut and spread on a cooky sheet.

Boil the liquid to 230°, or until it forms a very soft ball in cold water. Let it cool; then store in a jar for future use.

Place the coconut shreds in a slow oven (about 280°) until they dry and turn light brown, stirring occasionally during the process to prevent sticking. For added crispness, let the oven cool a little, then put the coconut back in and leave there overnight. Store in a dry place.

Makes about a pint *each* of honey and chips, if the coconut is good sized and contains plenty of milk. To serve, pour the syrup over the ice cream and sprinkle with the lightly browned crisp coconut shreds.

Melvin L Chase
Retired
Pasadena, Calif.

CHOCOLATE NUGGETS

Chef Mel Schwartz has invented a stout cooky that is absolutely foolproof. When you eliminate baking, you remove any possibility of error.

36 vanilla wafers
1 pound powdered sugar
1 cup chopped nut meats
¼ cup cocoa
½ cup muscatel
2 tablespoons white corn syrup

Put the vanilla wafers through the food chopper or crush them with a rolling pin.

Add all but about ½ cup of the powdered sugar. Stir in the nut meats, cocoa, wine, and corn syrup. Mixture will be very thick. Form into small balls by rolling between your hands. Roll in the powdered sugar you held out of the mixture. *Do not bake.* Makes about 50 cookies.

Mel Schwartz
Pharmacist
Los Angeles, Calif.

GERMAN COOKIES

There's some German influence in this cooky recipe, which Edwin R. Coltrin of Concord, California, copied from one of his mother's, and made modifications. It is actually a little more like a cake, moist, and lightly frosted.

"During World War II," says *Chef* Coltrin, "cookies of this type were the only ones that could survive a six-week, 7,000-mile journey, to arrive as moist and tasty as the day my mother had packaged them."

4 eggs
1 package brown sugar (dark or light,
    I prefer dark)
2½ cups flour
1 teaspoon cinnamon
½ teaspoon cloves
    Dash of salt
1 cup chopped walnuts

Cream eggs and sugar. Sift flour, measure, then sift again with cinnamon, cloves, and salt into egg mixture. Mix well. Add chopped walnuts. Spread on greased 12 by 18-inch cooky sheet. Bake in a moderately hot oven (375° to 400°) for 20 minutes, or until done. Immediately spread glaze (1 cup powdered sugar mixed with ¼ cup water) over top. Allow to cool, then cut into 2 by 3-inch squares or finger strips. Makes about 5 dozen squares.

Edwin R Coltrin
Concord, Calif.

PEANUT BRITTLE

Joseph Hovsepian is known at the California State Fair in Sacramento as a prize-winning amateur candy maker. His secret: use top quality ingredients. This recipe for peanut brittle lives up to his reputation. (You'll need a candy thermometer.)

    4 cups sugar
 1⅓ cups corn syrup
    1 cup water
  ⅓ cup sorghum (optional)
    2 pounds shelled raw Spanish peanuts
    1 cube butter
    1 teaspoon salt
    3 teaspoons vanilla
    2 teaspoons baking soda

Combine sugar, corn syrup, water, and sorghum and bring to a boil while stirring. Cook to 245° (firm ball in cold water). Add peanuts and cook to 290°, stirring while cooking. Add butter and cook to 310° (very hard crack stage if tested in cold water). Remove from fire. Add salt and vanilla and mix it in. Then add baking soda. Stir the whole mixture vigorously and then pour on a stainless steel counter or a chop plate well oiled with mineral oil. With your hands stretch the candy as thin as possible. After it is cool, break in appropriate sized pieces. Keep in a closed container. Makes approximately 5 pounds candy.

Jos. Hovsepian

Employee, California State Motor Vehicle Department Sacramento, Calif.

JUMBLES

  ½ pound butter (2 cubes)
   1 cup sugar
   3 eggs
   2 teaspoons nutmeg (or ½ a nutmeg, grated)
   3 cups flour
     Rosewater
     Sugar

Beat the butter and sugar to a cream. Add the eggs, well beaten; then add the nutmeg, and then the flour. Chill. Dust board and rolling pin lightly with flour. Roll out the dough very thin, down to about ⅛ inch thickness, if you can handle it that thin. Cut out circles with a round cutter, then take out centers with a smaller round to form rings. Dip in rose water and sprinkle with sugar. Bake in a moderate oven to a very light brown. Makes 3 to 4 dozen depending on size.

E. K. Roth.

Life insurance Portland, Oregon

JOE'S DOUGHNUTS

When J. S. Howard makes doughnuts, he combines dough with a nut. He builds up his doughnut like a baseball.

Starting with a walnut half as the core, he wraps a pitted date around it, and folds the dough around both.

"builds up his doughnut like a baseball"

We recommend a slight pre-cooking of the dates. Bring barely to a boil in a small amount of water, drain, and then proceed according to his directions.

  3½ cups flour
   4 tablespoons baking powder
   1 teaspoon salt
  ½ teaspoon nutmeg (preferably freshly ground)
 1½ cups sugar
   2 eggs
   2 tablespoons melted butter or margarine
   1 cup milk
     Grated peel of 1 medium-sized lemon

Sift flour, measure, then sift again with baking powder, salt, nutmeg, and sugar. Beat together eggs, butter or margarine, and milk until foamy. Pour into dry ingredients and mix thoroughly. Stir in lemon peel.

Deep fry, and sprinkle with powdered sugar (with or without cinnamon added).

J. R. Howard

North Hollywood, Calif.

SOURDOUGH DOUGHNUTS

We present the following recipe for the special benefit of *Chefs* who are sourdough enthusiasts, doughnut lovers, or who just enjoy the old-fashioned, rough and ready kind of cooking appropriate to the chuck wagons, ranches, mining camps, and lumber camps of the West.

Frank E. Blacklidge, of Tucson, Arizona, says, "I first 'dreamed up' this recipe while batching on a ranch about 20 years

"For the benefit of Chefs *who are sourdough enthusiasts or doughnut lovers"*

ago. As far as I know, it is original with me. Everybody who has sampled the doughnuts says they are the best he has ever eaten."

        2 cups flour
        2 teaspoons sugar
        1 teaspoon salt
    1⅓ cups warm water
        2 eggs
    ½ teaspoon shortening or salad oil
    1⅓ cups sugar
        1 teaspoon *each* cinnamon, nutmeg, and salt
        4 level teaspoons baking powder
    ¼ teaspoon soda
        3 cups flour (approximately)
        Shortening or salad oil for frying

Put the 2 cups flour, 2 teaspoons sugar, and 1 teaspoon salt in a crock or glass container and mix dry. Add the water. Mix and set in a warm place until the mixture sours and begins to work—usually in about 2 days.

Transfer sourdough mixture to a mixing bowl and stir in well beaten eggs and shortening. Dry mix together the 1⅓ cups

sugar and the cinnamon, nutmeg, salt, baking powder, and soda. Mix thoroughly with the sourdough. Add the 3 cups flour gradually until the dough is the right consistency for rolling and cutting. Roll, cut, and fry in hot deep fat (365°).

This makes a doughnut about halfway between "raised" and "cake." Makes approximately 5 dozen doughnuts.

F. E. Blacklidge Sr.

Tucson

WELL DONE BANANAS

We've tasted some mighty good bananas cooked fast in a skillet. But John Sills makes out an equally good case for cooking them long and slow. For best results, get bananas that are as ripe as possible.

Take as many ripe bananas as you can fit into a heavy aluminum frying pan (avoid black iron, which will turn the bananas purplish-black). The bananas may be so ripe that they are slightly translucent (the skin will be mottled with brown dots); just remove any dark spots on the banana flesh.

Place bananas in pan with melted butter (4 tablespoons butter to 8 bananas). Cover tightly and cook over *very* low heat for 20 to 30 minutes, or until the bananas are puffed up and soft. Then uncover and, if necessary, brown at a slightly higher heat, using honey or brown sugar to caramelize. When they are browned on one side, turn over and brown the other side. Serve hot, either as a "vegetable" course with dinner or as a dessert. They go very well with ice cream.

John S. Sills

Ceramist and designer
Woodside, Calif.

RODGROD (RED MUSH)

"Rodgrod," literally translated, means "Red Mush." If "mush" rates low on your scale of taste appeal, just call it "Red Pudding."

For the main ingredient, use fresh fruits in summer, canned fruits or fruit juices in winter. "We like Satsuma plums best," says *Chef* Jespersen, "but in Denmark a mixture of currants and raspberries is the most popular. However, you can use any kind of berries, plums, or tart fruit. We can also recommend nectarines."

    3 to 4 cups fruit or berries
    Water
    1 large cinnamon stick
    Sugar to taste
    ½ cup cornstarch
    ¼ cup cold water
    2 teaspoons vanilla
    Powdered sugar
    Table cream

Wash and clean fruit. Place in pan and cover with water. Add cinnamon stick. Cook until fruit is tender. (If you use canned fruit, add enough water to syrup to cover fruit; simmer long enough to bring out cinnamon flavor.) Remove cinnamon stick. Press pulp and juice through a sieve. Sweeten to taste and bring to a boil. Slowly add cornstarch—dissolved beforehand in the cold water—and stir continually. Cook until thick and clear. Remove from stove and add vanilla. Pour into serving bowl and sprinkle with powdered sugar to keep top from crusting. Serve cold with cream.

Mechanical engineer
Menlo Park, Calif.

BRANDIED RUSSE

Here's an ambrosial mixture that should please almost any guest with a well developed sweet tooth, provided you get the macaroons well soaked with juice. You will probably have to fill out with ordinary canned peach syrup to get the quantity of "peach liquor" specified. Bernard P. Fisher of Honolulu suggests brandied apricots or litchi nuts as alternates for the brandied peaches.

    (per serving)
    3 almond macaroons
    1 tablespoon whipped cream, slightly
        sweetened
    1 brandied peach
    4 tablespoons brandied peach liquor or
        peach syrup
    1 teaspoon whipped cream

Line sherbet dishes with the macaroons, put the tablespoon of whipped cream in the center, and the brandied peach on top. Pour peach liquor over the top and place sherbet dishes in refrigerator for 1 hour before serving. Just before serving, decorate with the additional whipped cream. Serves 1.

Optician
Honolulu, T. H.

PEARS HENRI

Robert Bard contributes a showpiece he learned from the illustrious French epicure and chef, Henri Charpentier. The only additional instruction we have to offer concerns the poaching of the pears. They will remain white if simmered very slowly in a covered pan immediately after peeling. The pears will be done when they acquire a translucent appearance and are tender to the tines of a fork; this takes almost 2 hours.

    6 selected firm pears, peeled
    1 cup muscatel
    6 heaping tablespoons vanilla sugar
    1 cup apricot jam
    ¼ pound very soft butter
    ¾ cup brandy
    1 quart vanilla ice cream

Place pears upright in a deep, heavy pan or roaster. Pour muscatel over them, and sprinkle each generously with vanilla sugar. (Granulated sugar kept in a covered jar with strips of broken vanilla bean in it makes vanilla sugar, usable in all desserts.) Cover and simmer until the pears are tender and well impregnated with the resulting syrup. Set aside and chill. In a separate mixing bowl, blend apricot jam with soft butter, mixing with a wooden spoon. Add a dash of the chilled syrup from pears. Pour this mixture over pears which have been placed in a serving bowl. Heat brandy in a saucepan, and when warm, ignite. Pour flaming brandy over pears, basting gently until flames die out. Serve each person one pear with sauce on vanilla ice cream.

Interior decorator
Palos Verdes Estates, Calif.

CHERRY CRISP

Ray F. Holmes from Monument Valley, Utah, joins the ranks of the elect with what he calls Cherry Cobbler. Newly initiated *Chef* Holmes may refer to this as a cobbler if he wishes, but we think it deserves a more descriptive appellation. Our nomination is *Cherry Crisp*. The crust isn't baked with the filling of cherries; it comes out of the oven alone and doesn't even meet the cherries until just before you serve the dish.

Filling

    1 can (No. 2) pitted sour cherries
    1 cup sugar
    3 tablespoons cornstarch
    ½ cube (4 tablespoons) butter or margarine
    ¼ teaspoon nutmeg
    1 teaspoon vanilla

Pastry

    3 cups flour
    ¼ teaspoon sugar
    Salt
    1 cup cold shortening
    ¾ cup lukewarm water

Cook the cherries only until heated through. Combine sugar and cornstarch and stir into the cherries; cook until the mixture thickens. Add butter and nutmeg and cook for 1 minute longer. Remove from the heat and add vanilla.

Sift flour, measure, then sift again with sugar and a pinch of salt. Mix with shortening until like coarse meal. Add lukewarm water and stir in lightly. Roll into thin sheet and cut in strips. Lay strips on a baking sheet and place in a hot oven (400°) for about 10 minutes, or until pastry is golden brown. When pastry is cool, break it up in small pieces and place in dessert dishes. Pour the cooked cherry filling over the pastry and serve. Serves 6 to 8.

Ray F. Holmes

Monument Valley, Utah

PEACH PERFECT

"This is an excellent fruit dish for Sunday brunch," says *Chef* Wharton, "and quite edible any other time (we recommend enthusiastically for dessert, with or without ice cream). Be sure it 'cooks' long enough for the sugar and wine to develop the most flavor from the peaches."

    Large ripe fresh peaches (figure 1 to 2 per
       person)
    Sugar
    Dry white table wine

Into a shallow bowl, slice peaches in moderately thin segments until the bottom of the bowl is covered. Cover the peach layer with a moderate sprinkling of sugar. Repeat layers of peaches and sprinklings of sugar until all peaches are used up. After the last layer of peaches has been sugared, pour in enough wine to barely cover peaches. Cover bowl and place in refrigerator for at least 6 hours; overnight is even better. Serve ice cold.

Wallace S. Wharton

Farmer and Civil Defense Director
Turner, Oregon

BAKED PEACHES FLAMBE

    6 large, perfect freestone peaches
    1 cup applesauce
    ¼ cup raisins
    ¼ cup finely chopped pecans
    ¼ teaspoon salt
    Sugar
    Cinnamon
    Brandy

Cut a slice from the top of each peach. Remove the pits, being careful not to break the peaches in so doing. Combine fruit, nuts, and salt, then fill hollows of peaches. Place stuffed peaches in a well-greased baking dish, sprinkling lightly with sugar and cinnamon. Scatter any remaining mixture over peaches. Bake in a moderate oven (350°) 10 to 15 minutes. Transfer peaches to chafing dish. Heat chafing dish with flame and pour in small amount of preheated brandy. Pass spoonful of brandy through flame under chafing dish and carry flaming liquor into dish to ladle over peaches. Serve at once with cream.

Kenneth Raymond Wight

Petaluma, Calif.

WINE STRAWBERRIES

We believe that the advantages of wine with fresh fruit are lost unless the wine is one which has a natural affinity for the particular fruit, and is used with restraint so that while it stays in the background, it also points up the fruit flavor.

Dry red wine, as Frank Petrucci uses it, does something worthwhile to strawberries. The filip of whiskey is an afterthought which could be omitted. But the important point is that it, too, plays a supporting part and never dominates the center of the stage.

    2 baskets strawberries
    5 tablespoons sugar (more or less,
        depending on sweetness of berries)
    1½ cups red table wine
    2 teaspoons whiskey

Wash berries in cool water before pulling off stems and small leaves. Cut all large berries in half, so wine will soak in. Place in a bowl, sprinkle with sugar, and pour wine and whiskey over. Put in refrigerator to chill for an hour or more until ready to serve. Serves 8.

Frank Petrucci
Menlo Park, Calif.

BEAN POT APPLES

To top off a meal, *Chef* W. A. Dyer suggests Bean Pot Apples. Since some of our taste testers found the dish almost too sweet, we suggest you cut back a little on the sugar if you use bottled cider. Another alternative is to use a tart, lemony sauce as a topping.

    8 apples
    1 cup sugar
    1 teaspoon cinnamon
    3 cups cider

Peel, quarter, and core the apples. Place a layer in the bottom of a bean pot; sprinkle with sugar and cinnamon (combined); continue putting in layers of apples, sprinkling each layer with cinnamon-sugar. Pour over cider—should be enough so apples are barely covered. Cover and bake in a slow oven (300°) for about 2 hours, or until apples are tender but not too mushy. Serve either hot or cold. Sug-

gested toppings: cream, thin custard, vanilla ice cream. Serves 8.

W. A. Dyer
Secretary
Seattle, Washington

APPLE GUFF

    2 packages (2¾ oz. each) dried apples
    6 cups water
    1½ cups sugar
    ½ lemon, sliced
    1 teaspoon cinnamon, or to taste

Stew the above ingredients for about 30 minutes until they become sauce. Transfer to shallow baking pans. Prepare the following topping:

    ½ pound margarine or butter
    1½ cups quick cooking oatmeal
    1 cup granulated sugar
    1 cup chopped almonds

Combine the margarine, oatmeal, and sugar and cook together until the mixture just begins to stick to the pan. Sprinkle it on top of the applesauce in the baking pans. Spread chopped almonds on top. Heat all in an oven (or reflector oven) until the topping turns to a deep brown. Can be served hot, warm, or cold; serves 12 generously.

Edward G Thompson
Van Nuys, California

SOUR-SWEET APRICOTS

    1 large can (No. 2½) whole apricots
    1 cup syrup from apricots
    1 cup cider vinegar
        Few grains cayenne pepper
    1 tablespoon whole cloves
    1 teaspoon white mustard seed

Drain syrup from apricots and measure out 1 cup of the syrup. Bring the syrup and vinegar to a boil, add the spices and boil for about 5 minutes. Add the apricots. Remove from heat and let steep in the spiced juice for at least 24 hours. Serves 6 to 8.

Hod White
Executive vice president
Honolulu, T. H.

DRIED FRUIT COMPOTE

"Have spent a good many years munching on this compote, both at home and when camping or fishing," says *Chef* R. F. Williams. "It's extremely simple to make, keeps well, and holds the inner man still when the outer man is busy—but very hungry."

"... inner man still ... outer man busy"

It's a version of an old-fashioned candy substitute that many of us used to know. Its sweet fruit-nut blend doesn't make you too thirsty on the trail.

    1 pound dates, pitted
    1 pound dried prunes, pitted
    1 pound seedless raisins
    1 pound walnuts, shelled
    1 pound almonds, shelled

Mix in a large bowl and run through a meat grinder two or three times, or until well mixed and finely ground.

Form into one large or several small loaves, wrap in waxed paper, and store in the refrigerator. Makes four 8 by 2-inch loaves or rolls.

"I don't suggest any other dried fruits because their higher moisture content makes for spoilage. Any other nuts may be used, however, to vary the flavor, although the taste of these two never gets old.

"Sliced thin, it even makes a good sandwich filling. But why gild the lily? This stuff will stand on its own."

R. F. Williams

Landscape contractor
West Los Angeles, Calif

CRANBERRIES AFIRE

Flaming food is good drama any time, but the timing is especially right for the holidays. Use this one as you see fit.

"For how many generations this dish has been served after midnight mass at Christmas time in our family I don't know," says *Chef* Moise Penning, "but it goes on and on as the center of our early Christmas morning brunch, served with many holiday treats."

    1 quart (1 lb.) cranberries
    1 cup honey
    ½ cup hot water
      Rind of 2 lemons (either in thin strips or
      grated)
    ½ cup 100 proof brandy, heated

Place cranberries in a 3-quart casserole. Add honey diluted with hot water, then the lemon rind. Cover and place in hot oven (400°) until the mixture boils well. about 20 minutes, then reduce heat to moderately slow (325°) and bake for 45 minutes, or until really thick. Then spoon into chafing dish so you can bring to table hot. Just before serving, pour over brandy, light, and serve "afire." Serves 8 to 10 with about 2 tablespoons apiece.

Moise Penning

San Lorenzo Village, Calif.

FIGS A LA BALLARD

If you like fresh figs (some people don't), you have vivid memories of standing under a fig tree where you could reach out and pick all the figs you could eat. *Chef* Ballard has discovered a treatment for figs that places them in very high company indeed. He combines just four ingredients to create a dessert along classic Continental lines. We agree with him thoroughly that this dish is "simple, but fit for a gourmet." For our money that's the best kind of all.

"Ginger gives it an excellent snap," puns one of our taste testers. For further experimentation: Try preserved ginger instead of the candied type. We also see no reason why this dish shouldn't be good with canned figs when fresh ones aren't available.

(proportions for each serving)

½ teaspoon finely chopped candied ginger
2 tablespoons sour cream
⅛ teaspoon salt (optional)
4 to 6 fresh black figs, peeled and sliced

Mix ginger into sour cream, and add salt if desired; then use it to top each bowlful of figs before serving. I prefer the contrast of figs at room temperature and chilled sour cream, although others· may like both chilled.

Charles L. Ballard

Banker
Pasadena, Calif.

MINTED WALNUTS

2 cups sugar
½ cup water
3 drops oil of peppermint
2½ cups whole walnut meats

Dissolve sugar in water and boil for 5 minutes. Remove pan from heat and beat the syrup until it starts to get cloudy. Then add the oil of peppermint and the walnut meats. Stir the nuts through the syrup and turn them out on waxed paper.

PHILBRICK McCOY
Superior court judge
Van Nuys, Calif.

CRUSHED FRUIT ICE CREAM

2 cups sugar
1 quart well-crushed fruit: strawberries, raspberries, peaches, apricots, Boysenberries
Juice of 1 lemon
1 pint coffee cream
2 large cans evaporated milk
About 3 cups milk to fill container ⅔ full

Sugar the crushed fruit. Add lemon juice. Stir fruit evenly through milk and cream. Pour into chilled container of a 1-gallon hand freezer. Adjust dasher and cover. Pack tub with mixture of 8 to 10 parts cracked ice to 1 part rock salt. Turn crank slowly and steadily until mixture starts to get firm. Drain off brine from tub, remove dasher, and close opening

with a cork. Repack with ice and salt (about 4 to 1), and let ripen before serving.

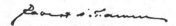

Pediatrician
Seattle, Washington

BARR'S PEACH ICE CREAM

5 cups sliced peaches
1 lemon
3 cups sugar
4 eggs, separated
Pinch of salt
1 quart milk
½ pint whipping cream
2 teaspoons vanilla
A few drops red coloring

Prepare the fresh peaches, cover with juice of 1 lemon and 2 cups of the sugar. Mash and then set aside.

Beat the egg whites with a pinch of salt until stiff. Add ½ cup sugar and continue to beat until mixture resembles a meringue. Set aside.

Beat the egg yolks well, add ½ cup sugar and continue to beat until light and lemon yellow.

Now, add the milk, cream, and peach mixture to the egg yolks. Then fold in the whites, and vanilla. Taste, flavor, and color until it suits you.

Freeze in a 1 gallon freezer, being sure to use plenty of rock salt. Pack and let sit 1 to 2 hours before serving.

Barr Olson

Manufacturer's representative
Seattle, Washington

CHERRY SOUP

Thaine H. Hahlbeck calls his dessert a Cherry Mousse—"not technically a mousse in the purist's sense, but far too unusual and interesting to be called a pudding. It should be served slightly warm; I usually put it in sherbet dishes. It's an ideal dessert to make just before starting to serve dinner. In the ensuing hour, it has cooled to just the right temperature. The secret of the preparation is to almost (but not quite!) burn the butter.

The more the butter is browned, the better the end result."

We agree on all points except the name. We believe that it qualifies completely as a fruit soup of the type that the Scandinavians make. For variations you might top it with a little sour cream, whipped cream, toasted almonds, or toasted coconut; you might also use it as a sauce over a sponge cake or ice cream.

> ½ cube (4 tablespoons) butter
> 5 tablespoons flour
> I pint pitted fresh sweet cherries, cooked in ½
>   cup water until slightly tender, or I can
>   sour pitted red cherries
> ¾ cup sugar
> 5 drops almond extract

Brown the butter in a skillet over high heat until it is almost burned, stirring constantly. Stir in the flour and cook the resulting roux for a minute. Add cherries, with their liquid, and sugar. Bring to a bubbly boil and cook for a minute, stirring as little as possible—you damage the cherries if you stir too vigorously. Add almond extract, stir once, and transfer to serving dishes. Serve while still a little warm. Serves 4.

Personnel manager
Redondo Beach, Calif.

CHOCOLATE MINT SUNDAE

Top each serving of French vanilla ice cream with 1 tablespoon crème de menthe, and sprinkle on one teaspoon grated unsweetened chocolate.

San Francisco

ORANGE ICE CREAM

> 2½ cups strained orange juice
>   Juice of one lemon
> 1¼ cups sugar
> ⅛ teaspoon nutmeg
> 1½ pints (3 cups) whipping cream

Combine orange and lemon juice with sugar. Let stand about 10 minutes, stirring occasionally or until sugar is dissolved. Stir in nutmeg and whipped cream. Pour into freezing trays, turn controls to lowest possible point, and freeze until firm. Stir twice during freezing, but do not beat. Makes 1½ quarts.

Orchardist
Escondido, Calif.

INSTANT MOCHA ICE CREAM

Frederick H. Polt of Santa Barbara, California, wins a tall white cap for his very simple trick involving instant coffee in the preparation of this "instant" mocha ice cream.

"A tall white cap for his very simple trick involving instant coffee"

> I pint slightly softened vanilla ice cream
> I teaspoon instant coffee
> ½ teaspoon ground chocolate

Mix all ingredients well and serve immediately or put back in the freezing compartment of your refrigerator for later use. Serves 2, more or less—or how long does ice cream last at your house?

Lawyer (retired)
Santa Barbara, Calif.

index TO CHEFS

EDITOR'S NOTE: These are the *Chefs of the West* whose "cooking bold and fearless" is reported in the pages of this book. We regret that we did not have space to include all the *Chefs* who have made significant contributions to cookery.

index TO RECIPES